Leading an
Emotionally Intelligent Life

Leading an Emotionally Intelligent Life

Expanding Your EI to Make Courageous Decisions and Transform Your Life

Patrick Kilcarr

ROWMAN & LITTLEFIELD
Lanham • Boulder • New York • London

Figures of EQ-i Comprehensive Reports copyright MHS Multi-Health Systems Inc. used with permission.

Published by Rowman & Littlefield
An imprint of The Rowman & Littlefield Publishing Group, Inc.
4501 Forbes Boulevard, Suite 200, Lanham, Maryland 20706
www.rowman.com

86-90 Paul Street, London EC2A 4NE

Copyright © 2022 by Patrick Kilcarr

All rights reserved. No part of this book may be reproduced in any form or by any electronic or mechanical means, including information storage and retrieval systems, without written permission from the publisher, except by a reviewer who may quote passages in a review.

British Library Cataloguing in Publication Information Available

Library of Congress Cataloging-in-Publication Data

Names: Kilcarr, Patrick J., author.
Title: Leading an emotionally intelligent life : expanding your EI to make courageous decisions and transform your life / Patrick Kilcarr.
Description: Lanham : Rowman & Littlefield, 2022. | Includes index. | Summary: "Emotional intelligence is necessary for facing life's obstacles as well as for cultivating inner calm and well-being. Here, emotional intelligence expert Patrick Kilcarr provides a master class in building emotional intelligence in all realms of daily life"—Provided by publisher.
Identifiers: LCCN 2021056002 (print) | LCCN 2021056003 (ebook) | ISBN 9781538143742 (cloth) | ISBN 9781538143759 (ebook)
Subjects: LCSH: Emotional intelligence. | Self-actualization (Psychology)
Classification: LCC BF576 .K555 2022 (print) | LCC BF576 (ebook) | DDC 52.4—dc23/eng/20211220
LC record available at https://lccn.loc.gov/2021056002
LC ebook record available at https://lccn.loc.gov/2021056003

Contents

Chapter 1	An Instrument of Hope	1
Chapter 2	The Landscape of Emotional Intelligence	33
Chapter 3	The Competencies as Levers for Change	75
Chapter 4	EQ-i Map: When Strength Is a Weakness	103
Chapter 5	The EQ-i Map: Finding the Pattern	129
Chapter 6	Struggles on the Journey Forward	167
Chapter 7	The End and the Beginning of This Journey	195
	Index	217
	About the Author	229

CHAPTER ONE

An Instrument of Hope

I am one of the countless invisible wounds walking around and participating in this campus, pretending to be a smart, whole human being.

Smart I am.

Whole I am not.

These profound words resulted from an emergency phone call. A faculty colleague who taught a large Intro to Philosophy class at our university had asked her students to write an essay about overcoming a difficult experience.

Now she was on the phone, and a bit frantic. No fewer than 50 of the 250 essays reported experiences of suffering, pain, and disillusionment—both past and present—exceeding anything she had previously encountered in her many years in academia. Because she had mentioned that they could write about something that might not be known by anyone else, many used the essay to describe something they had rarely—or never—discussed before.

She asked me to speak to them and share my perspective on growth, pain, and healing, assuring them it was all confidential and that I didn't have their names. They agreed. Then, I addressed this gifted group of young students who had won admittance to an elite university:

You look at one another and draw various conclusions: Smart. Did a lot of extracurricular activities in high school. Probably top of their class. Pretty motivated. Achievement oriented.

What you don't see are the emotional mountains that many in this room had to summit to be here today. What you don't see are the struggles that many continue to battle because of situations over which they had no control. Yes, this is a room filled with people whose talent knows no limit. But what can, and often does, limit talent is unremitting pain and hidden suffering.

So, what can we do about what has happened to us? Carry the weight until we simply can go no further? Carry it until what is left in our wake are broken relationships, obsessions, addictions, and mere fragments of what was possible—all based on incomprehensible internal and external woundedness?

A window of opportunity has opened. Your professor created it by sharing your thoughts with me and inviting me to share mine with you. Our opportunity is to find a safe place to tell your story, own what is yours, and learn to discard what is not. It is a process for survivors, and each one of you in this room who has suffered and made it here is precisely that: a survivor. Imagine for a moment that you are no longer white-knuckling it in relationships, you are not relying on substances or something outside of you to ease the pain. Imagine you feel emotional balance, you feel—yes, you feel—in control of your life. You champion your life with all your varied talents and abilities. This is the process of transitioning from surviving to flourishing!

So how do we really begin to flourish? Sharing our stories is a start. However, learning to work with a trained therapist and understanding the fifteen coompetencies of the EQ-i 2.0 is an essential tool for flourishing to continue.

The Heart of This Book

We hear and read a great deal about emotional intelligence (EI) these days. It's a popular concept that leaps at us from the mainstream press and business consulting. It has emerged through research journals and psychological theory. But it's more than just buzz. It also has a real application in our lives, and it can be an index to what's happening within us when other measures don't identify the problem. The reason emotional intelligence has attracted so much notice is simple. It is the best index I know of to evaluate our aggregate sense of well-being.

Well-being is born out of four very specific competencies: Self-Regard, Optimism, Interpersonal Relationships, and Self-Actualization. The questions emanating from the interaction of these four competencies indicate the socioemotional balance we feel in all aspects of our life . . . Do we treat ourselves and others with respect? Do we manage the array of emotions we feel in our daily lives, and can we navigate the emotions that others present to us? If we do these things, we forge strong, lasting, and generative relationships. Breaking down the walls we have created to survive is the definition of courage. You will meet brave people in this chapter and in this book.

The survival mechanisms and strategies that we used to get through childhood and adolescence become arrows in our quiver, and we continue to rely on them as we grow older. Other arrows are available to us, and we can learn to use them to create interpersonal connection and balance. But doing so requires desire, motivation, and a vision for what we want. Otherwise, we rely on the strategies we learned to count on in childhood.

Our early childhood and adolescent experiences significantly influenced the degree to which we are emotionally intelligent individuals. Those of us who have been emotionally scarred can find that shifting our perspectives, enhancing our self-awareness, and embracing change can be challenging, yet exhilarating, moments. This is when our coping strategies put us in a position where we feel as if we are walking on the wing of a 747, and we don't dare take another step. This book offers a solid and helpful template for identifying what we want and what it will take to get it.

Often, in an intimate relationship we respond to our partner's anger by emotionally withdrawing. Conflictual feelings are generally met with the coping strategies we adopted while growing up. Have you ever seen someone when angry or upset retreat into an internal cave, or have you done it yourself? "My mother was so volatile and unpredictable that . . . once she started spinning up, I retreated into myself out of self-protection. And this is what I now do as an adult; my husband starts getting angry and I emotionally disappear." Other responses are aggression, passivity, or passive aggression. Any of these indicate a lack of consistency in finding and utilizing our voice in the workplace and in relationships—a voice we did not or could not use when growing up. This anger/retreat switch tends to be binary, on or off.

The hardest part is reconciling our knowledge—our experiences—with our actions and building the bridge between knowing and doing. For example, what happens when someone is angry, but instead of reacting with anger or retreating, we offer a thoughtful and nonaggressive response they did not expect? This response requires us to not be carried downstream by our emotional reflexes. It requires being measured in our responses as we express and take care of our emotional needs. For most of us, this requires a dedicated and committed approach to changing our response style when we are in the center of negative feelings/anger.

Most of us possess an innate knowledge of emotional intelligence. We see it in others. It feels right when we follow it. Under stress, however, we usually revert to what we know best. It is the path of least resistance, one which distances us from ourselves and from others. But it doesn't have to be that way.

Our emotional intelligence is environmentally and interpersonally learned and taught. Even when we don't have role models by displaying strong emotional intelligence, we can still reshape it. We don't have to continue guarding ourselves from imminent attack.

But knowing isn't doing. There is a balance between recognition and change. Awareness or insight into our behavior does not necessarily translate into change. Recognizing what binds us takes us only part of the way. The rest of the journey requires us to change in ways that are illustrated in this book. Woven into these two elements—recognition and change—are four specific criteria:

- *Know ourselves*: This comes from recognizing our behavior and emotional reactions and utilizing the information we hear from others about how we manage stress and feelings. Children represent a river of ever-present cascading needs. These needs often intersect with us feeling tired, overwhelmed with work and life, and trying to post-up for all of it. How can we find our own time in an environment that precludes it? A client once said to me, "I know that what is about to spill out of my mouth will wound my

daughter. I know it and yet do not pull back. I blanket my child with the same dehumanizing and heart-breaking responses to her behavior that my mother foisted on me."
- *Advocate for ourselves*: This is especially necessary for moving in the direction we want to travel. If others avoid us or gossip about us, then we must reconfigure our social and emotional maps. External criticism, even gossip, is like getting a performance review at work. It may be fair or unfair, but we can't dismiss the information we receive about our overall performance. Self-advocacy becomes imperative.
- *Develop a plan for sustained change*: This requires seeking out and establishing support structures. These will help us sustain motivation in achieving the type of attitude and behavior we want. "I really envy my sister who is in recovery . . . Going to meetings regularly, hearing people share what it takes to live a responsible and accountable daily life and directing her life toward what has clearly been emotional and behavioral success."
- *Activate change within an environment that allows us to flourish*: If we can't stand a job or a living situation, finding the right environment within which to flourish is critical. Achieving this has its own inherent and predictable challenges. If as adults we are in a relationship or professional setting that lacks emotional health, nurturing, and stability, and extricating ourselves is not immediately possible, we can start taking slow, yet incremental steps toward our own liberation. "I am the poster child for being held hostage by golden handcuffs. I get up in the morning and dread going to work. I make too much money to even consider leaving my job. Yeah, people would look at my life and if I said this to them, they go 'boohoo.' I feel imprisoned. You just can't see the bars and the 8 by 4 foot cell holding me captive."

Personal balance emanates from the choices we make, which serve to expand or contract (inhibit) our emotional intelligence. Forging a more fulfilling life must start with believing things can be different (perspective), experiencing clarity in the direction you want to pursue, and setting clear markers along the way to affirm we are moving in the right direction.

From Shutdown to Engagement and Optimism: Paul

An expression of low emotional intelligence often has its roots in the degree of sustained stress we encountered growing up. Seminal emotional and physical pain does not go away as we age. The almost unbearable feelings and stress that accompany the trauma are meted out in our emotional responses toward intimate partners and friends. If we are fighting for survival, it is nearly impossible to enter into a place of sustained well-being. To give you an example, I'll introduce you to Paul.

Paul was referred by two professors and an academic dean at my university. He was frighteningly bright, with extraordinary academic ability. Yet despite his intellect, there was something in his demeanor that others found troubling.

For someone who was so capable in the classroom, Paul often displayed a severely disaffected and removed persona. They worried that Paul suffered from depression, masked a deep emotional pain, and might act rashly, even suicidally. Paul never gave them any tangible reason to believe it, but they felt it intuitively.

I asked Paul what concerns he had during his first visit.

"None, really. I am doing well in school. I have a girlfriend. Everything's okay."

I asked Paul if he understood why he was referred to me.

"They think I'm depressed."

Our conversation shed little light on what was going on with Paul. I asked if he could describe what his deans and professors were seeing.

"I am not really sure. You'd have to ask them."

"Imagine, if you did know . . ." I pressed.

"Like I said, you'd have to ask them. But they said I sound or look withdrawn, whatever that means."

"So, their impression is you're not connecting in the class?"

"I guess, yeah."

"Is that what you want?"

"I want to get good grades, which I am doing. My goal in class is to achieve academically, not demonstrate social connection."

"Who else worries about you?"

"No one."

"How would your best friend respond to the concerns of the dean or your professors?"

"I don't really have a best friend in the way you probably mean. I focus on school and my girlfriend. That occupies most of my time."

"And your girlfriend would be your best friend? Meaning, she is the one who knows you best?"

"I guess."

"If she were here right now, sitting next to you on the couch, would she express any concerns?"

"I don't know! I don't ask her what she is concerned about."

At this point, Paul grew annoyed—fidgety and impatient. His girlfriend brought him out socially, he said, and he helped her keep academic focus. The positive experiences with her showed him life could be good.

Paul wouldn't accept that he might be depressed. However, he humored me and took the Beck's Depression Scale and the Connor Depression Scale. I was somewhat surprised when both results indicated he was not depressed, although it is quite easy to mask depression on these instruments. Even so, our session made it clear to me that Paul was just barely holding on.

Paul came back three more times. He said he found the sessions helpful but wanted to limit them to thirty minutes. He told me that he was too busy to afford more time for "this."

After the fourth visit, I shared with Paul the concept of emotional intelligence and asked if he wanted to take the EQ-i 2.0., a tool I have found extremely helpful in working with clients. He did. At our next session, we discussed his Comprehensive Feedback Report.

I find it best to wait until the fourth session to administer the assessment. If someone comes to four sessions, it means they are engaging in the therapeutic process and likely to continue coming back.

Paul's EQ-i 2.0 results clarified something important. His Self-Regard and Optimism score were exceedingly low. Paul's Well-Being Indicator was 54, three standard deviations away from the norm in a negative direction. The EQ-i 2.0 assessment results begin with a total EQ-i 2.0 Score. For now, it's enough to know that a score of 100 indicates you are doing okay. I'll explain in more detail later.

Under the umbrella of each composite there are three competencies for a total of 15 competencies. These allow us to gauge how we navigate our life emotionally and relationally. How do we manage strong emotions like anger or fear? Do we connect emotionally to those whom we consider important in our life? To what degree are we aware of our feelings and compassionately recognize when someone is "just holding on"?

Figure 1.1 shows page 3 of Paul's EQ-i 2.0 Comprehensive Report, which visually captures the strength, or lack thereof, of each competency. The client feedback report of the EQ-i 2.0 is in color. This book shows them in black and white. While the colors are useful to separate the different composites/competencies, they really are not necessary. Whether in color or black and white, you can see the breakdown of the competencies. In order to understand the significance of an individual's score, 85 and below is low; 100 is the mid-range, suggesting the competency is okay; and 115 and higher indicates the competency is very strong. The scores give us an immediate sense of whether a particular competency is underutilized, working well in the person's life, or overutilized (suggesting the competency is so strong it has the capacity to have a negative impact on self and others).

Paul's results indicated he had dealt with profound emotional disappointment and pain by controlling his environment as much as possible. This explains his 122 score on Impulse Control. Paul wanted to control everything and leave nothing to chance. If he couldn't control it, he wouldn't deal with it.

He also managed emotional pain by learning not to care. His Flexibility score of 110 suggested he would just let things roll off his back. He wouldn't deal with anything. When emotional problems arose, he would consider an appropriate emotional response, but only to a point. This is indicated in his Problem-Solving score of 96. He managed stress just enough to keep his head above water.

Paul directed his strong empathy toward his girlfriend, with very little directed anywhere else. This made him seem tougher and more disaffected than he actually was, for he actually had a deep sense of Emotional Self-Awareness, although he also felt unable to express his emotions.

My first meetings with Paul confirmed what the EQ-i 2.0 showed. He was so guarded and tentative. When he did sit down, what tumbled forth signified a great deal of Emotional Self-Awareness. However, this combination of high Emotional Self-Awareness and Empathy was largely dormant, and a prevailing sadness and pain overtook everything.

In two key areas, Self-Regard and Optimism, Paul's scores were among the lowest I had ever seen. Usually, I send the feedback report

Figure 1.1.

to a client in advance. But I did not know how Paul would react, so I waited until he came to my office. I handed him the feedback report and asked him to go over the results. He took twenty minutes. I asked Paul if the results appeared accurate. He said yes, so I asked him to analyze more:

"Help me understand what is really happening with you. After we first met, you took two depression assessments, which indicated you were not depressed even when my behavioral observations indicated you were. The results of the EQ-i suggest the opposite, however. They say that you are depressed, with extremely low Self-Regard, Optimism, and Well-Being Indicator. Which is real?"

"When you described the EQ-i 2.0 instrument to me, you mentioned it was an instrument of hope!" he replied. "So, I took you at your word and answered the questions as honestly as possible. I am tired of feeling like I am carrying a two-hundred-pound man on my shoulders everywhere I go. If hope is what you offer through this instrument, then it is hope I am after."

In that session and beyond, Paul discovered that his depression was—as he put it—"not a label I want to wear anymore." He told me how he had been "unmercifully bullied" in Catholic grade school. He was uncomfortable in organized sports, received little support from his parents, and even "dumbed down" his academic performance in school to appear less intelligent.

His intelligence and need for self-protection led him to reading. Paul spent hours, at home or in the library, losing himself in stories: "They were tales filled with magic, sorcerers, and occasional aspects of redemption. It was the only time I could suspend the pain in my life and feel like I may make it out of this inferno alive. I felt similar to an outlaw in the Old West, living with a price on his head. If you have ever seen the movie *Matilda*, where, because of her crappy home life she literally was invisible, her place of true solace and comfort was in literature. It has been the same for me." (This was the second time a client mentioned *Matilda*.)

Paul dismissed the notion that these scenes from his youth were in any way formative. "I don't even want to think about it," he said. "It's over and done, right?"

"Though those tortuous moments are fortunately gone," I replied, "their profound emotional effect continues, often in ways that look nothing like the original abuse."

The first issue we tackled together was Paul's difficulty in seeing how his depression and problems establishing close and loving friendships had roots in these experiences. Those who have suffered must undergo a process of healing, and the EQ-i 2.0 suggested that the abuse had eclipsed his ability to form solid and caring relationships, especially with men.

Paul looked down. His eyes welled with tears.

I moved closer to him. "The years of keeping this to yourself, suffering in silence, believing either no one cared or no one could possibly fathom what you went through, has already begun to change. You have begun the process of healing, though initially you did not know it or call it that. You decided to come back to meet with me, even though you didn't have to. Your obligation was to meet with me once. The process of healing began when you chose to come back after that. While there are many things I don't know, Paul, what I do know is that you never deserved an ounce of this suffering, and now, with the right supports and challenging the pain, you can move toward liberation."

"How do I even do it?" he asked, quietly. "It feels so hopeless. You know, this is just who I am. And I don't know if I am up for confronting this."

"It is big, Paul. But I don't believe it is bigger than you. To have traveled this far with all that pain, experiencing the levels of success you have, suggests to me you are a survivor, a man of great courage, and within the right environment, a man of vision. This did not happen overnight and will not disappear overnight. You can, however, begin to extinguish the pain with the promise of moving toward precisely how you want to live your life."

As a result of analysis from the EQ-i 2.0 assessment and our work together, Paul began to put himself first. He learned to take more social risk, with less emotional cocooning, a concept we'll discuss later. Yet years of abuse, with all its attending doubt, did not immediately or easily dissipate. A significant part of the abuse had been witnessed by teachers or administrators—who actually laughed with the kids imparting the abuse. Kids can be cruel, and adults were not trusted.

"Academics are easy," he told me. "Socializing is not. I literally take zero social risk. No clubs, minimal involvement in group activities, and never speak in class. Regardless of how smart I feel, when it comes to taking social risks, I feel handicapped. One of the most difficult things to see was my Self-Regard score on the EQ-i, accompanied by a complete lack of Optimism. I will no longer buy into this crap that has been foisted upon me since grade school. I am not awkward! I just think awkwardly considering what has been said and done to me."

Paul had to forge a plan, and he did. He was well aware of how he had lived his life up to that point and became clearer on what he wanted instead. He began to engage in social activities he typically would avoid. He learned to get information about his options for joining clubs. He was able to raise his hand to ask or answer questions in class or to speak with students he hadn't met previously. All of these things that had made him anxious before, he was now engaging with as new skills.

One breakthrough came when his girlfriend asked Paul to bartend with her. She had to cater an event because a colleague canceled at the eleventh hour:

> I felt like I was watching myself in a movie. My girlfriend was blown away by how I connected to those at the party. I can't really explain it other than I simply wanted to have fun and enjoy people. I lay in bed that night imagining precisely what I wanted, how I want to be treated by others, and seeing the path as clear and uncluttered. The way I was treated growing up filled my mind with such disbelief in people. I became convinced that everyone would either be a bully or out for their own gain at my expense. I can tell this is shifting. I really feel alive.

Why I Use the EQ-i 2.0

While a number of assessment instruments gauge varying degrees of emotional intelligence, the one with the most longevity and vetting is the EQ-i 2.0. It is also the most popular and useful subjective test of emotional intelligence.

The EQ-i 2.0 is often administered in professional settings, such as big corporations or organizations, or in academic environments for students, faculty, and staff, to strengthen personal and collective interactions. However, as you will see, my experiences in using the assessment tool as a key element in my practice indicates that the EQ-i 2.0 has important uses far beyond work and school.

In this book, I will share with you the 15 competencies that are the essence of emotional intelligence, as measured by the EQ-i 2.0, and I'll show you how I use them in my practice. This isn't just a book about the tool itself, but about how I use it and how I connect with people like Paul. By the time you finish reading, you will have a deeper knowledge and emotional connection to these competencies as well as a sophisticated grasp of their impact and influence on your day-to-day life. You'll have me working alongside you as you consider the possibilities. Understanding the power of these competencies, which are the backbone of emotional intelligence and well-being, can be so much more than a tool for enhancing your business, building a successful team, or encouraging students to strive toward their potential. Knowing these competencies will unlock their transformative potential in life!

The 15 competencies do not simply measure emotional intelligence. As a therapist, I have discovered they are powerful tools to help clients know themselves and create a plan for personal change. The feedback provided by taking the EQ-i 2.0, combined with a plan based on that assessment, become essential elements in a therapeutic relationship. Together, they offer the support to make the journey toward establishing more consistently fulfilling relationships and developing a deeper sense of calm, stemming from reduced anger and stress. We are going to peel back the competencies to see what makes their existence and interplay such a rich and fundamental element in our socioemotional growth.

When trainers and employees explore the EQ-i 2.0's 15 competencies in a corporate or educational setting, consultants do not have the time to harvest the full narrative of what competencies are saying, nor the time to follow up with individuals. When a person receives a brief overview of the results, it can whet their appetite to know more. However, it misses out on the full-course meal that actually could exist and the potential for meaningful and sustained personal change.

That is the nature of the beast in giving organizational-level tests. The amount of time to offer feedback to clients is very limited. Consultants who offer access to an individual's 15 competencies simply do not have the leeway to excavate the power of the competencies to their full potential. It would be comparable to buying a Ferrari and never taking it out of first gear!

Even if you have never heard of the EQ-i 2.0, or the competencies that it measures, learning about the foundations and mechanics of emotional intelligence, as told through the stories of those striving to improve their life, can provide hope for changes in your life's trajectory.

I use the EQ-i 2.0 as a fundamental tool within my own practice with individual clients because it is the only way to comprehensively observe and utilize the power these competencies provide. Strengthening one competency will, by necessity, impact other competencies.

This book offers practical information on how to interpret the complex interplay of various components and competencies of emotional intelligence. This is an actual "what-to-do" rather than just a "what-you-should-consider" book. The more we learn about emotional intelligence, the more we see the world in a fundamentally different way.

The extraordinary personal narratives of individuals who have taken a deeper dive into the social and emotional competencies that make up our daily interactions and emotions provide all of us opportunities for personal growth. Using this comprehensive knowledge about the landscape of their own emotional intelligence, they were able to leverage the type of change they wanted and find what had been previously missing in their lives. Their journeys challenge us to explore what binds us to outmoded or destructive patterns that hold us back from our potential.

This work is a mining expedition of sorts. The competencies resemble different sedimentary levels, and our goal is to travel deeper into those layers to find the treasure we are after. Initially, we are face-to-face with the darkness of our stubbornness, unsatisfying recurring habits, disillusionment, inertia, stasis, and feelings of being unloved or unlovable. The knowledge gleaned from the 15 competencies of the EQ-i 2.0 generates light that guides us through caverns of immediate, situational, and historical pain.

Searching for what's valuable requires sifting and digging through quite a bit of sediment before you find something of real worth to bring back to the surface. This effort is directed toward discovering the treasure of a more fulfilling life, which is, of course, what we are all after. It is the reward for the effort put into the journey.

The student who challenged us all to look at one another differently at the beginning of the chapter and Paul's story above both help explain the role that competencies can play in understanding where we are in life and how to get to where we want to go—even if we have tried to get there many times before. The competencies are particularly powerful when woven into a conversation that is guided by a strength-based and solution-focused model of personal change. The competencies are a map, but that map only works when we choose a route and begin following it. We have to learn its terrain as we venture forward.

Here's an example: I attended an Alcoholics Anonymous (AA) meeting with a student a number of years ago, and a member of the group began sharing. One participant sitting next to us said, "Oh, here we go again. This guy says the same damn thing over and over at every meeting."

The student looked him in the eye and replied, "Sometimes, to get past whatever tried to break us, we have to talk about it a lot."

Healing means telling our story. Finding our voice. In telling our story, we can see all the possibilities we may have missed before. It moves us ever closer to a place of engaging our own personal courage to transform our life. The stories in this book provide remarkable clues to follow as we journey toward flourishing.

People wear their brokenness beneath their clothes like a medallion, trying to hide the fact that it is cast in the shape of a skeleton key as many search to unlock whatever has been holding them back. I see this when they bring it to therapy. They bring a deep desire to make things better. This is where our emotions—and our emotional intelligence—play such a vital role in charting the life we want as we learn what it will take to actually live it.

Listening to what the competencies say about us, as Paul did, gives us the opportunity to assess our social and emotional landscape and decide how we want to continue this expedition. What character do we want to be in this play called life?

The impressions left by others permits us to develop a solid vision of what has been missing for us, socially and emotionally, and what precise resources would help us achieve a sense of personal and interpersonal wholeness. The EQ-i 2.0 paints a three-dimensional picture of how we utilize our emotions and the impact they have on those around us. It also suggests new paths to arrive exactly where we want to go. The map keeps us on course toward what we want to socially and emotionally achieve in our life.

In organizational settings, clients usually receive a 45-minute overview of what the assessment tool says about the emotional intelligence of the individual. This is simply not enough time and space to leverage the power of the competencies to achieve change. Because it frequently signals a need to change that was not on a client's radar, the meaning of the results—and how the competencies function—must occur over time to achieve opportunities for personal growth that accrue exponentially.

As we dive deeper, we will discover the intricacies of how the various competencies of emotional intelligence interact, reinforce, and at times, even *work in opposition* to one another in ways that are startlingly complex.

The Full, Transformative Power of the Competencies

I operate out of a strengths-based and solutions-focused model related to clients' therapeutic goals. We work on understanding their strengths, respect the emotional traumas that have created such far reaching pain, while devising solutions to achieve their goals—first and foremost of which is diminishing the pain. My method requires them to change perspectives and abandon negative voices, images, and beliefs that have sabotaged their ability to find contentment. Fear is born out of pain, and pain is often unavoidable. Losing someone, being fired, not getting into the school or program we so desperately wanted, losing out to someone else who got what we wanted, and so on. These are natural pain points we encounter on our journey. Take all of this and add it to someone who was physically, emotionally, or sexually abused in their most tender years. They are then bombarded by unremitting pain. The competencies allow us to recalibrate how we see ourselves, others, and what we want to accomplish in the world.

Honoring a client's pain is foundational. At times, it is difficult for me to grasp the pain and suffering individuals have endured at the hands of adults and others who were supposed to love and protect them. In spite of brutality, abandonment, fear, neglect, an array of abuses, and every other imaginable wound inflicted upon them, these children somehow grew through adolescence and into varying stages of adulthood wielding the sword of pure courage. Discovering how they accomplished it soon becomes a central focus of our work together. Are the strategies they used sustainable, like hyper-focusing on school, an athletic talent, or mastery of a musical instrument? It is also easy to adopt a coping strategy that adds new strata of pain like alcohol or other drugs.

My clients have experienced so much emotional and, at times, physical and sexual, abuse that regardless of what they achieve, they always see themselves as failures. Together, we learn the truth that tolerating and moving past attempts to crush their spirit can actually lead to a path of lasting strength and change. Their accounts bear witness to the transformative impact of this combination of focusing on the EQ-i 2.0 competencies from a strength-based therapeutic perspective in order to establish lasting change. If we spend significant parts of our life swirling around in the antimatter of social and emotional intelligence, it is a challenge to find—and maintain—an antidote or cure. Remember, our default setting is the behavior that preceded any change or growth. When stress increases, so does the reflex to rely on old behaviors and responses.

Emotional intelligence is not a one-time achievement. Amid all of life's stressors and disappointments, it is something we continually work at building and maintaining.

The roots of this work can be found in understanding how the 15 competencies are reflected in the way a person thinks and acts. It is essential to have a strong working knowledge of the competencies as we begin this journey. Below are five composites. They break down into 15 competencies. Each composite describes what its three competencies measure. All of these will be described at length later.

> **Composite 1. Self-Perception** (The three competencies below systematically move us toward healing.)
> Competency: Self-Regard
> Competency: Self-Actualization
> Competency: Emotional Self-Awareness

Composite 2. Self-Expression
  Competency: Emotional Expression
  Competency: Assertiveness
  Competency: Independence
Composite 3. Interpersonal
  Competency: Interpersonal Relationships
  Competency: Empathy
  Competency: Social Responsibility
Composite 4. Decision-Making
  Competency: Problem-Solving
  Competency: Reality-Testing
  Competency: Impulse Control
Composite 5. Stress Management
  Competency: Flexibility
  Competency: Stress Tolerance
  Competency: Optimism

We use all of these composites and competencies, to one extent or another, in our daily lives. They are the sinew and bone that support the strength of the larger and more comprehensive field of emotional intelligence.

Most of us can recognize an emotionally intelligent person when we meet one. However, accurately describing emotional intelligence is more difficult. These 15 competencies break down our generalized view of emotional intelligence into manageable processes or aspects of our life that would benefit most from change. Knowing the competencies not only helps us articulate the constituent skills and capacities of emotional intelligence but also helps us see how they interact, overlap, and work together.

Some people underutilize particular competencies that need enhancement, for example, in the statement, "It would be better if I were consistently more assertive." Other people overutilize certain competencies, or express them too strongly, for example, "Being emotionally independent means I often don't take into account what other people say. I think I already know what is best for me, my employees, or my company, and that is exactly what I do."

Consider the executive who recognizes how his high impulsivity and low emotional problem-solving lead to his explosive anger. Or the student who discovers how being overly stress-tolerant, high in social responsibility, and empathic can hinder others from recognizing her needs because she asks for so little. In each case, the competencies offer a unique lens to understand the emotional intelligence landscape. This understanding invites us to see how emotional and social thoughts, feelings, and behaviors unfold in our lives, and their resulting impact.

From Responding to Others' Needs to Articulating Her Own: Zara

Zara summarized her problem as always feeling less than. She tried different therapies with different people over many years. Yet even when these therapeutic interactions allowed her to feel better, the improvement never seemed to last. The puddle always seemed to fill back in, bringing with it persistent feelings of being minimized, emotionally frozen, and socially stuck.

When I asked what the other therapists had missed in working with her so that what I offered didn't replicate the same disappointment, she replied that therapy seemed like a waste of time. She didn't want to continue to feel like "a piece of lint on someone's blouse." She wanted to matter.

No one yet had asked about her strengths, survival skills, and ability to keep moving in the face of change and chaos. When I initially asked her to identify her strengths, her responses were amorphous and noncommittal—much the way she experienced herself in the world. Because she did not recognize any personal strengths, she could not deploy them to change.

Knowledge of how the competencies worked in her life gave her verifiable strengths to use as tools to construct the type of life that had been so elusive for her. Zara noticed that her competencies of Social Responsibility, Empathy, Emotional Self-Awareness, and Emotional Expression were very strong. She reflected first on how those strengths helped others in her life. But then she noticed what was missing in her results. The competencies in which she demonstrated so much strength were all centered on others. She imagined what it would be like if she were kinder toward herself. What if she cared for herself as much as she cared for others? What if she began to use her strong Emotional Self-Awareness to meet her own needs? In doing so, it would not be in a selfish way, but rather as a way to clarify and announce what she needed from others, as opposed to only anticipating and responding to their needs.

Zara's competencies became a catalyst to reframe her strengths and better align her needs with those of others. It was a shift that she originally believed to be unattainable.

Well-Being after Growing Up in a Violent Home: Aaron

I could have done without seeing him beat my mother and my sisters.

These are the words of Aaron, who told me about a life-altering event involving his father. "At the age of five, I crouched in fear, unable to act—and then unable to cry."

Aaron said that gender was at the center of why his father never beat him. "I was a guy," he recalled, "who needed to see how to keep women in line. I knew his way of thinking was so broken and wrong, but I felt completely helpless."

Aaron used humor to ward off the pain. "I made my father laugh, which kept him at a distance. I felt this terrible sludge seeping through my veins. He would laugh at me, but in the next breath backhand my sister across the kitchen table. I was such a fucking pussy. I never said a thing." Things became less violent as Aaron grew older. But the damage was done:

> At times I feel like I am drowning in guilt, not for what I did, but what I didn't do. What I couldn't. For God's sake, I couldn't even tie my shoes. As I grew older, my father expressed less of an appetite for cruelty and one more laced with apathy toward the women in his life. I don't know if there is anything worse than going through life feeling tolerated. Like the gum on the bottom of a shoe that needs to be scraped off. I am not sure what that man got out of life other than making others miserable. I have always felt completely off balance.

As Aaron explored the map of his competencies offered by the assessment, he began to see a way out of what has dogged him all his life. Since he was young, he kept everyone in his life at a distance, because he didn't want to think about his perceived lack of courage. As he unpacked more of that experience, however, he remembered how important his sense of humor was to his sisters and mother. It carried them through many a tough time. He remembered connecting with his

Figure 1.2.

mother and sisters in a way he had forgotten. This realization resulted in them talking more and distancing less and less. They explained to him that they never fully understood why he was so distant and unapproachable. He wasn't mean or cruel like his father, just emotionally unavailable.

Healing emerged from reconnecting and his desire to take more social risk. He also had the capacity to withstand a great deal of *stress* (one of his higher competencies was stress tolerance), which was not healthy for him. As he found his voice in telling his story, the burden of unspoken stress and his perceived lack of courage diminished. He also developed a sense of hopefulness in the world, although his competency score in Optimism was understandably initially very low.

At one point, Aaron, his mother, and his sister went away on a retreat for a week. It was an opportunity to tell each other their stories. While difficult to do and hear, Aaron felt lighter and more hopeful after the retreat. He started moving toward well-being and stronger emotional intelligence and away from fear, regret, and isolation. He certainly grew in Self-Regard, feeling better about who he was as a person.

Up until he discussed his life in therapy, Aaron never considered what he needed or what would make him feel good on a day-to-day basis. He directed his attention toward others whenever he could. His high empathy, born out of his childhood experience, made sure he would routinely help and think about others. This was also verified in his Social Responsibility competency.

Taking his needs into account every day and doing something daily that would allow him to embrace self-care was a herculean shift for Aaron. As he told me: "You know it felt like beginning to write with my opposite hand or kick with the opposite foot. It felt very unnatural." The competencies consistently gave him a visual of how he wanted to live his life and what it would take to make that happen.

The Varying Roads to Substance Recovery: Damien

Occasionally, you meet someone who challenges you to your core. A person whose philosophical beliefs drill down deep into the human spirit, dredging up inescapable honesty, accompanied by the possibility to live well for at least a day. Damien was precisely that sort of individual. He had the mind of an ancient philosopher, the musical talent of a modern rock star, and the humility of one of the great religious prophets.

Yet Damien also grappled with an intense addiction to substances. His addiction kept him off balance. He doubted everything good and pure about his wise and formidable spirit.

Addiction saddles us with optics that lie to us about who we are and what we can achieve. These wayward beliefs push everything off kilter. We see reality as the enemy or as a foreign agent sent to kill us. The axis of addiction spins in a direction far different than most. When a person stops using mind-altering substances, it allows for greater normalcy and balance.

For Damien, such normalcy and balance seemed to be located in far-off lands when we started our work together. But his recovery tells a story about his immense capacity for change and how assessing the competencies identified his variable currents of emotional intelligence.

Damien possesses a rich and fertile mind, cultivated by the ideas of our society's deepest thinkers. Even in his addiction, he read Carl Jung and Hermann Hesse voraciously. His professors saw so much promise in him but couldn't understand why such a bright mind produced such uneven academic results. He also practiced music with passion. Yet none of these things helped him earn an academic degree. It was a void he felt deeply, especially as he watched his peers graduate from college and find gainful employment.

When a job was available to him, he worked hard. But those jobs were often far below his ability. After getting high, or moving into various stages of inebriation, he would identify with the characters in a book, or find solace in Jung's theories about archetypes. He expressed his inner musings through music, making sense of what he read in masterful songs that captured the longings of his heart.

As is the case with most addicts, Damien knew he was lost, trapped in a self-imposed prison. He wrapped himself in impregnable excuses that only lengthened his purgatory, further fueling the addiction. Before ever seeing his competencies, I could tell just from meeting Damien that his Self Actualization competency (which captures our goal-directed behavior as related to personal motivation and personal drive) was likely severely limited.

Damien's initial competencies—revealed six months before he entered treatment—confirmed this and so much more. The results showed a man fraught with uncertainty, self-ridicule, low emotional independence, and low stress tolerance. His total EQ-i 2.0 score was 71, well below the 100 that we noted earlier as the baseline for healthy emotional intelligence.

There were other unusual things as well. Damien's interpersonal relationships were his strongest area, which made sense considering how much he loved to perform in front of people. His second strongest area was impulse control. This was rather odd, considering that he lived with ADHD and was also an addict. But it indicated that he was aware of the stranglehold substances had on his life, and, therefore, he exerted as much control as possible over everything else.

This control had the paradoxical effect of heightening his stress, which he did not manage well. In turn, his stress further amplified his addictions, like the snake eating its own tail.

While emotionally aware and expressive when playing his music, Damien did not share that strength when it came to understanding his own emotional processes and related responses. Addiction stalled his movement toward any particular goals or abilities outside of playing music. And, though he was gifted, his talent also hit a ceiling above which he couldn't ascend. He often left songs unfinished, his improvement slowed to a crawl, and his friends found him more and more unreliable.

Damien had other hurdles as well, which caused real physical and emotional pain. He was diagnosed with ADHD in grade school. He had a physical disability that often left him reeling from the pain. His mother and father divorced when Damien was young, devastating him and sending lasting ripples of doubt and emotional angst through his development.

Because of the divorce, he lived far from his father, whom he saw infrequently and on an irregular schedule. Below are Damien's first competencies. I offered the test to him six months before he entered treatment to give us a map of where he was socially and emotionally. He liked the idea of being able to see where his social/emotional life was headed. I offered it again to him 10 months after ending treatment.

As the results indicate, the addiction and his attending state of mind kept him in a negative feedback loop, which foreclosed the option of sustained forward movement. The longer the substance use, the more it whittled away at his native ability and talent. Dealing with the substance abuse first is the only way to open the safe and bring out all the remarkable wealth inside him.

Figure 1.3.

Every substance abuser gets to the point of diminishing returns, usually referred to as "rock bottom." For each person that point is different, but the state is inevitable. The cure is to stop using. This is torturous for the person who is dedicated to using the substance and addicted to how it makes them feel.

Damien's movement toward emotional and personal freedom was expedited by both timing and his own personal readiness. Prior to entering a month-long treatment program, he told me: "I am pissed, I don't want to go. Why is this happening to me? I also know if I don't go, I'll be left aboard the *Titanic* without a lifeboat. I will sink and with it my abilities and dreams." Although Damien agreed to go to treatment, he did so begrudgingly.

It helped that Damien's mother also laid down the gauntlet regarding his substance use. "In some ways, this is his last chance with me," she told me. "I love him. He is such a talented young man. But I can't continue to be an accessory to this crime. If he doesn't go, he leaves my house. I am clear about this."

Before he agreed to enter treatment, I asked Damien something shocking but necessary. I asked him to imagine those he loved and those who loved him gathered around a grave site. Inside the grave were all his talents and the things he treasured. These were the things that represented who he was in the world. His humor, his gifts, his gentle touch, the competencies we talked so much about, and so on. I asked before writing the eulogy that he be completely sure of what things are in that grave.

> If you believe in our supreme uniqueness, as described by Buddha, Plato, Socrates, Aristotle, the varied interpretations of the Christian faith, and Confucius, then death is the extinction of a species, never to be duplicated by anyone again. And it is also a death at your hands. All those standing around grieving the loss of what is in that grave know this and are angry.
>
> What will your eulogy be?

Although it took four tries and my constant challenges to really engage Damien, he finally described the objects in the grave to me in detail. It is the first and only time I saw tears well up in his eyes and words evade him. As he spoke, I wrote his words on special parchment paper, which I gave to him in our last session.

The eulogy he ultimately wrote was haunting and honest. It began the process of him surrendering not to the addiction but rather to the hold the addiction had on his life for many years. This surrendering culminated in his entering treatment and seeking a new life.

Damien told me later about the beginning of his sustained recovery:

> It was what it must feel like for a rescue team to fight their way into the compound that has been holding you captive for months on end. You are worn out, consumed with fear, exhausted by captivity's monotony, anxious, waiting and hoping, wanting to be rescued, though having no idea what that would look like, considering the sheer strength of your captors. Then, after the smoke clears, and for me, it was the culmination of a 30-day treatment program, you stumble out a free person, clueless on how to relate to a world you barely recognize as a sober person, unable to really explain what you have been through, while only finding temporary solace when you meet for one hour a day to tell your story with the other captives who were released with you.
>
> When I was drinking or smoking, I was armed with limitless excuses as to why my using wasn't the problem; it was a nagging mother, girlfriend, boss, or band member. They were the problem, not the pollutant I kept dousing my system with day after day after day. You have to learn to both recognize and deal with your emotions in a completely new and authentic way. You are now living out in the open, with other surviving captives who also no longer wish to stumble about in the shadows.

The fellowship of Alcoholics Anonymous has been central in Damien's recovery. This process does not work for everyone to extinguish the raging fire of addiction. But for Damien, AA buoyed his belief that recovery was possible. Its 12 steps were instrumental in both getting him there and keeping him there.

Reconnecting with his Catholic faith also helped Damien. "The treatment program has its foundations in faith," he told me. "If you wanted, my treatment program offered daily Mass and prayer, along with the traditional aspects of recovery and AA. Something just happened where I felt so much comfort in reconnecting with my faith, going to Mass, and steeping myself in prayer. It feels like a miracle happened in me—going there and getting everything out of the program I did. I feel as if I escaped a rope tightening slowly and consistently around my neck."

I asked Damien to tell me about the last time he felt so connected to his faith:

> I can't say I really ever have. There was something in the way church, prayer, and recovery were offered that just completely worked. You know I am somewhat of a wordsmith, and I have little ability to verbally explain this. It is a deep existential yearning that has been answered. It is not so much what was done to me, per se. It is what I did with the opportunities presented. There were many people in the program who were not Catholic and had no interest in Mass or the prayer. It was offered, not mandated, which made it very appealing to me. There were also some optional daily discussions weaving together the concepts of faith, Catholic faith, spirituality, and recovery. I felt and continue to feel the presence of God in my life, which is profoundly comforting to me.

Choosing sobriety means learning how to write and do everything with your opposite hand. It does not feel natural, and the temptation to return to using the other hand pulls on you with an indescribable gravity. Entering recovery is a remarkable feat to witness, and for most who do not knowingly struggle with an addiction, we can all learn significant life lessons from those who find strength in "the fellowship of AA," or whatever it personally takes to sustain their recovery.

Where does this intersect with the competencies that comprise our emotional intelligence? The concept of Smart Recovery, which focuses on retraining our brains to think differently about virtually all facets of our life, has significant parallels to my work using the competencies as a guide to therapeutic treatment.

Determining the triggers to drinking and working diligently to neutralize those triggers is a significant part of both AA and Smart Recovery. There are also people who enter recovery through their specific faith, finding it unnecessary to look outside of their faith for strength and direction. Addiction and recovery are not like seeing one squirrel, which looks like all the other squirrels. The process is unique for each person, as they must find what works to restore a sense of balance in their respective lives.

Damien's second set of competencies tells the powerful story of his recovery and its link to emotional intelligence. Remember, his first total assessment score six months before he entered treatment was 71.

His second assessment was taken 10 months after treatment. It's a key moment to determine whether or not someone will continue on their journey of recovery or tumble into some form of relapse, resulting in living an unfulfilled life until the possibility of recovery reappears.

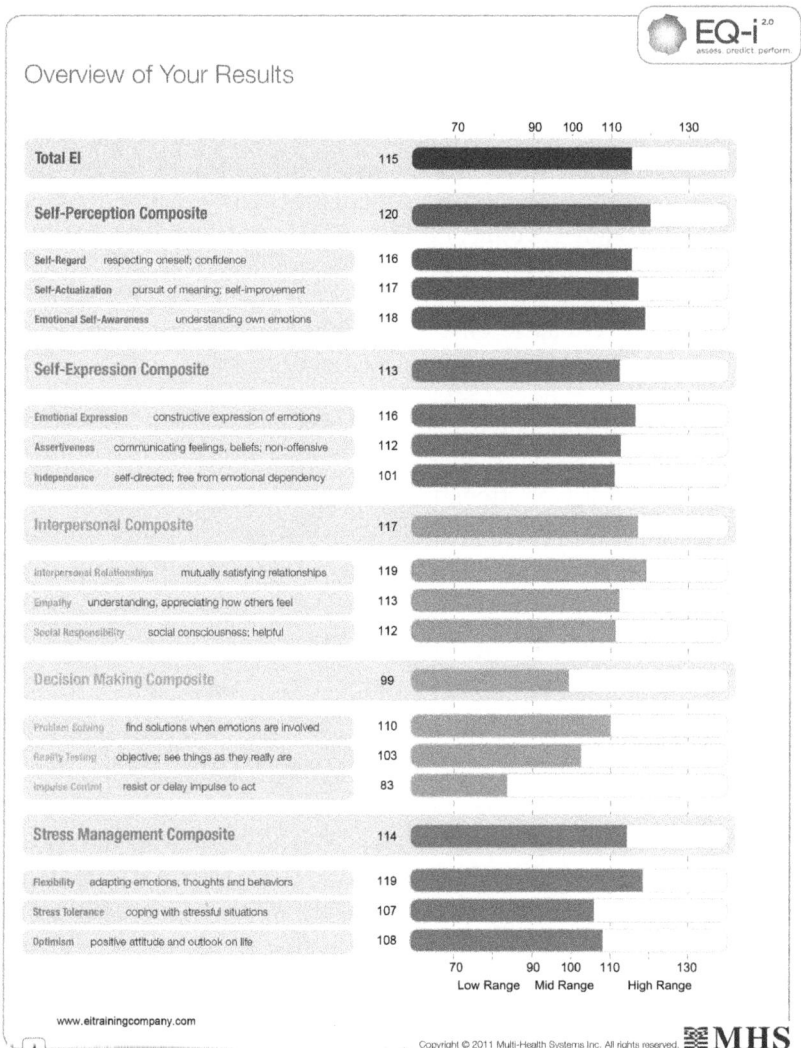

Figure 1.4.

Damien's score on the second assessment was 115!

This score also reflects the reality that Damien did not slip back into substance abuse. That happy fact continues to be the case today, more than six years after his treatment program.

I asked Damien what the biggest difference was between the person he was when using and the person he is today:

> For one, I am back in school, dialed in to what I want to accomplish, following through on what I say—you know, actually being reliable. I'm making great contacts, playing better than I ever have for sure, and I have reclaimed my vision about what I want . . . I was a shadow of that previously. Not using means not losing. It really is that simple for me. Through our relationship, I have learned to understand the role of ADHD in my life and how it can be disruptive if left unchecked. I've plugged new coordinates into my GPS, and if . . . I stay true to the route I am on, it will lead me to what I want. Which is living out what I am capable of. I am no longer in some maze I can't get out of.

Once Damien truly entered sobriety, the demons that ate his talent and corrupted his emotional agency began to subside. They were replaced by a consistent strength, desire, and emotional balance that once felt fleeting to him. As he said, "something that's healed contains more joyful wisdom than something that's always been healthy."

Beginning the Work

I have seen many people in therapy grow wings. They come to understand that if one side of the coin is pain, the other side must hold healing. This belief creates hope, which in turn leads to optimism from which healing then emerges. Like a flower blossoming, healing is a process that must follow its natural course. The more belief and effort that are directed toward healing, the more healing that takes root, allowing for an individual to begin moving toward feeling a greater sense of wholeness.

There is sustained power in knowing we do not have to live with regret or feel broken and uncertain about the strength of our relationships. There is a deep desire in all of us to experience our own emotional and social competency, which again is commensurate with personal well-being. Though the path to attaining this at times is uncertain, knowing the path we are on and want to remain on is half the battle.

I received a note from a client named Chloe, who was moving to another city for a new job. Before moving, she had spent time in therapy exploring what it would look like for her to live in the zone of well-being in all aspects of her life.

Chloe had a number of strengths, but in the key competencies of Self-Regard, Optimism, Interpersonal Relationships, and Self-Actualization, she scored in the low range of 85 and below. She had been in a series of bad, if not destructive, relationships that had taken a toll on her self-worth. Even though she grew up with a loving father, her mother was physically and emotionally abusive. Despite this, she continued into adulthood trying to have a "normal" relationship with her mother.

In therapy, she began the process of surrounding herself with healthy, respectful people by examining her relationship with her mother. What had previously been porous, inappropriate boundaries became fortified, strong, and clear. This began her process of healing. Her note read:

> I wanted to let you know what I have done with what we started in therapy. Both fortunately and unfortunately, I am no longer speaking with my mother. It runs along the sweet path rather than the bitter. I gave her ample chances to step up, show up, and be kind. As you know, in the past, it is not that I just sat there and took it. I would make one-dimensional threats she pushed aside. They are no longer threats. As you would say, "I said what I meant and meant what I said" about how she would treat me. Be kind or be gone!
>
> Having the courage to be strong in her presence has changed the way I feel about relationships. . . . I have been dating someone for six months, and this does not resemble at all my past relationships. When we argue, which isn't often, we hear each other and resolve the conflict without either one feeling like we lost. I remember the exercises we did about seeing the exact type of relationship I wanted in my life, and, well, this is it. I know it is not luck or magic. It is a reflection of how I feel about myself in the world. . . . My goals and achieving those goals have continued to move "toward my potential . . ." What I started by leaving

for this job has only gotten better. I have a new template in my brain for what I want and how I want to achieve it. And, I am following it! I don't think it gets much better than that.

With a sense of these possibilities, as we saw in the stories of Paul, Zara, Damien, and Chloe, together let's begin the work of examining emotional intelligence, learning how to cultivate it in ourselves and others, and creating lasting change by using the competencies in daily life.

CHAPTER TWO

The Landscape of Emotional Intelligence

Emotional Intelligence When You Should Feel Happy, but Don't

Everyone wants to feel both balanced and whole. Complete. Our personal histories and the relationships that flow into and out of them often deter us from moving toward our better selves. This is an outgrowth of social and emotional pain and disappointments that invade our life, often through no fault of our own.

When we have been emotionally wounded, we have a tendency to overcompensate in order to create a buffer or distraction from what has been—and still is—missing in our lives. I have witnessed the problems that arise when a person focuses on one specific element of emotional intelligence, for example, Self-Regard, without noticing how this influences the other aspects of the way they feel about self and other. People with overutilized Self-Regard can resemble self-consumed know-it-alls, the type of person you try to avoid at all costs.

Emotional Intelligence and Childbirth: Rena

There is a strong interplay between joy and anxiety. The beauty of witnessing the birth of a baby is generally something we look forward to with great joy (and understandable trepidation). However, weaving in and out of the post-birth experience is a level of fatigue that feels endless. This can lead us to feel—and express—less-than-ideal emotional responses. As we are attentive to and cradle this beautiful baby in our arms, our emotional needs go into suspended animation.

It is the nature of this experience. All of our energy and that of others is understandably directed toward creating a safe place for the little one. We sacrifice our specific needs and desires for a period of time. When this doesn't happen, and when parents continue to put themselves first at the expense of the child's development, the emotional intelligence of both the child and the parents is wounded.

Rena came to see me several years ago shortly after having a baby. She described her life before as vibrant and full of rich relationships. She was attentive to her sleep habits and felt balanced and lively, particularly during her pregnancy.

After giving birth, however, she experienced postpartum depression. Life lost its sheen, and she felt terribly guilty because she wasn't enjoying the baby the way she felt she should. She isolated from her partner, family, and friends. Another client, Gwen, described this conundrum beautifully when she told me:

> Having a baby sets the stage for things never being the same, yet never being as good. It also put me under intense stress, starting with two months of bed rest, having to leave work much sooner than I expected, and a baby that was in the NICU for six weeks. I was a pissed-off bear to live with. My emotions were all jumbled and I . . . wiped my negative emotions all over my partner without regard to what he was experiencing. Based on the circumstances, I know I had every right to feel upside down. What I didn't have the right to do was make the man I love pay for this imbalance.

Four specific competencies (Self-Regard, Self-Actualization, Interpersonal Relationships, and Optimism) create our sense of well-being. But each of these competencies alone, even if high, does not suggest we are basking in happiness and health. It is truly a gestalt where the whole (well-being) is greater than the sum of individual competencies.

For instance, if I have appropriately high Self-Regard, yet my Self-Actualization is low, my sense of well-being is hindered because I have no real direction in life. Like a pinball, I bounce from one thing to another—elevating stress and decreasing motivation.

Think of the composites we saw in chapter 1 as five seed pods, or green beans. Each pod contains three social and emotional competencies. Now, we'll examine each composite and its constituent parts. If we can identify and understand these concepts and effects, we will become skilled readers of the EQ-i 2.0's comprehensive feedback report. We will be able to interpret it with nuance and sophistication.

Part A

Self-Perception
This composite explores how comfortable a person is in their own skin. It also reveals the degree to which they understand the impact and movement of their social and emotional intelligence. What creates her particular feelings? Do they have a sense of purpose in life? Is life moving in the direction they want it to go?

Self-Perception is the foundation upon which all other competencies build. If someone doesn't feel good about who they are, or has no real sense of purpose or direction, the effect can be pronounced. The weaker areas can negatively affect the other competencies as the person overcompensates.

Let's examine the three competencies within Self-Perception:

1. Self-Regard

Self-Regard is really about the strength of our identity. This competency captures how we balance our given strengths with areas in need of enrichment. The latter are commonly known as weaknesses, although I don't use that term. We all have areas that could be enhanced or that we rely on too much. For instance, someone with low Self-Regard may overutilize Social Responsibility, giving to others at the person's own expense.

Some evaluate their life in the rearview mirror, rather than focusing on what they are seeing—and all the beauty around them—as they live in the present moment. We may rely on past experiences, things done by us or—as is often the case—things done to us, determining the depth of our self-worth or the degree to which we will accomplish anything in life.

Self-Regard also measures whether we are embroiled in an unrelenting battle between how we see ourselves (self-esteem) and how we believe others see us (self-concept). These skirmish lines are often invisible to others.

There is a strong confluence between how we see ourselves and how others see us. It is important to synergize these two perceptions. If people see us differently than how we see ourselves, problems emerge in response to the discrepancy between the two.

Imposter syndrome is a good example of this. Someone may be doing extremely well by measurable standards, yet the individual feels like a fraud and imagines they don't deserve the praise they receive. The feeling of being an imposter begins early in the person's development and grows stronger over time. A young African American football player at my university talked about the stark cultural difference between where he grew up and the prestigious university. He felt he was a "poser," which refers to someone pretending to be something they are not.

Strong Self-Regard does not mean we have somehow escaped the sharp sickle of trauma or pain. It simply means we have learned not to evaluate ourselves based solely on the past. People with balanced self-worth both acknowledge and lead with their strengths, attaining more and more of what they want. They freely acknowledge past mistakes and make amends when and if appropriate, with the freedom to make the choices they feel are best for themselves and others.

2. *Self-Actualization*

Knowing ourselves is essential. But how do we translate this knowledge into our daily experience? How do we embody our better selves and actively move toward things we find personally rewarding?

Self-actualized people choose things in harmony with their native potential. They tend to pursue things they find both personally satisfying and emotionally advantageous, whether it be volunteering, taking classes, pursuing advanced degrees, changing professions, starting their own businesses, or going on other adventures. On their journeys, they may make mistakes. But they harness and learn from errors while moving closer to where they really want to go. These people remain on their journeys until they achieve their goals.

Naturally, goals can shift and change and give way to other opportunities. True joy is always in the journey as well as the destination. Persistence in Self-Actualization can be an invigorating force that takes us closer to the goals a person established in therapy.

Embodying Self-Actualization: Kal My client Kal loved the outdoors and also enjoyed working with his hands. Kal worked in a warehouse most of the time, but on weekends he was a landscaper doing everything he could to remain outdoors, bathing in the sun as he accomplished his clients' goals.

To become as fluent as possible in the language of landscaping, Kal read books about landscape architecture and watched videos about building retaining walls, fountains, and structures made with railroad ties. Three years after working at it part time—which was more like full time in terms of the hours he put in—he left the warehouse and opened his own business.

Well-meaning friends thought Kal was crazy. Landscaping was too competitive of a business. They said he should stick to supply chain analysis, something he knew well.

Today, five years later, Kal owns three nurseries, employs 40 people, and loves what he does. He treats those who work for him with deep respect. He epitomizes what it means to lead by example from the perspective of Self-Actualization.

3. Emotional Self-Awareness

The central element of this competency is understanding the sources of our inner feelings. Understanding the subtle differences among certain feelings is challenging, however, because emotions emerge in a nonlinear fashion. A feeling, or its attendant response, can be the product of a complicated series of states and emotions typically left unaddressed until certain events bring them to the surface.

Here's one example: How do you manage growing uncertainty about how to complete your varied tasks, both desires and responsibilities, when you are pressed for time?

Most of us can appreciate those moments in home or work relationships when Mount Vesuvius erupts, reducing our opportunities to ash. How we begin rebuilding the ruined city of Pompeii is vital to growing our emotional intelligence.

Emotional Self-Awareness allows us to know what we are feeling regarding a specific event or interaction with someone particularly when strong or even negative emotions overwhelm our awareness. My client Jenny said it well:

> The way I grew up, I learned to keep feelings locked up tight. I didn't talk or share unless it was superficial, or I was drinking. Most fights with my boyfriend happened when we both were drinking. When we weren't drinking, we rarely fought. However, there was always a tension resulting from the previous fight. My unaddressed feelings would stack like Jenga blocks and tumble down when my emotional resolve was threatened. Learning to talk more, drink less, and say what I was feeling has allowed me to be so much more aware of my feelings and emotions, and to express them in a way that is constructive.

Emotional Self-Awareness, when utilized as a strong competency, attends to inner rumblings before there is an eruption. We see it when a person speaks clearly with their significant other about not having enough time, even if the outcome of the conversation feels a bit uncertain. We are often reluctant to verbally step into our thoughts and feelings because we can't anticipate the other person's reaction. Many people are quite aware of what they feel emotionally but are constrained from fully expressing that awareness. Conversely, they may also express their emotions often but inappropriately, without understanding their feelings fully. This seems like communication, but has the unintended outcome of throwing relationships off track.

Self-Perception: Steve

Steve came to therapy skeptical that his life could change, because "Life has been profoundly hard."

> My parents taught me to tolerate ridiculous behavior, because, in many ways, the way they lived was unacceptable to anybody with an ounce of sense and who was not held captive by biology and familial obligation. They were alcoholic and pretended to be the perfect parents, until 5:00 p.m., of course, after which, and with uncanny precision, alcohol took possession not only of them, but of me and my younger brother.
>
> The house had to be impeccable. This was my mother's way of compensating for an anorexic emotional life. When we sat down to dinner,

I had this throbbing knot in my stomach. I could hardly eat. Just before I went to sleep, I felt the knot unfurl, at which point I ate crackers and junk food I stashed in a locked box under my bed.

My father came home at 5:00 p.m. on the dot and poured a scotch. He never said hello to us, asked how the day went, or anything. He read the paper until dinner, when he did nothing but bitch about my mother spending money.

I never remember my father hugging me, complimenting me, or knowing anything about me. I was invisible really. I learned to put my needs second, at best, to others. Demand little, expect even less.

My brother Tim had a very jubilant personality, and he would do things to make my father laugh. He would tussle Tim's hair, hold him close to him with one arm, and give him a little pat on the butt as he went back to whatever he was doing.

My mother was more like me, withdrawn, sullen, and serious. Tim could make her smile. She would go, "Oh Tim, you are such a joy." He made me smile as well. He was a genuinely happy kid. He seemed to exist in the bubble where all the tension and humiliation I felt never passed through to him.

Or so it seemed. At 23, he would be dead, and my only hope of having any family died with him. As joyful as he was, he also was very sensitive, and he must have absorbed the sorrow that permeated our family.

Steve wanted to feel a sense of lightness. He said much of his life felt like "trying to walk on a ship in gale force winds." When something positive occurred, he called it luck and did not expect it to last. He would not allow himself to entertain what it would be like to have a fulfilled life. The potential for heartache and disappointment was simply too great if his expectations went unfulfilled.

He could not immediately see the difference between simply having vague expectations and becoming the architect of the life and future he wanted. He expected disappointment in relationships, and often, disappointment was exactly what he got.

In order to achieve some semblance of success, Steve had walled off his feelings to reduce the pain. He observed that this walling-off allowed him to go through life not feeling that familiar ache in his stomach from childhood. The death of his brother created unimaginable pain, so we discussed how the death of his pain could then lead to exceptional freedom, believing this required resetting his way of looking at himself and others. Our process together would begin with a clear vision of what Steve wanted.

Looking at the results of his EQ-i 2.0 in figure 2.1, a story began to unfold about the way Steve was raised and how that gave birth to the way he thought in his present circumstances.

From the vantage point of Self-Perception, the three competencies in this composite tell an interesting story. Steve is successful at work. He is on a team but works in a virtual office at his home in Virginia. In essence, on a daily basis, there is no one around him or interacting with him. His interaction involves mainly text messages, occasional phone calls, and tri-weekly team video meetings. He is alone to solve the intricate problems of his profession.

Until examining his competencies, Steve saw the ability to work in solitude as a strength. He now sees it afforded him the opportunity to remain isolated from others, while minimizing social interaction. As one colleague said to Steve in his previous job during a work retreat: "It's like you are there, but not really. Though you are arguably the smartest on our team, we know nothing about you as a person." He remembered precisely what this man had said, because it was far too accurate. He operated like a hologram, and he let no real substance out.

Steve wasn't someone who felt good in his own skin (Self-Regard). He questioned his goodness, as his parents did on countless occasions through their silence and lack of recognition. As he said, because of this he felt invisible, leading him to make an assumption: Letting people in would introduce them to the ever-widening cracks in his plaster.

All of Steve's efforts and direction in life were directed toward his professional development. He set goals and did everything he could to achieve them (Self-Actualization). Not personal goals or relational goals. Rather, he set goals where he felt he could direct the outcome through pure persistence. He directed his energy toward what he could control and nothing else. He did not take any relationship risks.

Considering what Steve had been through in his life, and the way he had shut out the world, one would think that he would be limited in his Emotional Self-Awareness. Quite the opposite. It was one of his higher scores. He had a 100 on Emotional Self-Awareness, which suggests he was doing well.

The Landscape of Emotional Intelligence ~ 41

Figure 2.1.

Steve's challenge was not in recognizing emotions but in learning how to express them. Sharing his feelings, telling his story, and understanding his narrative felt like walking into quicksand. His Emotional Expression score was 65. This is extremely low. It is a cautionary tale in that the discrepancy in his Emotional Self-Awareness and Self Expression advances the idea that Steve has surgically cut himself off from the world. Before seeing his competencies, he never considered the impact of having a flatline in relationships.

Self-Perception sets the pace for what type of journey we will have. One would think that with high Self-Actualization and high Emotional Self-Awareness, the competencies to follow would also probably be as strong. Yet a markedly low Flexibility, aligned with very high Assertiveness, is the hallmark of a person who has no time for the thoughts, feelings, desires, or needs of others. A person with this combination of competency scores can become easily agitated, or even aggressive, when someone does not see the world as they do, cannot follow their train of thought, or requires more of them then they are willing to give.

Steve had one girlfriend as he worked toward his MBA. When asked to reflect on what his girlfriend would say to him during their relationship, he did not miss a beat: "You can't be pleased. You are negative, harsh, aloof, and unyielding. I mean, WTF, this is kinda how I would describe my parents, right? You would think once I got outside the blast radius I would begin treating people the way I wanted to be treated. I am just perpetuating the [expletive] cycle."

After seeing his EQ-i 2.0 results, Steve imagined the type of life he wanted and stripped away layers and layers of old paint from his childhood. Stripping it off took effort and a reconstructed belief system. He had the blueprint for this already in the vision he performed when he was trying to get a promotion or achieve something specific in the workplace. In those circumstances, Steve could clearly see what he wanted, what he wanted to do, and what it would take to achieve it.

"Oddly enough," he told me, "I took this Silva DVD course years ago and found it to be very helpful with work. Funny, I just never even considered it for my personal life. My focus has been so work-oriented, everything else was less significant."

Slow and subtle changes began to occur in Steve's life. In therapy, he began talking about the pain, joy, and uncertainty. It was the place where he could practice what it would look like to foster and maintain a healthy relationship. He also realized his high Stress Tolerance competency was overused, and thus, not actually a strength. It allowed him to take on a lot of stress and just keep going, long after most people would buckle under the strain. He said,

> Years of shouldering so much negative energy and behavior was the epitome of either sink or swim. I swam; my brother sank. I would have thought early on it would have been the reverse. It was like that eighties movie, *Ordinary People*, where the weaker brother survived a boat accident in bad weather. The stronger and preferred brother drowned. The mother resented the son who lived even more.

Steve joined a local soccer league and played twice a week. Previously sports weren't enjoyable. He got so caught up in winning and fairness that he ultimately quit soccer in college, though he was apparently talented. His overutilized Assertiveness competency, which indicated a real aggressive streak, created a "win at all costs" mentality.

In the spring season of his second year in a local league, he met a young woman on another team at a barbeque after a city tournament. The first thing he said in therapy was, "She is everything I am not, or everything I haven't been." He began to describe these qualities, but I slowed him down and asked key questions. How are you both similar? What can she teach you over time? What good qualities does she see in you?

Steve worked on casting away black-and-white thinking to find the subtle shades and hues within himself and others. Through our work together he was able to create new social and relational memories. As he did this, his persistent pain receded. He said that growth and change inside him was more available than he anticipated. "Literally, Doc. I just could not have imagined this for me, in my life."

Part B

Self-Expression
How do we express what we feel? Do we treat colleagues or classmates with respect, or do we misuse the intimacy and familiarity of our loved ones to unload misdirected negative feelings—demonstrating a lack of tolerance and annoyance with people we supposedly prize? Do we express natural anger appropriately and fully in a measured way, with balance and perspective? Or do we throw temper tantrums in front

of our friends, family members, or coworkers? Or emotionally retreat where passive-aggressive attitudes and behaviors are born?

If Self-Perception is about being aware of our emotions and understanding them, Self-Expression is about how we act on this knowledge. This composite is not merely about being perfectly calm or happy or at peace; it also informs those moments when we feel bad about ourselves or our feelings, or about things transpiring in our life. Are there friends in our life with whom we can talk in an unfiltered way? Do those conversations move our well-being in the direction we want it to move? Can we build from our strengths and come closer to personal healing and emotional intelligence?

Patterns of positive or negative Self-Expression can permeate our lives. Do we exhibit healthy behaviors? Do we acknowledge when we are hurt, angry, uncertain, or frustrated? Does this occur in such a way that those on the receiving end can actually hear us—and possibly even adjust their behaviors in relation to our needs? Or do we do the opposite, becoming so exasperated that we walk out of meetings, away from relational discussions, without actually speaking our minds? Do we spend the day pissed off at a significant other because we "perceive" a slight from them? Do we treat our children like mini-adults, and rake them over the emotional coals for underperformance, without remembering that they are only children? This is my concept of the three competencies of Self-Expression:

1. Emotional Expression

This competency involves how we express what we feel, both in a verbal and nonverbal manner. Your child asks if you are mad. You say no, but the child can see anger in your face and body language. Which of the two of you is most on target?

At times, expressing our emotions can feel like walking through a minefield. Candor and honesty about what we are experiencing allows us to achieve emotional sustenance and balance. Emotional expression is about presenting the truth of what we are feeling. It is not social etiquette, or offering the right compliment to someone on their wardrobe or latest selfie. It is instead a balance between honesty about what we are feeling and presenting it in a way that draws the other person toward you, instead of pushing them away.

Say two people are out on a date. One of them has a scrunched-up expression (or maybe they're on their phone, looking bored), but answers, "Yes, I am having a great time," when the other one asks how the date is going. How does the person interpret such a response? It may be obvious that the sour-faced one is looking for an escape route. Despite the words, the questioner will inevitably pick up that signal on internal radar anyway. My client Deb nailed the essence of honest emotional expression and had a better date instead of suffering.

> I told him I just wasn't feeling it. We had a drink before dinner, and even though he seemed to be a nice guy, I didn't want to string it out. He really appreciated my honesty and said it was refreshing. From there we started laughing, telling stories, had dinner, and remain good friends to this day. Before therapy, I would never have said what was on my mind. I told people what they wanted to hear, which was usually at my expense. It is liberating to be upfront with people in a way that isn't hurtful.

She had been in therapy with me for a while and had learned an emotionally intelligent way to balance how she felt with what she said. She grew up in an environment with limited touch where feelings were rarely discussed. Her parents were very attentive to her physical needs, not her emotional ones.

2. Assertiveness

An open and honest disposition is essential if others are going to perceive us as authentic. But sometimes there can be too much of a good thing. As we saw in Steve's report, Assertiveness was his highest score. But was it really assertiveness, or just plain old aggression? After all, Steve pushed his way through things either when he sensed injustice or when he simply wanted to win. EQ-i 2.0 Assertiveness, by contrast, is respectful and socially appropriate. It is the old adage: "You say what you mean and mean what you say."

Imagine you are at a self-checkout station. The scanner says you need age verification to buy cough syrup, a substance that adolescents are known to abuse. You ask an employee why you need approval, since clearly you are over 21. However, the employee is busy helping another customer and shrugs you off with a noncommittal answer, not even making eye contact. What is your response? If you berate the employee, then you're engaging in Steve-style aggression. But if you apologize for the interruption but press on and find another employee to help you, you're assertive. Assertiveness is all about appropriately taking care of the self but not at the expense of others.

3. Independence

An emotionally independent person is confident in their beliefs and opinions, as well as their personal code of ethics or morals. However, a person like this will still seek out and process feedback. Independent people maintain a balance between their foundational beliefs and strategies and hearing how others approach certain issues. Emotionally independent individuals do consider other people's beliefs to be important and consider them in their own decision-making calculus. A former client was very much in love with her partner. A couple months into the pandemic her partner wanted to move down south. Lin had been in Washington, DC for 15 years and did not want to leave. She solicited outside advice, took in everything she heard, and held it all in front of her like a puzzle. She decided to remain in DC. Her partner's emotional reaction, which came very close to abuse, solidified her decision.

Emotionally independent individuals strive to create emotional interdependency in relationships. Their strength resides in the capacity to self-govern. They welcome the counsel of others as they deliberate. People often feel heard when interacting with an emotionally independent person. This type of person makes decisions based on their personal understanding of the issue, available information and data, and the impact it will have on others. They also reflect on how they will feel after making a decision. They are well aware of their needs and how they want those needs acknowledged by the larger world.

Part C

Interpersonal

To what degree can we actually feel what it is like to walk in someone else's shoes? Understanding what someone else is going through is central to the Interpersonal composite consisting of Interpersonal Relationships, Empathy, and Social Responsibility.

Attempting to grasp someone else's experience is the essence of empathy. Being around someone who has experienced trauma or loss is emotionally difficult, largely because we often don't know what to say. The competencies measured in the Interpersonal realm allow us to approach our fellow human beings with tact, compassion, and empathy.

This can be as simple as finding someone who has suffered a loss or hurt and gently saying: "I wish I had words right now that would somehow make you feel better or lessen this pain. I just can't imagine!" We can always offer this level of compassion, even if we can't fully fathom someone's pain. Or, if we have experienced similar circumstances, then we have the capacity to offer even more in the way of solace.

These are situations in which we can deeply and personally connect with each other. To offer comfort during times of sorrow allows us to share hope. The Interpersonal composite offers us a chance to explore the relational qualities of trustworthiness and compassion.

1. Interpersonal Relationships

Do people feel they can trust us? And if so, why? Do we feel genuine compassion for those we love? If so, how do we convey it? The Interpersonal Composite reveals the depth and strength of our friendships and love relationships.

We all strive to have mutually satisfying relationships that possess a healthy rhythm of ebb and flow, give and take. The most balanced relationships create a consistent cadence in which neither person is overburdened. The relationship flows down a river of equality. They bring out the best in us, challenging us to grow emotionally and take appropriate risks.

We've all had relationships that drain us and leave us feeling off balance. These can cause us to doubt our judgment and our intuition.

As they say in AA, if it walks like a duck, quacks like a duck, and looks like a duck, then it is a duck. But how often do we see it waddling along, with its colorful duck feathers shining in the sun, only to be told it is "really nothing at all"? If you feel that you perform most of the heavy lifting in a relationship, covering up for another person's problematic behavior, or if you feel as if you are walking a tightrope with no safety net below, then most likely you are!

Living with Someone's Disorder: Jerome After Jerome married, his wife began acting strangely. She often became hyperemotional, and as her feelings spiraled upward in intensity, she would say extremely hurtful things. Yet the more Jerome offered her support and strategies to regain balance, the worse things got. He tried to get her medical help, but she refused to see a doctor. The only person she said could help her was Jerome. Not one to shy away from a challenge, he kept at it.

His wife's parents told Jerome that she would have similar bouts while growing up. But she wouldn't go to the doctor then either, and her parents didn't force it. They would wait for the situation to burn out on its own, like a receding fire. Often this could take quite some time, leaving destruction in its wake.

Jerome's wife's behavior began to negatively affect his quality of life. He lost weight. He lost sleep. He even began losing his hair. He finally let her know he loved her, but that he couldn't love her more than she was willing to love herself. If she chose not to see a doctor and figure out what was going on, he would leave. In fact, he wanted her to see three specific doctors. He meant it and was prepared to leave if need be, though it left him feeling hollow. He also made the connection between what was happening now and how he was the principal caretaker of his mother while growing up. She had a progressive form of ALS (Lou Gehrig's disease).

Jerome's wife finally consented and made the fortuitous discovery that she had undiagnosed and untreated premenstrual dysphoric disorder. She wasn't crazy at all, but something actually physical happened to her metabolically every month that could now be treated. Once she accepted the diagnosis, she followed a treatment protocol that saved their marriage and possibly her sanity.

2. Empathy

True empathy is not mere sympathy, where we imagine how tough a situation must be. It is, rather, that famous notion of knowing what it feels like to "walk a mile in another's shoes." Empathy allows a deeper connection with someone traveling through a particularly challenging life event.

Yet even in empathy, we must seek balance. Empathy does not mean accepting other people's pain as our own. We also need helpful emotional distance. This is both protective and necessary, so that we can offer the most strength possible to people in need. If we feel the wounds as they do, then we are unable to be strong in a sustainable way.

This interplay is the fundamental definition of Empathy: We are able to partner with, and be strong for, people in their hours of challenge, while maintaining our own emotional balance.

3. Social Responsibility

This competency draws significantly from Empathy yet blazes its own unique trail. Socially responsible people actively strengthen their families, social groups, communities, and professional relationships. We give our best and add value to an enterprise, but without feeling depleted.

The essence of Social Responsibility is putting others—and the greater good—*appropriately* before your own interests. It represents a capacity to elevate people among our Venn Diagram of connections. It requires us to rely upon our empathy and commitment to guide others toward their potential.

In practice, Social Responsibility often asks us not to immediately take charge in a group, although that may eventually happen. It also calls on us to offer our talents to members of the community who may be more vulnerable, and benefit from our contributions to their own journeys.

Social Responsibility goes beyond just being socially conscious. It involves action. The word "responsibility" means actively doing things that effect change.

Interpersonal: Jennifer Jennifer, a woman in her thirties, described so poetically why she came to see me: "There is an aching in my heart that is calling me to something. I'd say it is more of a haunting, like a long-forgotten voice constantly tugging at the essence of who I am."

She connected her aching to the work of the photojournalist Shelby Lee Adams, whose photos you may want to view online before reading this section. Like Jennifer, Adams was born in Appalachia, yet he truly grew up among the photographs he had taken of that region through the years. His art allowed him to feel the impact of the lives represented in his art.

Adams's photography played a pivotal role in Jennifer's consciousness and identity formation. As Jennifer put it,

> Shelby Lee has spent decades sharing with the world the courage, honor, and dedication of the mountain people. He does this because these people are his people and his roots—his identity. He proudly chronicles for the world a life that is often overlooked and swept aside as minimally relevant and often perverse. What I have not done since leaving the holler is share my story with people. I have had countless opportunities to dispel these longstanding myths about the mountain people of Appalachia. I just quietly sidestep any discussion of my heritage and past.

Although she has not returned home since leaving at the age of 18, Jennifer inherited certain gifts from her family. For example, she considers her knowledge about the value of hard work to be their legacy. She also shared their allegiance to a personal vision and a sense that whatever she wanted could be achieved if she was willing to work for it and make the necessary sacrifices. She was often struck by the wavering values of others whom she met or worked with in the military. They seemed to base their behavior on what immediate situations dictated, and not on a fundamental sense of right or wrong. She expected more of her service experience. "You would think in the military that values, or 'positions,' if you will, would be more cut and dried. [Instead] what I learned was: 'No. We live in a society where virtually everything is relative and permissible, to a point.'"

Jennifer's parents divorced when she was 11, and she had three younger siblings. She described her father as a good and reliable man. He moved for work to a town 50 miles away, but every Thursday he would gather up the kids after school and take them to his friend's house. They would go on long hikes in the forest and set traps that his friend would check on the next day. Then they'd come back to cook a great dinner.

Jennifer left home before she was fully formed and before she could appreciate who her father was. She became emotional and tender as she talked about loving him but never really showing it.

> I was what you would have called a brooding, cynical teenager. I always thought he had more in common with my brothers and that I was [unwanted]. Looking back, that inaccurate assessment was always on my

mind. It was manufactured in my mind. He was gentle and kind to me, giving me room to be unappreciative. He would say, "the sun hasn't risen on appreciating me yet." You know I just feel overwhelmed with regret. And I hate myself for it. And I don't know what to do about it. On one hand, I feel like the biggest fake even though I have accomplished so much.

I told her that it was obvious to me that her father instilled in her some critical values that had grown and taken shape over the course of her adulthood. I said it to her this way:

As an adolescent, which you were when you left home, there was an inward awareness of your needs at the expense of realizing the needs or desires of your parents. Adolescence is a very self-serving time, where friends are most important and the adolescent feels fundamentally unknown and misunderstood by his/her parents. You left before being able to feel a sense of your own stability, which in turn would have allowed you to understand more the individuality of your father. I am struck by how loving your thoughts are toward him.

Jennifer considered this. She responded thoughtfully:

If you look at any community, there are problems. God knows I realized that after joining the military. I did notice that there was a difference between people who felt strong in their body and comfortable in who they were, and those who were more posers . . . the individual who adjusts to his or her environment to get by or be accepted! I remember talking on the phone to my father after my first deployment, and I was complaining about not really feeling connected to anyone. After listening, he said, 'you know, you never let anybody get to know you when you were here. You would keep your distance, and make excuses not to join in on things.' At that moment, it occurred to me that I was fenced off from those around me. I wouldn't extend myself in relationships or reach out to people for fear I would be discovered.

Jennifer feared being judged by where she came from rather than who she was. She told a compelling story about a time in North Carolina when her rental car had a flat tire. She had no idea what to do, where the equipment was to fix the flat, or even who to call besides the rental company, which, by this time, was long behind her.

She sat on the guardrail. Eventually, a young Black man wearing a hoodie sauntered up to her car and said to her, "I noticed you are like stuck here. You know, nowhere to go. I don't know a lot about cars, but want me to see about the tire?"

At first, Jennifer felt uneasy and tense. She profiled this guy, just like hundreds before her have done and likely will in the future. She didn't know him, but he was willing to help. She said thanks and explained that she didn't have a lot of money but could give him something. He looked at her for a long, uncomfortable moment and then asked her to pop the trunk.

He pulled back some fabric on the bottom of the trunk to reveal the car jack and tools. He studied them for a bit, playing around with them, then searched under the side of the car with his hands. He asked her if she had a manual. She looked in the glove compartment and there it was. He used it to look up tire repair, and how to place the jack on the car. He then used the right tool to try and take off the lug nuts. When they wouldn't budge, he stood up and put all his weight on the tire iron, kicking it forward as he did. And then he smiled, and said:

> Funny, right? I remember my brother telling me this joke. A guy was driving through this really creepy area with fog and all, and, you know, he was getting creeped out, when, of course, like in a horror movie, he catches a flat. So, there he is alone, all nervous in the dark, with weird sounds all around him, trying to change this tire. Well, he gets all the lug nuts off the tire, and once he does, he puts them in the hubcaps. He moves to take off the tire, since it is dark, right, he kicks the hubcap by mistake, and it flies into the sewer opening. Like, gone. He goes from nervous now to terrified, not knowing what to do. Then high on the hill, this voice, like out of nowhere, says, "Instead of four, use three lug nuts for each tire, that way you can get out of here quickly." The guy looks up at the lone light breaking through the fog, in this big ass building, with like big fences, and the kind of wire you see in prisons way up on the hill. Then he notices a sign that says, like, "Saint Elsewhere Insane Asylum." Instead of being freaked out, and, like, losing it, he is puzzled.

He yells up to the voice, "Hey, what are you doing in a place like this? That was a brilliant solution! The voice came back, "I may be crazy, but I am not stupid."

That just makes me laugh you know. My brother was a piece of work.

She had initially judged this young man, but her judgment was completely wrong. Once the tire was fixed, he said: "Have a great rest of the day." She tried to give him some money. He looked at it both appreciatively and sadly, and said, "I was raised to help people out when they needed it. You needed it and I helped. That's always enough."

That is how Jennifer was raised, too. And in that moment, because of that young man, she started to remember who she was and how she had been taught. This young man never forgot what he was taught. He never turned his back on who he was, whereas Jennifer had done just that. Now she knew she wanted to balance the ledger.

Creating a new vision of ourselves is not easy or quick, but with some strategy we can accomplish it. Jennifer looked back on her life as a road map, showing all the paths she had taken to this present moment, as well as the routes she hadn't taken. There were many possible ways she could have gone. Some were scenic and open. Others were congested and frustrating. The beautiful part for Jennifer, and for all of us, is that the choice was up to her. It's up to any of us.

So how does this connect back to Shelby Lee Adams? Well, that path led her back to the holler. It shaped her thinking, feelings, and behavior. There is nothing magical about this. It requires bringing the pictures of our journey to life and making them as real in our minds and hearts as Shelby Lee Adams likely intended in sharing his photographs.

I asked Jennifer about the Adams photos. What sort of album would she create from these pictures of growing up in Appalachia? How could the collection depict her strength, the durability of the values she held so close, and the importance of family relationships that shaped her early development?

I invited her to consider creating her own album. What type of pictures would she use, or what would she want to go into her album? It is an opportunity to acknowledge what you have accomplished, who you are, and where you came from. This is an album of celebration!

"Explaining is cognitive," I told her. "It's a rational exercise, if you will. However, *showing* is emotional and linked to what is most important in your heart." This is the power of using pictures instead of words. Shelby Lee's photos connected with you emotionally.

Even though Jennifer was successful in the military, she did not internalize her success. By shifting her goals and visualizing specifically what life she wanted, she could start with a new, blank canvas on her easel. Having measurable goals and a clear vision is essential for all of us if we hope to capitalize on our innate talents. Afterward we continue to add touches of paint over time, adding to the picture as it emerges.

Looking at Jennifer's initial EQ-i 2.0 results in figure 2.2, and her competency scores, was not a surprise. As imagined, low Self-Regard kept her from celebrating who she was in the world. When I listened to her tell her story, however, I knew she also had strong Emotional Self-Awareness. Similarly, her robust Emotional Expression meant she could talk about her feelings.

She had such clear strengths but an accompanying deficit in her ability to feel emotionally independent. This was a bit surprising, considering that Interpersonal Relationships formed her strongest composite. While she took care of herself financially and made good life decisions each day, she did not feel emotionally independent.

Jennifer's insecurity about her Appalachian heritage loomed large. Dodging or lying about questions related to personal history reinforced her feeling of being emotionally stuck. Instead of being herself, she watched what others did and mimicked them. This reduced her sense of Optimism and her ability to solve emotional problems.

Jennifer's low Independence and Self-Regard competencies contributed to an unwillingness to speak up and speak out about her feelings. Yet her Flexibility score suggested that she copes fairly well with change and unpredictable situations, which is how she was able to handle two tours in Afghanistan. Considering that she left home at 18, knowing so little of the larger world, this Flexibility makes sense. Since Jennifer had a positive and decorated career in the military and is now a consultant for the Department of Defense, her high Self-Actualization score was also not surprising.

We developed a plan to leverage her strong Empathy and Social Responsibility while also nourishing her emotional needs. This would strengthen her lower competencies, while providing a path to visualize the exact type of intimate relationship she yearned for. While she had good friends, what she did not have success with was maintaining an intimate relationship. Although she had been in combat and traveled the far reaches of the world, her Stress Tolerance was low because she was not honest about who she was. Her worry about making a mistake and being "found out" cast a long shadow in her lived experience.

Toward the end of therapy, Jennifer shared these observations with me:

> I had dinner the other night with a guy I have had my eye on for a while. Those kind of initial relationship moments usually include questions like "Where are you from?" "What are you about?" I shared with him my background. He was intrigued and wanted to know more. I asked him if he had preconceived notions of Appalachia. He said the usual brewing moonshine and cousins marrying one another. He also said hearing my story changed, in an important way, his perception of what he now realizes are a proud people. I felt like a superhero at that moment. I mean what he said felt great, but even if he didn't say anything, I would have felt the same just because I let him know who I was.

Jennifer has not deviated from this course since sharing this story!

After eight months of meeting with me either weekly or bi-weekly, and working hard to construct the life she wanted, I asked Jennifer to take the EQ-i 2.0 again. Figure 2.3 shows the results. Everything moved in the direction Jennifer wanted it to go. She became even more aware of her feelings and felt empowered to express them when appropriate. Her hard work, determination, and belief in what she wanted is evident in the 15 competencies.

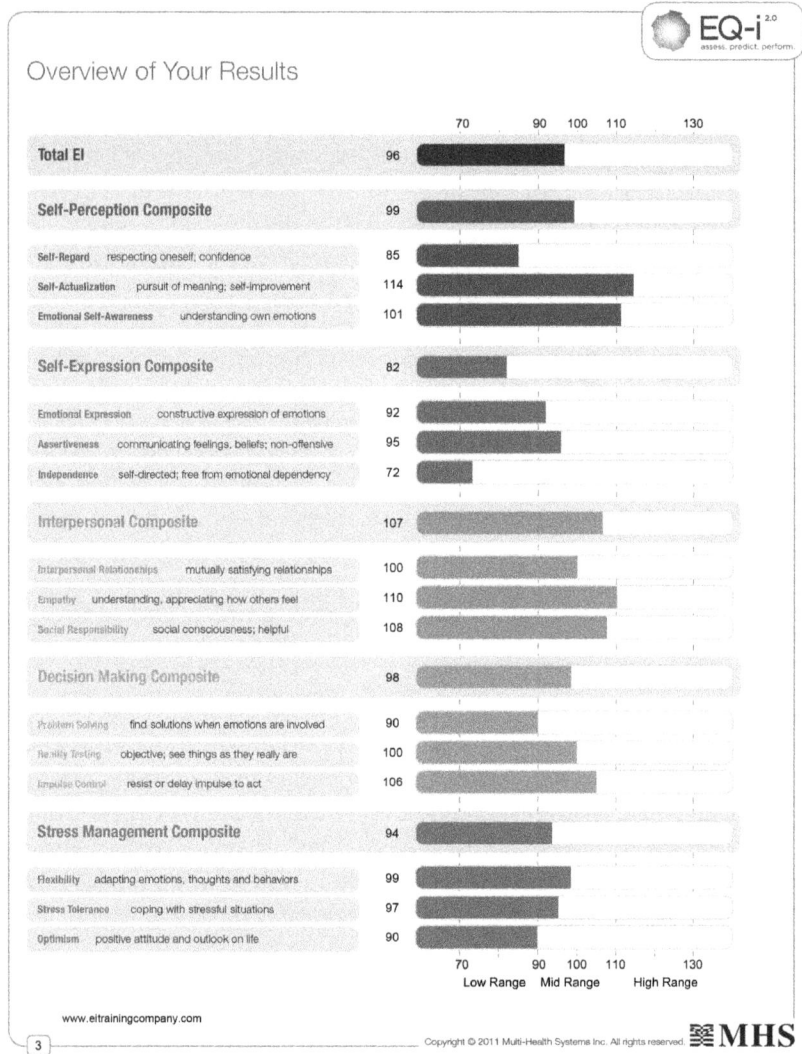

Figure 2.2.

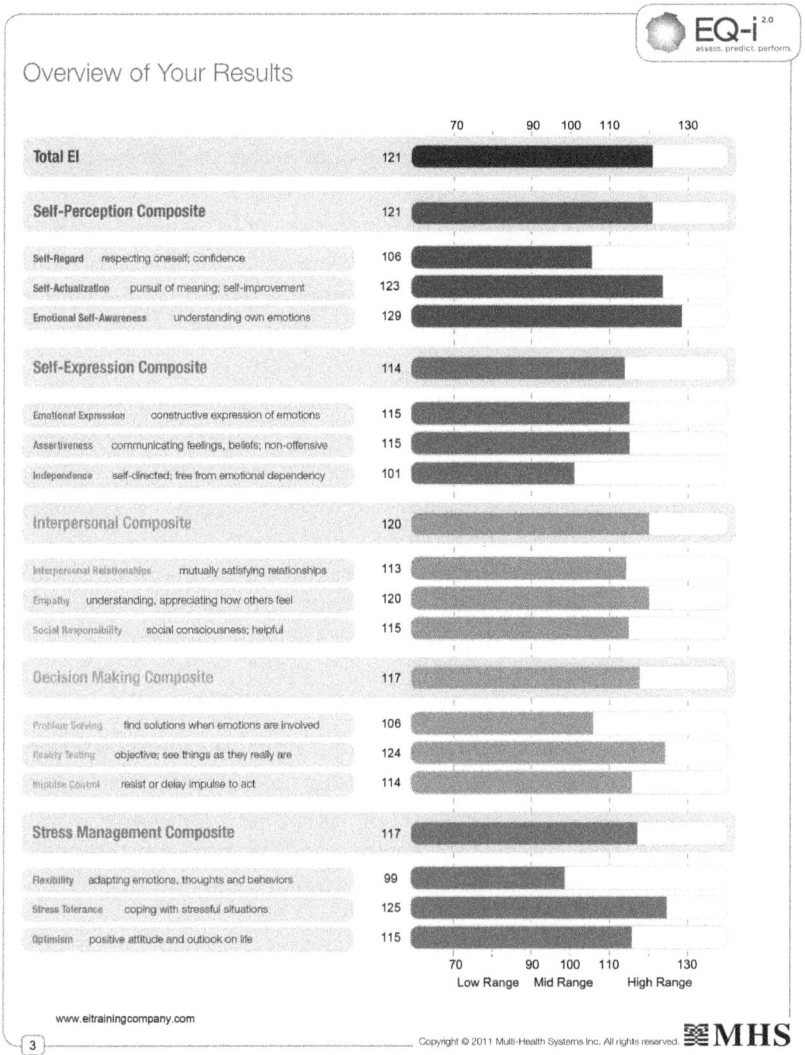

Figure 2.3.

Part D

Decision-Making

How well do we understand how our emotions influence the decisions we make? The Decision-Making composite measures how well we use and balance our EI competencies when we ponder something and then act upon it.

Our decisions are intimately tied to our states of Emotional Self-Awareness and Emotional Expression. In many ways, the Decision-Making composite bridges our contemplation of a challenge and the action that follows. Decision-Making engages an active interplay among our problem-solving, reality-testing, and impulse-control competencies. They measure the reliability of the bridge that we build between our emotional awareness and our subsequent expressions and actions.

The information in this composite permits us to gauge our ability to slow things down and digest the details of a situation. It also offers clues to how accurately we interpret information (Reality-Testing). What we think is going on with another person may well be inaccurate. Checking out our feelings, assumptions, and observations will allow us to know where we stand with the varied relationships in our life. Learning to pump the brakes and slow things down is particularly important, especially if we tend to be impulsive.

1. Problem-Solving

How effective are our self-regulation techniques against emotional tailspins? The intensity of the forces pushing against us fluctuates based on how we perceive the events. How steady and reasonable are we when the heat is on? Do we race headlong, without specific strategies? Or do we stop to understand what we want to accomplish and what potential risks lie ahead?

The objective is not to vanquish difficult emotions. Rather, we can use them as leverage to achieve desired outcomes. This Problem-Solving competency also allows us to slow down enough to engage our critical-thinking skills.

Say you are running an important meeting. What do you do when attendees saunter in late and unprepared, or when they do not achieve your stated goals? Do you become authoritarian and yell? Do you resort to passive-aggressive behavior? Or do you slow down the emotional process and steer the ship? Acknowledging your frustration, with an eye toward what could be achieved, may facilitate a better direction for the entire group.

These are moments when our emotional side and rational/thinking side engage in a choreographed dance. We have seen how this is true of children. Think of a morning when you are trying to get out the door with the kids, and they are dawdling, playing with toys, and chasing each other around the house. Do you explode? Or do you employ a method from one of the positive parenting books out on the market? Or do you shepherd them toward what you want via threats while unraveling emotionally?

The point is not to pretend you are not angry! You can be angry and still convey what you are experiencing in a measured way that people can hear. Leading with anger—or its disguised sibling, passive aggression—can bring out the angry adolescent in others. This is often counterproductive and even more maddening.

On the positive side, though, harnessing emotional problem-solving skills can strengthen relationships. This competency gives us a sense of security—both with ourselves and with others—by demonstrating that we can weather emotional turbulence.

Problem-solving often is not linear. Problem "A" does not always lead to emotional response "B." Emotions are like tributaries that flow into a river, one that can easily overflow its banks. Stepping back from those rising waters can enhance our perspective and protect us from being swept into the depths. Perspective gives us scope and the opportunity to reach higher ground.

Emotional problem-solving strengthens our personal relationships. In turn, there is an essential mutuality, as strong personal relationships reinforce our emotional problem-solving skills.

2. Reality-Testing

Do we seek clarification during uncertainty? Assessing our capacity for Reality-Testing reveals our ability to remain objective in emotionally trying circumstances.

Let's say you are speaking with your partner about something you think is important. As you talk, you feel emotionally frozen out. Your partner gives clipped answers and lacks interest in what you say. Instead of being hurt, however, you conduct a reality test by sharing your feelings and observations about this situation. You may learn that your partner simply feels depleted, or that they have been stretched by unrealistic time demands at work, which serve to fully distract them.

Checking your feelings and observations this way directly prevents us from relying on faulty assumptions. It also prevents the possible unhealthy reactions we have to a perceived slight. I think of these as clarifications where these reality tests light the unlit spaces within relationships. I call this the "in and out" aspect of relationships. One person is in, wanting to talk, share, and connect with their partner. But the other person is out, with focus and attention somewhere else completely. This happens to all of us at one time or another in relationships. The key is to know how to acknowledge what you are experiencing at the moment it happens. Then you can learn what's really going on and not take things so personally. It also keeps the typical negative escalation in check.

3. Impulse Control

It is hard to avoid the temptation to have a "knee jerk reaction" to upsetting situations. Measuring the Impulse Control competency gives us a window into our capacity to act with prudence and balance.

All of us have an ability to slow things down and gather more facts before making important decisions. For some, it comes naturally. But for most of us, it is a skill we must develop. Even though many don't possess this skill because it is acquired, it is essential to our emotional balance. No one wants to feel controlled by instinctive responses.

Healthy impulse control helps us establish predictability in our relationships. Say you have had a long day, and work was stressful. Things did not come together the way you anticipated, and you felt mounting degrees of disappointment as the afternoon progressed. However, when you get home you find that your partner is not there, which is unusual, and you're now all alone. When your partner does come home, they can't even get past a greeting before you erupt: "You know, you are just like all the other unreliable people in my life. You can't even do something as simple as being here for me after I had a grueling day!"

What you don't know—and didn't take time to learn—is that your partner's best friend was experiencing a crisis. The disappointment of not seeing an expected loved one after a long, tough day is understandable. Taking time to gather some facts, including sharing your mutual frustrations, strengthens the relationship. This allows you to spend time together as you share both of your experiences of that day. Like anything else, our emotional responses can get stuck in patterns; these patterns then present themselves as triggers.

The key is slowing things down. You can learn breathing techniques to accompany you as you reflect on what you are experiencing. Now, you're able to imagine what your partner may be going through, all outside of your own awareness.

Decision-Making: Marsha

Marsha was filled with monstrous self-doubt, and this gentle person existed within a mountain of sadness. She wanted to believe her woundedness was hidden from those around her, including herself, but others could see it whether she acknowledged it or not.

She came by this doubt quite honestly. What she worked so meticulously to conceal from the world was a tortuous childhood. Marsha's mother was a functioning alcoholic, at least initially, who tried to compensate by creating the impression that nothing at home was awry.

Everything seemed to be in order. This attempt to create external order while the interior walls are splitting apart is something I have heard from many clients. The house was always clean. Her father had a solid management position. Her mother was always publicly running errands. But no one knew the brutality Marsha's mother leveled against her when she returned from school. Her mother would ridicule her. She often allowed Marsha's brother to beat her by not interrupting. When they wanted her gone, they would lock her in a windowless, cramped powder room. Marsha's mother often justified this by accusing her of lying, though Marsha had no idea what she was supposed to have lied about.

The feeling in Marsha's stomach coming home each day was indescribable. Her mother barred her from extracurricular activities, including working. She could not socialize with anyone. Her mother thought of her as different and awkward, and she described her to others that way. Yet Marsha's good friends in school thought she was great. They could not understand why she never met them to hang out after school or on the weekends, and she could not talk about it. She felt disloyal even imagining what it would be like to share this with a friend.

Marsha was intellectually gifted and graduated high school at 16. For the first time she felt relief because she would be able to leave home, and this kept her going. She received a full scholarship to a local university, but she wanted to attend a private school. Because that would require her parents to pay some of the expenses, they refused. When she said she would take out all the loans to attend the school, they refused.

So, Marsha had to attend the local school, and her parents made her live at home. It was one of the most devastating episodes in a life so full of them. Instead of crumbling or giving up, she lived at home the first two years. Since her parents didn't really know her schedule, Marsha stayed away from home as much as possible. When she turned 18, she got a job to pay for her own housing off campus and never looked back. She trained for a career as a therapist after getting a sizeable grant to attend a graduate program in social work in another state after graduating college.

Marsha mentioned that she was already developing an emancipation plan at just six years old.

> I almost felt like the little girl in the movie *Matilda*. I certainly felt Matilda's level of emotional abandonment and the feeling that she was a burden to her mother. I have always been a very nervous person, a nervousness I have not been able to shake. It is also hard to acknowledge, but I married my mother. The man I married treats me almost identically to the way my mother treated me. I suppose there is no rest for the weary, and I feel so . . . worn out.

After hearing her story and considering the model utilized throughout this book, I asked what she considered her greatest strengths:

> My strengths, well, I am not completely sure. I think I am a good therapist, though it is often psychically hard for me to hear people go through so much turmoil. I tend to carry it home with me like leftovers after a meal. It has a tendency to magnify my nervousness and anxiety. I had a client once say that I seemed so ill at ease in our session because I have so many body and facial tics. My body just keeps moving in almost an uncontrollable way.

I kept trying to bring Marsha back to what she saw as her strengths, although it was difficult to do so. Repeatedly, she tried to move the conversation to something else. It was exceedingly uncomfortable for her to talk candidly about her strengths: "Talking about the positive parts of me is like imagining it is beautiful and sunny out during a rainstorm. The image doesn't match reality."

"That is a great analogy," I said. "What I suggest is not to pretend or bend reality. I am suggesting taking a bit of distance from where you are right now, like stepping out of your present situation and acquiring a 100-foot view, to see parts of yourself that are there and often underrepresented in your perspective."

When she tried this, Marsha saw how she had been marginalized in every way imaginable. After the difficulties of life with her parents, her husband was gaslighting her relentlessly. You may already be familiar with gaslighting, in which a partner makes you question your own sanity by demanding that the things you observe about the relationship aren't true. He told her that she had not accomplished the many things she had achieved, from starting her own business at 25 to obtaining her Master of Social Work degree, let alone surviving soul-crushing cruelty at home. The world from which she came whispered that she should accept this cruelty, rather than challenge it and get away. Because of Marsha's doubts and fears, the best parts of her were hidden in plain sight.

Take her entrepreneurship, for example. Once, in my office, she shared two remarkable ideas for internet-based businesses. Yet she was barely audible as she whispered them to me. That whisper became a metaphor for how she had been trained to live her life.

It was truly impressive to see her talent and intellect weave together over future sessions. Her husband thought it was all "smoke and mirrors," and even denigrated her knowledge of the internet. But she became committed to building a new business, embracing her strengths, and in doing so, challenging the ever-present emotional pain.

The results of Marsha's EQ-i 2.0 are in figure 2.4. Her competency scores shed light on the depth of her suffering, both at the hands of her family and her husband. Because of sustained abuse, she felt little, if any, Emotional Independence. Announcing her thoughts was tantamount to exposing herself to public shaming. Because she felt so irrelevant, her ability to emotionally Problem-Solve with any accuracy was limited. She did feel positive about herself as a person (Self-Regard). This was related to her self-perception of being a good therapist, which is a testament to the strength of the spirit and her ability. She also was able to find and hold on to trusting loyal female friends (Interpersonal Relations).

Marsha's impulsiveness often materialized as saying the first thing that entered her mind. She did not think about it, or emotionally problem-solve a situation (her lowest competency), but always relied

Figure 2.4.

on her feelings. She had a network of childhood friends. However, others with whom she interacted daily concluded she was internally disorganized or ditzy. Those years of systemic abuse did lend an air of emotional disorganization to her self-presentation.

When she reflected after the fact on what she said to clients, Marsha was disappointed and would even cringe. We helped her adapt her clinical practice with a new strategy. She would ask clients to tell her what they had tried to do about whatever problem or situation they discussed. As she outlined what she had done thus far, she would have time to slow things down in her mind, coming up with a response that honored the depth of her Empathy and Social Responsibility. That question became the fulcrum around which she consistently managed her impulsivity. She used that same strategy in her daily interactions, with ever-increasing success.

As we can see with the Reality-Testing competency, Marsha was acutely aware of her pain, the dysfunction of her past, and the role she had played in it all. According to her, remaining in her marriage was one reflection of this dysfunction. She became a lightning rod for those too shallow and mired in their own pain to see the pain they caused her.

> I suppose I don't know what it is really like to be free. I have always felt incarcerated. Although, no one could really see it. I just looked like this privileged white woman in the world dreaming up worries to excuse away my good fortune. It is funny what really counts as good fortune in this world.

I was not surprised when one of Marsha's big ideas eventually blossomed into a successful business. By applying her talents and determination, she freed herself from years of enslaved beliefs and habits. Eventually she also freed herself from a suffocating marriage. Marsha's nervous tics subsided conspicuously as she adopted meditation and mindfulness strategies, and her accomplishments grew.

Part E

Stress Management
Many threads weave together to form our Stress Management composite. It measures our competencies of Flexibility, Stress Tolerance, and

Optimism. It explores our response to change, how well we manage challenges in our lives, and how hopeful we are that we will achieve our goals and live purposefully.

It also measures our capacity to align priorities. You often hear people comment on the number of tasks they juggle. Their workload requires enormous concentration and energy. Aligning responsibilities properly means we take on what we can—and, at times, what we have to. Forecasting the impact of those responsibilities is a step toward managing stress effectively.

For example, if you want to have a child, with or without a partner, how will this impact your life? What effect will moving from one job to another have? No one can know with certitude what the eventual impact of such decisions might be. But one *can* align perspective with probability.

Stress Management also requires we identify—and seek out—support to make specific transitions easier. Those of us who manage stress well also manage ourselves well. We feel good about who we are and where we are going. This allows us to accommodate detours when they crop up. We do not rely on things outside of ourselves to make us feel consistently better or to drain away stress. Our internal coping strategies operate synergistically to keep us in balance.

1. Flexibility

Most people like to feel rooted in the familiar. However, when a deviation from our routine occurs, it can move us from feeling unbalanced to becoming emotionally unhinged.

Navigating inevitable changes requires solid strategies to address disruptions in our emotional force fields. Taking stock of our Flexibility allows us to assess how accurately we find the sweet spot to balance changes, both anticipated and unanticipated. Most parents can relate to anticipating a busy day at work, while also discovering the phone volume was set too low to hear the alarm, and that the other shoe is missing. Throw in a sick child, a spouse who's out of town, and the sudden need to stay home to take care of it all. On days like these, flexibility counts.

The more intentional we are regarding specific strategies for managing change or stress, the greater emotional flexibility we possess. Perception is one key strategy. If we think we always "know" a certain level of change is going to be disruptive and throw us off kilter, then we will be right! That old adage, "whatever you believe is true," usually proves accurate. A young man was in the final stages of Qualifying School (Q School) to become a special forces Green Beret. They were doing river training, when, after a few days in the river, he got out of the water and began taking off his gear. An instructor came up to him and said, "Pardon the pun, however you're about to wash-out of Q School with only a very little time left before wearing the beret. When you step into the river, what are you thinking?" The soldier asked to talk freely and said, "I can't stand the water and I know if I find myself in the water, I'll figure out a way to get out. This sucks for me, pure and simple." The instructor said, "Yeah, that is what we are seeing." He began walking away. He stopped on the top of a berm and said, "You may want to ask yourself what that river can teach you." He then walked away. The next day, river training was over, and the soldier was taking off his gear when the same instructor came up to him and said, "I don't know who got in that river today, but it sure was a different person than the past few days." So, what changed? Not the river, not the soldier, not the training, and not the requirements. What changed was the soldier's perspective. Our perspectives determine so many of the outcomes in our life. The healthier and more grounded our perceptions, the better the overall outcome in terms of what we want and what we want to achieve.

We often stress about things either before they happen or before we know the outcome. Feeling secure in your skill set, surrounding yourself with trustworthy people, and planning the things you want to accomplish with respect to change, all enhance our sense of Flexibility. And flexibility is about having the right perspective.

2. Stress Tolerance

By now, you should be able to see interplay among discrete competencies. While each is individually necessary, they are insufficient in themselves to move someone toward strong social and emotional intelligence.

Stress Tolerance relies upon our strengths in multiple competencies. It requires a strong belief in self (Self-Regard). We must also possess confidence (Optimism) that we can manage emotional challenges. Attention to our emotional constellation (Emotional Self-Awareness), and how we want to govern our emotions to address the stressor (Emotional Expression and Flexibility) is also necessary and completely up to us.

The interplay among these competencies creates sturdiness within us and a personal resilience. When we experience anxiety, we are often in the midst of the storm without a viable survival strategy. It is not that we don't try to stabilize the anxiety. We do. Yet we often find ourselves falling into patterns of thinking and feeling that keep us stuck and continually resuscitating our anxious feelings.

3. Optimism

Optimistic people feel emotionally and socially equipped to deal with life's inevitable challenges. They are not optimistic because they had it easier growing up. Often, they did not. Instead, along their life path they noticed people who approached life with a sense of hope, irrespective of personal trials. In the face of setbacks, they remain confident that the sun will rise again. This quality personifies resiliency.

Optimistic people focus on what is possible. On a regular basis, they reflect on how they want to feel and what they want to achieve. They seem positive about who they are and assert themselves to achieve their desired goals. This optimism within resilient people can be both contagious and maddening. Their hope bolsters our hope while making us wonder how they are able to rise above the fray. Emotional and social competency indeed does leave clues to how it is achieved and maintained. It is up to us whether or not we want to follow the stones that have been sprinkled on the path before us leading to emotional intelligence.

Stress Management: Ray

Ray was an 18-year-old college freshman when we first met. His first-year colloquium class at Georgetown University required taking the EQ-i 2.0. The students examine their results in class as I go over a sample report on an overhead projector. I guide them in analysis, pointing out how to utilize the competencies in ways that make sense to them, improving the possibility that they will refer to their competencies beyond class.

If a person measures strikingly low in certain competencies or possesses a low "Well-Being Indicator" (as noted previously) the combined score of Self-Actualization, Interpersonal Relationships, Self-Regard, and Optimism), I send them a note inviting them to come in and talk about how to use their strengths to raise the competencies that need enrichment.

I want to share Ray's competencies in figure 2.5 before describing his story.

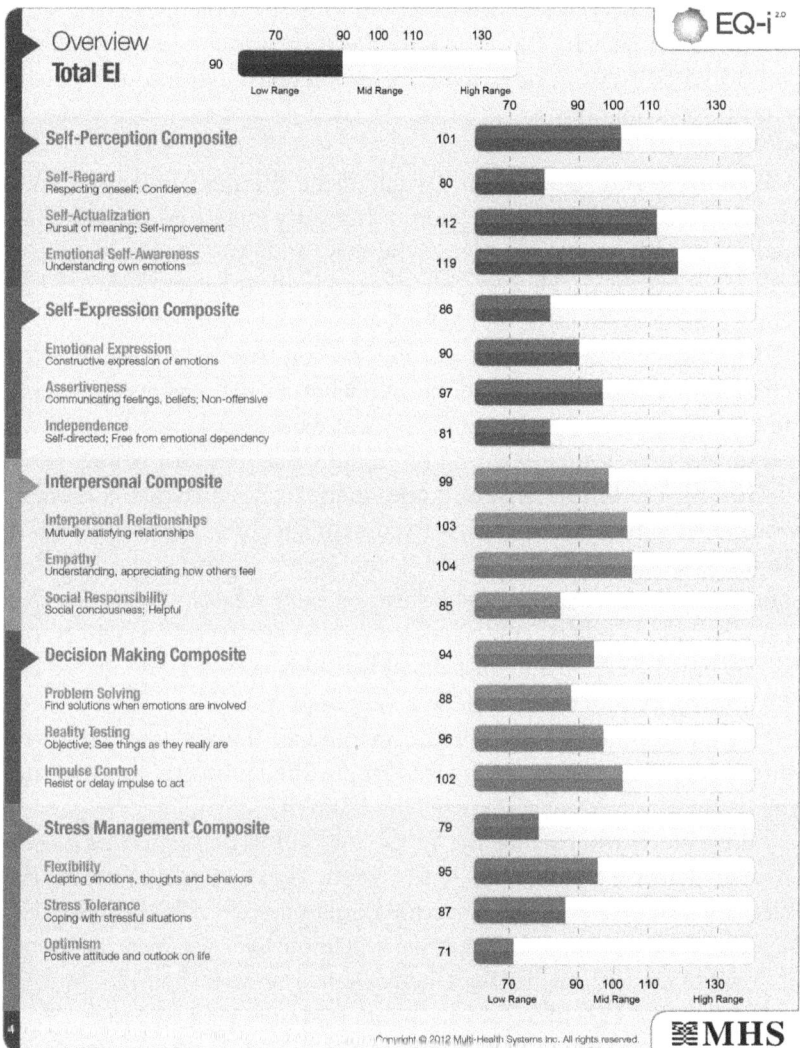

Figure 2.5.

Now that you have become more familiar with how the competencies interact and what they specifically mean, how would you describe the way Ray saw himself and the world?

Five of the 15 were in the "Area for Enrichment" category, with the others varying in strength. His Self-Regard, Independence, Social Responsibility, Optimism, and Emotional Problem-Solving were exceedingly low. His Emotional Expression was far lower than his Emotional Self-Awareness, which is problematic because the person is aware of what they are feeling, yet they do not take advantage of talking about it.

Looking at Ray on paper, you would think this guy has what it takes to excel. He was the valedictorian of his fairly large high school class, graduated with several academic honors, and was an accomplished high school wrestler. He certainly worked hard to accomplish what he wanted and had the skill set to do it.

What was glaringly absent was any feeling that he mattered in the world. Ray reported never feeling like what he did was good enough. He failed to measure up to standards that existed only in his mind. Of course, the question here is measure up to what? And for whom?

This self-incrimination was omnipresent in Ray's thoughts no matter what he achieved. He always lived with a feeling of being less than. He was the youngest of three boys, the oldest of whom was killed in combat in 2006. Ray was just beginning high school, and up to that point he largely played the class clown. His parents and teachers said he was unfocused. A therapist diagnosed him with ADHD at the age of eight. As he described it, he was very high in H.

"I was pretty much untethered," he told me. "I just floated from one thing to another, leaving in my wake unfinished projects, chores either half done or not done, you know, you name it."

I understood what he meant. In the mid-1990s I co-authored a book about it! Patricia Quinn, MD, and I wrote *Voices from Fatherhood: Fathers, Sons and ADHD*. We examined only boys who "had the big H," meaning they were both hyperactive and impulsive. We were interested in how fathers with highly hyperactive sons parented their children.

Historically, kids like Ray are the most challenging to parent. They take up so much emotional and physical space at home and in school, requiring a substantial outlay of energy and dedication by both teachers and parents. We wanted to know what type of father was successful in both perspective and attitude. We also wanted to know what happened between the father and son with kids who did not thrive in school and at home.

Fathers who had success with their big-H kids did so with a great deal of thought, patience, and partnering. They either instinctively or purposively relied on Positive Parenting. They also had a vision of what they wanted to accomplish. These were highly emotionally intelligent men, who realized they would either positively or negatively contribute to their child's growth. As one father said:

> I just wasn't going to let the ADHD be a distraction from loving my boy fully and totally. Because of me and my wife, this young boy grew to be a good man, a loving person, and contribute positively to society. My father saw the opposite in me and, in spite of him, I turned out okay. My little guy did not have a very bright prognosis. The doctors said he would struggle in school, experience consistent social tension, and be someone more suited for the trades, like carpentry or plumbing. According to them, this would be less demanding than college for reasons I still can't figure out. Our plumber puts me to shame with his fund of knowledge and the amount he makes. If he was going to be a carpenter, then it would be because that is truly what he wanted, not because that was his default setting. He went on to do masterfully in college and land a remarkable job in hospital sales.

I remembered what we had learned from this book when approaching Ray and his needs. In terms of living with his ADHD, Ray told me:

> You know I was a time gobbler. I really was like a wound-up Jack Russell terrier. Just moving all the time, saying stupid stuff to people, and getting a lot of eye rolls. I rarely finished what I started unless it was a video game. And video games would make me so angry that it really wasn't worth playing. I know being around my dad really pissed him off. And, because he didn't like being around me, I acted out even worse. I mean, go figure. Why would I want even more distance from him? He was a good dad. The problem was I was compared to my older brother who was calm, considered in his interpersonal relationships, said the right things, was going to West Point after the military. He was just a really great guy who had patience with me. Patience I didn't have with myself. I remem-

ber before he deployed, he said: "Listen, if you don't start controlling this, it will control you. Like a prison guard controlling the prisoners. It will keep you under its thumb. You are such a smart kid. Start showing it. People see you as a goof. That is not what I see." He hugged me for a long time. I didn't want him to leave. He was my ground wire.

Except for a satellite phone call here and there or an email, that encounter was Ray's last memorable moment with his brother. The memory of that last hug was emblazoned in his heart and soul, like getting a tattoo.

When his brother was killed, the world's axis began spinning in the opposite direction. No more screwing around, no more "dipshit pranks," as he would say. Overnight, he woke up a different person, one who seemed to have been bitten by a creature that sucked out all the venomous ADHD. He became serious, deliberate, and sullen. His freshman year in high school he did nothing but homework, except for wrestling.

Why wrestling? Well, his brother loved it and took him to high school matches. His brother didn't wrestle, but he thought Ray should.

"He was right," Ray observed. "I was very good and put all my angst into each moment on the mat."

The death of his brother became, in many ways, the death of Ray's family. Everyone closed off, went to their respective corners, and never came out to take on the world again. His parents' emotional abandonment was another death in the family. His older brother started getting into and selling drugs—an occurrence no one noticed until he was expelled from school.

> My mother saw a big difference in me and often expressed concern because even though I did well in school, I didn't really have any friends. Life just felt too harrowing and unpredictable, so I just kept busy on what I could control.

After his brother's death, that idea of control became his guiding premise. If he couldn't control it, he ignored it. Meanwhile, his dad began working more and coming home less. His mother went back to work full-time. Everyone poured themselves into something other than one another. Family life became an active and deliberate quest for distraction.

After Ray's brother's funeral, there was no celebration of a life well-lived. His brother was really never spoken of again. It was too painful to talk about him. He had really been the glue in the family. Ray recalled:

I overheard my dad saying to him that there were many ways to serve his country. Fighting in combat did not have to be one of them. He felt obligated and also felt that would facilitate him getting into West Point, which it did. He was accepted to USMAPS, the preparatory school for the Academy. However, instead of attending the preparatory school, he wanted to show his ability *in vivo* rather than in the classroom. You know, I wish I could go back and get a redo on junior high. He so believed in me. But we don't get a redo. It is what it is.

We discussed Ray's transition from being that self-styled "Jack Russell terrier" to a steely-eyed watch dog. It happened almost reflexively and outside of his awareness. All these things lined up to push him in a different direction. His description of it and my response are key elements of this story:

Actively peeling all this back to examine it . . . feels like peering into a deep well. I wouldn't know how to approach it. Everything up until now just seems to have kind of happened, you know. It is like I didn't choose it. It was the logical outgrowth of losing my brother.

Even with all the noticeable changes, Ray still saw himself as this out-of-control middle schooler. "I have changed," he said, "but it is like painting a zebra blue. It is still a black and white zebra underneath." That's when I challenged him:

Even though you have changed considerably, in a way it seems Billy would be so proud of you, yet you won't cut yourself a break and acknowledge what it has taken to rise from the ashes of this out-of-control kid. It would be interesting to see you embrace your accomplishments and the choices you have made to get this far. Feeling like a painted zebra is based on all the messages and feelings you had growing up. Now, you can truly choose what type of animal you want to be. The only restrictions exist in how you think about you.

Guilt! It was guilt holding him back. Guilt that it took his brother's death for him to change. "Had he lived," Ray said, "I doubt I would be here speaking with you."

What he failed to hold onto was that his brother's memory began to liberate Ray from the stone Billy handed him in their last conversation. The stone was given to Billy by his instructor at boot camp. He said the stone reminded him of Billy. Billy said the stone represented strength, being personally solid and consistent. That is where it began, not at the news of his death. Ray was honoring his brother's life, not death. I told him:

> It seems his parting words to you were a gift. One you started opening after he was gone. Completely unwrapping the gift means beginning to love yourself the way he loved you.

Ray felt loving himself would mean relaxing, and that such relaxation would invite the crazy 12-year-old out to play. He gave himself no wiggle room to be human, which invariably meant that he made mistakes. That's why his Independence score was so low. He directed all his emotional energy into being what his brother expected out of him, and he never really owned what he was achieving.

Ray described his friendship with his brother, what he missed, and what that friendship gave him. He acknowledged he hadn't been very flexible or realistic with himself. He also imagined what it would be like to challenge himself more socially in college and to allow himself more personal Flexibility.

What would a more enriched sense of reality look like? It was a double-edged sword. The risk of letting people in or getting close to others meant they could leave him. He also might be exposed as a fraud if the old Ray were to appear.

The more that Ray was able to envision what he wanted and actually see it in his mind's eye, the more self-assurance he experienced, the more positive social risk-taking he pursued. We made the connection between believing in who he is now, and subsequently inviting people into his life. Taken together, they will reinforce the fact that he has grown past the out-of-control kid with ADHD, even though that outdated image plays such a prominent role in his mind.

His brother's death accelerated a developmental shift. Relaxing became associated with deeper levels of happiness. It also meant Ray began to believe in who he was as a person. I believe this developmental shift would have occurred at some point regardless. But now, thanks to him seeing it for himself in his competencies, Ray has a new lease on life orbiting around living a desired life—not avoiding one.

CHAPTER THREE

The Competencies as Levers for Change

Each client's competencies are unique. But there are discernible patterns that can assist in shepherding all of us toward a renewed and stronger self. If the Self-Regard competency was extremely low, we would begin looking at the other competencies to leverage and strengthen a negative self-image.

Reinventing a Self: David

David came to me hiding behind a make-believe persona that was slowly suffocating him. He was prone to lying about his past. And while he looked like a superstar to most people, a look at his EQ-i 2.0 in figure 3.1 revealed that his Self-Regard was extremely low and that it was accompanied by low Emotional Self-Awareness. Yet his Self-Actualization score was high.

One finding that really caught David's eye—and served as an initial catalyst to change—was his low Reality-Testing score. This meant even he had significant difficulties differentiating between fact and fiction in his own narrative. Once he recognized and owned the ubiquitous stranglehold that lying had on his life, David could inhabit tactical strategies to foster the emotional liberation attached to manufacturing an authentic life.

The EQ-i 2.0 measures competencies that provide words to the melody of our experience. They work in sync to create something neither one alone could provide. In David's case, his EQ-i 2.0 results inspired him to create change.

In our first meeting, he said, "I tend to overstate the truth or very occasionally engage in fabrication."

I replied, "Fabrication is the television show, *Pimp My Ride*, when they totally redo a vehicle on its last legs. You mean you tend to lie."

David put his head down a bit, then gazed to the left, sifting through his memories. "Yes," he said, "That feels un-redemptive to me. But since you aren't going to let me 'play through,' so to speak, yes. I tend to lie at times."

I suggested that his semantic distinctions were a way "to subdue, or tame, if you will, this wild beast called lying."

David's propensity to lie was woven into his background. His father was a set designer who had worked on many famous movies, and his mother was a talent agent. In reality, his father has been incarcerated since he was five. To this day, and against all the evidence, David's father claims he did not commit the crimes for which he was convicted. However, his actions were captured on CCTV. A distinctive item of clothing he was known to wear appeared prominently on the screen. His initials were even on it in big, bold letters. David's mother, who has never worked, had written off the relationship completely.

Skilled athletically and intellectually gifted, but surrounded by chaos, David coped with the stress by devising alternative stories about his life. He began in junior high school. Teachers and others were so impressed by these tales that he wove them more and more. Over time, these stories became his reality. At times even he believed them.

David was now in a great university with a scholarship. He had nothing but the wind at his back. Yet part of him felt like a ticking bomb. If it detonated, his life of deceit would come crashing down. Could he let go of a family tradition where everyone lied, even in the face of clear evidence?

"If it weren't so tragic," David said, "it would almost be laughable."

David's English teacher saw unparalleled promise in him, more so than any student he had taught. He introduced David to college professors and writing groups, which David lapped up hungrily. "Had it not been for my teacher," he said, I shudder to imagine where I would be today. He said athletic talent will someday slow down to an eventual crawl, often sooner rather than later, and if you have exercised your brain as convincingly as your body, [you can] achieve whatever you put your mind to.

Fortunately, David's competencies were a foundation for the course correction he desired. While he had a robust Self-Regard score, that was not the key to making change in his life. David felt good about who he was in the world only because he could create any scenario he desired. For David, Self-Regard was a sort of role playing. If he genuinely reflected upon the scope of his untruths, then he would have had a much lower Self-Regard score.

Rather, it was acknowledging his low Emotional Self-Awareness that defused the bomb. Lying, by necessity, had limited his Emotional Self-Awareness. Indeed, before therapy, David didn't even see himself as telling falsehoods. For him, lying was a creative survival skill that increased his ability to tolerate and move through his environment.

Since David's Awareness was limited, so was his Emotional Expression. He could talk a lot, but not about what he was feeling. His Self-Actualization also was lower than I thought it would be. David rarely considered the future, because he knew his talent and intellect would win out. Lying also helped him appear to manage stress well (Stress Tolerance) and develop strategies to prevent being found out that boosted his Emotional Problem-Solving score.

Yet the one competency that really caught his eye on the EQ-i 2.0—and served as the impetus to change his life—was Reality-Testing. This was among the lowest of all his competencies, showing significant difficulty differentiating between fact and fiction. Low Empathy and Flexibility were byproducts of his burning desire to live in the light, even if he had to create artificial lighting to do it.

So which aspects of David's accomplishments were genuine?

"I come from South Central LA," he told me. "I am African American. I have two parents who are not role models. I have an ability to surround myself with role models—my own age and older. I was valedictorian of my high school, I received a full ride to college, and I am a reliable friend with a bright future. I have unlimited potential."

Over time, David displayed more personal integrity and honesty. It was not easy to accomplish, and it required successive attempts, moving closer to what he wanted. When he found himself tempted to lie, David imagined an enormous clock that had only a second hand and 10 digits. He let the clock click off five seconds, which gave him time to slow the process and choose a more authentic response. This exercise stalled his knee-jerk reaction to pretend, replacing it with a different, better response.

The more truthful that David was, the more people admired his strength and resiliency. "Knowing I lied to people felt so heavy," he told me.

> I feel like I have more bandwidth to really live a credible life. . . . I can't do anything about the past and what has happened in my life. I can live each moment in the here-and-now, honoring what I can accomplish. This is my history, my story. It is a powerful one and each day I am becoming more excited about how I have handled getting to here.

While his past may have been scary and uncertain, attempting to live in truth allowed David to recognizes there are no limits to his future—other than those he imposes upon himself.

Recovering a Self

The road to recovery is a deeply personal journey for everyone. It is a case in which the map is *not* the terrain. Our way out is uniquely our own. The route that makes most sense to *us*. One of my clients captures it eloquently:

> I have known fear for so long that the thought of letting go of it is frightening. It is that special hiding place that generates some type of comfort. . . . But the work we are doing gives me confidence. It means taking full responsibility for my life—what I want and what I don't. And focusing on what I need and want . . . up until now, I have allowed for neither.

Recovering a self means taking responsibility. We do not have to subject ourselves to the desperate feelings others thrust upon us. This responsibility requires us to sculpt a vision of what is possible, based on our specific desires. It requires time, effort, and discipline.

Figure 3.1.

Sculpting a Vision: Chas

Chas is a former Army sergeant whose job was hunting down Taliban operatives in Afghanistan. He had been in the reserves for 10 years before the Army deployed his unit. During the 10 years, he acquired two advanced degrees and was working on a third when I met him. His use of language and storytelling was inspiring.

"The people I pursued in Afghanistan were individuals who had a mother, a father, siblings, maybe children, and a devoted wife," he told me once.

> These guys had friends that cared about them deeply. These men also lived with the singular purpose of killing as many Americans and those allied/aligned with the Americans as possible. So, if they could kill one of their own countrymen who were eking out a living by interpreting for the ISAF forces in the Eastern Province, then so be it!
>
> I was three blocks away from an open-air market where soldiers occasionally bought stuff from the locals, when all of a sudden it felt like the air was sucked out of my lungs. A car loaded with explosives was detonated. Seventeen people were killed. Not one was an American or member of the ISAF. The people responsible for such a heinous act killed their own people.
>
> This is what made my time down range so predictably horrifying. It is my job to kill people and, not in my wildest messed up nightmares could I imagine doing this to anyone. So, is the barometer of determination the degree of savagery [that] one is willing to exact on his or her neighbor? Kindness is synonymous with weakness, and brutality is the new normal.
>
> I mean, just look at the sorry ass state of affairs [in] our government. Everyone is sleep walking through an administration that is a step away from the way Assad thinks. Assad, Al-Qaeda, the Taliban, the Mafia, Israel, Palestine, gangs—all are bound by a willingness to kill everyone and anyone who disagrees with their God-given right to do whatever they please. If we were to track the life of just one of these faceless/nameless people killed in such a reprehensible manner, then maybe we would begin to connect with their humanity and start to care. And the problem is we just don't care.

Although Chas was swimming in rage, the anger was there before he joined the military. His combat experience metastasized it. He felt he had an important story to tell, and being unable to tell it was becoming repressive. He had a hard time sleeping. When other people talked, it sounded to him like drivel and noise, so he had little if any patience for it. His world got smaller as his rage got bigger.

What a lonely and volatile combination.

Chas shared with me a story of his chance encounter with a Marine at Bagram Airfield before leaving Afghanistan. "He was a real solid guy who seemed to have a lot of wisdom. . . . He said, 'It isn't that people don't care. They do care about the things directly related to them. Beyond that, it is just too damn big to do anything about.'"

The Marine related some of his own experience to Chas as an example. He was from a rough section of Chicago, but his mother worked hard to keep him on the straight and narrow. "We didn't have much," the Marine told Chas, "but [my mother] always talked about what I could have if I played it straight. 'Shortcuts get you a short stay on this earth,' she would say. My point is that I heard her. Did she change the reality of where I grew up? No. But she changed the environment in me. . . . I think that is what the Afghans are doing."

As Chas told me about the Marine whose observations so affected him, he said,

> I am not sure what will make me see things differently and siphon off some of this anger. I do know what the Marine said was pretty right on. I can't change it all. No one can. But I suppose I can put myself in a place to challenge what is happening around me, like that Marine's mother.

Dealing with his deep anger appropriately was the primary reason Chas sought therapy. It was becoming more unmanageable, finding its way into the large and small spaces of his life. Most of all, his anger was draining him of his optimism in what was possible at every level. This insight—and his desire to change—showed that Chas was emotionally intelligent. Emotional intelligence doesn't mean we don't struggle. It means we are aware of it and attempting to do something about it.

Fortunately, the pattern of competencies revealed in Chas' EQ-i 2.0 in figure 3.2 allowed me a glimpse into the inner workings of what had kept his anger machine running. His scores told me he could cope with a lot of stress. He possessed high Social Responsibility and tremendous

Emotional Independence. Indeed, Impulse Control was his highest competency. In the context of his other competencies, it was actually an overutilized strength. Chas focused so deeply, and with such meticulous precision, not only on what he thought and did but also on others' thoughts and actions. His desire to control his environment shut off spontaneity, appropriate social risk, and even the ability to experience joy.

The EQ-i 2.0 also revealed that Chas did not know the self he needed to recover all that well. His scores in Emotional Self-Awareness and Emotional Expression were very low. His lack of both qualities kept him in an unforgiving loop of anger and despair. It also drove down his competencies in Interpersonal Relationships and Flexibility.

And, as happened with David, a low score in Reality-Testing shook him up. It pointed to his tunnel vision. I pushed him about this during one session. "In many ways, your thinking right now is very much linear and unyielding—like the insurgents you used to track down." I asked him, "It is an eerie parallel, and I am wondering if this makes sense and if you see it at all?"

With his head bowed, and his hands placed over the top of his head, Chas simply said, "Yes."

It was a turning point. Chas recognized that he exuded a character trait he personally believed was repulsive.

His journey toward healing moved in an unanticipated direction. The world turns in funny ways, because his healing took a route I did not see coming. Chas began meeting with members of a local mosque who had anti-American sentiments. He wanted a discussion. He sought an exchange of views, and he was willing to listen to locate the tear in the fabric.

Chas visibly began to soften. He left his consulting work with a government contracting firm (in DC we call them "Beltway bandits"), and he moved to a consulting firm not connected to the military. He met an Egyptian-born woman Jasmin at his new job, and they fell in love. She was Muslim but only nominally practicing.

"It was Beauty and the Beast," he told me. "And she tamed me. She saw through my hairy and gruff exterior to the good man inside, and my liberation began."

The Competencies as Levers for Change ~ 83

He credited her with his freedom, but when they met it had already begun. It happened when Chas took the EQ-i 2.0, recognized his patterns of anger and control, and worked to change them.

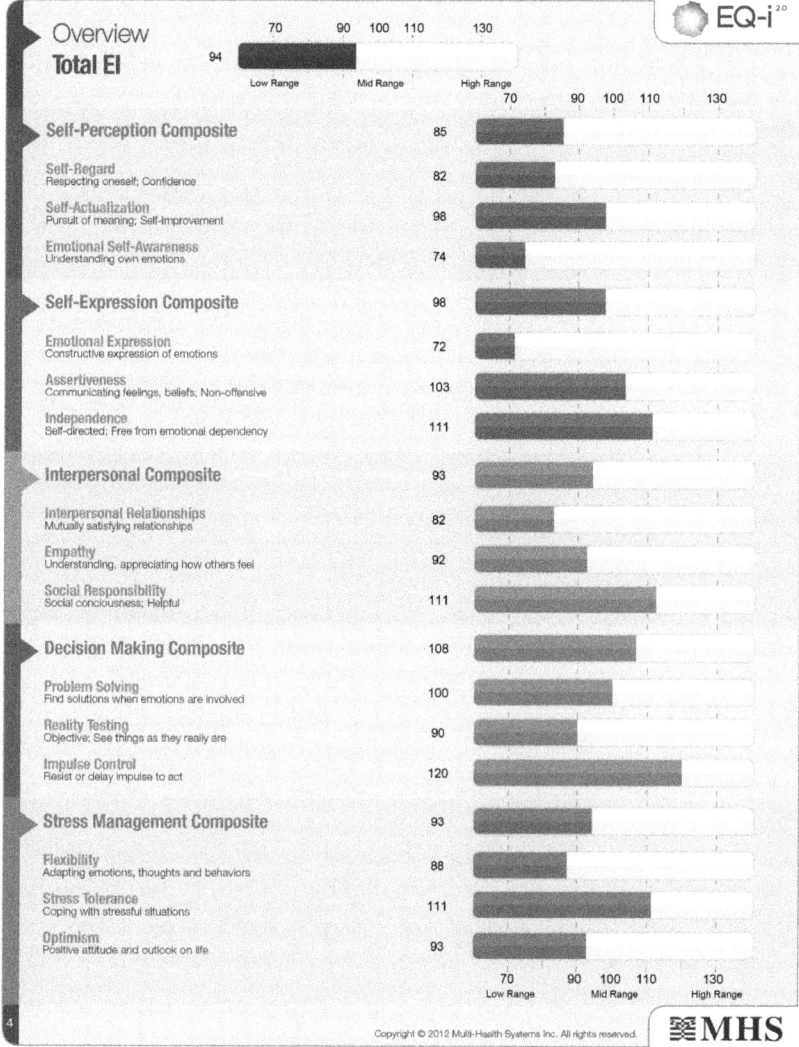

Figure 3.2.

A year later, I asked Chas to take the EQ-i 2.0 again. It was to be our second-to-last visit. In figure 3.3, you can immediately see the difference.

While Chas's Impulse Control and Optimism did not change, he told me, "I am far more realistic than before. There is no competency for that."

Chas added that his new relationship reinforced his belief that he was more realistic. "I have always been a guy who needs to have a sense of control," he observed.

> Jasmin allows me to control what I can and live with what I can't. I haven't had that before really. I am more aware. In love for sure, but in love with life, not just a person. I feel like I was a bear hibernating through the winter. . . When I woke up, I was lighter. Things were brighter. . . . I am one person among eight billion. One star in the sky. I will burn as bright as possible, cherishing Jasmin, accepting my back story, and enjoy scripting a new saga moving forward. . . . People in the recovery community talk about gratitude a lot, and I can see why. It is hard to be angry and pessimistic when you are shrouded in gratitude. I have turned the page to a new chapter. I am grateful for being here today.

It is no surprise that Chas's Flexibility profile showed the greatest change. It increased by 33 points. He had catapulted from being a rage-aholic with tunnel vision to an individual who lived to serve others.

"It would be safe to say I never would have set foot in a mosque, direct my romantic intentions toward a Muslim woman, and occupy a space outside my safety net where I did not feel fully in control," he told me. "In fact, it is impossible to feel fully in control, which inflamed my anger and intolerance."

Before therapy and the EQ-i 2.0 assessment of his competencies, Chas was walled off from his feelings. The result was that he pushed people away and avoided social risk. Now, he had become a very good listener and far more Emotionally Self-Aware. Chas created a life that he was proud of, along with the ability to establish lasting relationships.

Figure 3.3.

White Knuckling: Irene

"Something just feels wrong, or out of sync, in my life," she said. "I spend a lot of time thinking about it, rolling it over and over in my brain, and I can't make heads or tails of it. And it's been there for a while. At least since I was in college, and that was years ago."

Initially, the causes of her troubled feelings were elusive. This frustrated her immensely. "I am the kind of person that once I see something needs to be fixed, I fix it," she told me. "I help all my friends and even family, but I can't seem to help myself."

Invoking the notion of "Physician heal thyself" was interesting given that Irene is an oncologist who specializes in a particularly tricky form of cancer.

The first step in healing was having Irene take the EQ-i 2.0, her results pictured in figure 3.4. Her array of competencies suggested that she possessed solid emotional intelligence. She scored very well in 12 of the 15 competencies, with a 41-point difference between her highest competency score (Reality-Testing) and her lowest ranking (Assertiveness).

Yet examining how these competencies interact and fit together like a puzzle tells a bigger story not readily apparent from individual scores. Her three highest scores were Reality-Testing, Social Responsibility, and Emotional Self-Awareness. Her three lowest scores were Assertiveness, Independence, and Self-Regard.

Her initial response when looking at her competencies was to shake her head ruefully, with a raised eyebrow, that seemed to say, "What does all this mean? Although, it does look pretty good!"

Indeed, it did look good. So, what was troubling Irene?

Fortunately, the EQ-i 2.0 results held the keys to unlock that question. Irene was a medical doctor with an accomplished practice that offers cutting-edge treatment for those suffering with a frightening illness. She was attractive, though she worked hard to obscure that fact. She had close friends. She was optimistic. And she was extremely aware of her own emotional states and their impact on others.

Yet examine the assessment more closely, and three important competencies seem more problematic: Stress Tolerance, Social Responsibility, and Interpersonal Relationships. Like many doctors, Irene can tolerate a great deal of stress. Yet this strength proved to be a disadvantage because of her propensity to take on too much via Social Responsibility and Interpersonal Relationships.

If Irene's Social Responsibility score was low, she would have put herself before others. But instead, she had the opposite propensity. She put everyone else's needs (friends, patients, family) before her own. And in group situations? Irene would take on the full burden to make sure the group achieved its goals.

She told me what happened when three college friends who lived spread out across the country came to Washington, D.C., to visit her. The visit came during a particularly grueling time for Irene at work. Yet she got up at 4:00 a.m. to put a whole itinerary together for the weekend. She booked hotels and restaurants—and even a spa treatment that her friends would have to enjoy without her. Her Reality-Testing strengths were pushed to the maximum as she attempted to anticipate the needs of all her friends to make sure everyone was absolutely comfortable. Everyone, that is, except Irene.

Friends have grown to expect this from Irene. She will take care of everything. And if Irene is visiting them? The same thing. Her friends would just show up and enjoy. It was a world that held no surprises. No one, including a guy Irene dated for a year, ever surprised her, or planned anything for her, or even gave her a special gift.

Irene's high Stress Tolerance score indicated that she could keep on maintaining the same dynamic. But it took an emotional bite out of her every time it happened. She was even aware of these effects. But Irene felt trapped in a labyrinth of her own design. It was no surprise, then, that Assertiveness and Emotional Independence were the lowest scores in her assessment. She went along to get along—and rarely voiced negativity about anything she was feeling.

Our discussions left her visibly torn. Should she give to others only when they give to her? Create a balance sheet? That felt artificial. Stilted.

So, we talked about ways to make relationships bi-directional, with give and take throughout. "If [a relationship] is tilted in one direction," I observed, "it is like everyone in a rowboat standing on the bow. What happens?"

Irene said that the boat would fill up with water and tip over. That was the moment when she got it.

"You are not demanding that your friends and family shower you with gifts," I continued. "You are asking they share in the heavy lifting of the relationship."

Irene devised a plan that made a lot of sense. It required her to tap into her Reality-Testing competency. Her new reality urged her to stop once she came up with a good plan. No need to micromanage, or cross every "t" and dot every "i."

An opportunity for Irene to test her new reality knocked a few weeks later. Several friends were renting a place in the Florida Keys for winter break. They wanted Irene to come. They gave her the location and set the usual expectation that planning the rest of the trip was up to her.

Irene wrote everyone back. She would love to come. But she added, "I want to invite you all to take charge. I am wiped out and need some emotional convalescing. Whatever you choose will be great, that I assure you. Much love."

One friend's reply to Irene's note captured the group's sentiments: "Hell yeah, girl. You have been carrying our pathetic butts too long, and now, it's our turn. You rock!"

Irene was dumbfounded by their collective excitement and support. What she discovered was that we are all creatures of habit. Shifting gears in that moment proved to be the beginning of a process in which Irene could rely on others to help with fostering the relationship. She also felt better about herself and increased her Assertiveness in a way that also sustained her Emotional Independence. She began wearing clothing that complimented her natural beauty, along with jewelry and so on. She really had been anonymous. No longer.

Irene's story offers a good example of how the competencies interact and overlap with one another. Changing one competency can positively influence the movement of another competency.

Figure 3.4.

Achieving Balance: Denny

Living well means living without what I call the Big Three Emotional Black Holes, each pair of which represent opposite sides of the same coin: anger and rage, jealousy and envy, doubt and fear.

In the medical world, this isn't just about state of mind. Cardiac and cancer patients who enhance their social support and learn to manage anger and other negative emotions cut recurrence of a heart attack and death in half compared to those who do not.

Denny's story is a wonderful example of using our strengths as a lever to achieve emotional balance and relationship integrity. Similar to Irene, a look at Denny's EQ-i 2.0 in figure 3.5 reveals that all of his competencies rank in a high range. Yet his inability to deal with anger bordering on rage is what brought him to my office.

We have examined the ways in which a simple glance at an EQ-i 2.0 assessment doesn't always tell the whole story. But it's natural to wonder if the tool could be in some way faulty, especially when a client is not emotionally honest. After all, anyone can lie. So, can someone only pretend to be emotionally balanced and intelligent?

Well, yes and no. If a person is not emotionally balanced, it will become apparent fairly quickly, whether at work, at home, with friends, or alone. Someone will notice a crack in the ice. Since the EQ-i 2.0 always includes a Coach's Report, there is room for this outside data. The client doesn't usually receive this report. This lets the coach or therapist know the degree of honesty with which the client took the assessment. The therapist uses the Coach's Report to spot inconsistencies or inflation in the client's response patterns.

My Coach's Report for Denny showed zero inconsistent responses. It also indicated zero inflation, either positively or negatively, in his answers. His responses were about as accurate as possible. So why was Denny in my office?

The event that became his catalyst for change occurred at the grocery store. He was with his son, buying some last-minute things for Thanksgiving dinner. As he aimlessly pushed his cart, his son read off a list from his mother, looking for items she requested. All normal. When his son wandered away for a moment, a young man talking on his phone accidently bumped into Denny's cart. The man apologized, but Denny got in his face and pushed him.

As Denny's son came around the corner of the aisle, he saw the young man slam Denny on the ground.

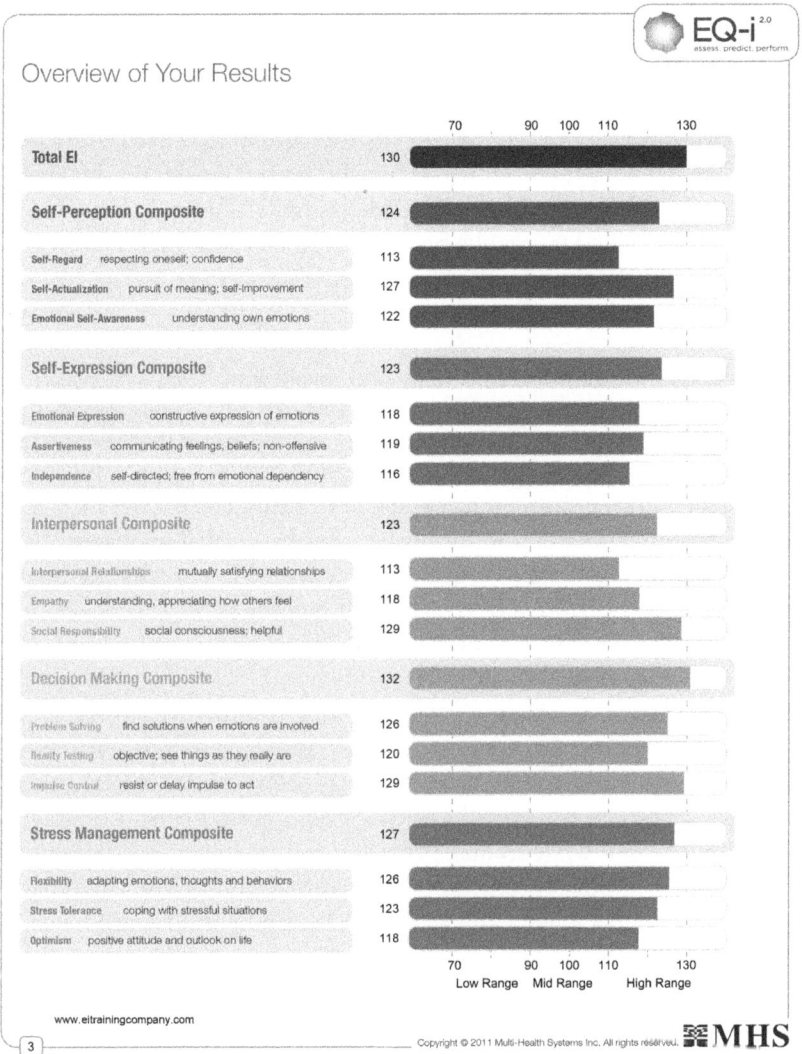

Figure 3.5.

> He did some kind of wrestling move, where he put my arm behind my back, and somehow twisted me, so my shoulders and head were . . . pinned on the ground. I couldn't move, let alone breathe. . . . My son was pulling on him, and telling him to get off, with no luck. He calmly said to my son: "Back off. It is up to your dad whether this ends badly or not." He leaned down and whispered in my ear, "Ask yourself, is this how you want to raise your son?" I shook my head no. He released his hold on me, and I rolled over, trying to catch my breath.

The situation was soon over. But the moment made an immense impression on Denny's son. When his son demanded that Denny call the police, he admitted that it was he who had provoked the incident.

Denny recalls that his son was beside himself: "'He could have killed you, Dad. He talked to me like he was in a library, not in a fight. If you had kept it up, I think he would have let you suffocate.'" And his son did not stop there.

> You know, you go from zero to 180 over stupid stuff, Dad. It has been that way for as long as I can remember. You are really a great dad. But your anger almost took my father from me and the rest of the family.

It was a turning point that compelled Denny to seek therapy and create the stable foundation for his life that he needed and wanted. A key element was getting in touch with his anger. Eventually, he began to understand it better, and to see how it had long controlled so much of his life. He came by it honestly, considering many events in his life story.

The strengths in Denny's EQ-i 2.0 also provided a lever for the change he wanted. One of his highest competencies was Self-Actualization. After the incident in the grocery store, his goal was to intuitively become the most balanced, well-adjusted person he could. Denny put in the work to make that happen. He exercises, eats well, meditates 30 minutes a day, keeps a gratitude journal, and regularly spends time with his wife and kids. He also hired an executive coach to be as productive and professionally balanced as possible.

Making a choice to stop drinking also made a difference. Denny's previous therapy sessions had pointed to links between his anger and its relationship to alcohol consumption. While he was not an alcoholic,

Denny was clearly dependent on alcohol to relax, unwind, and be more social. Oddly enough, drinking also did keep his anger bottled up.

Considering everything that crashes into our life on a daily basis, recovery requires some form of a breakthrough. It often requires a radical event to push us from choosing to live at less than our emotional potential to fully embracing all of our possibilities.

Denny's story is an excellent example. There is no generalized formula for finding such a moment. It is personal and unique to each individual. Sometimes, even the EQ-i 2.0 cannot pinpoint what qualities we possess that will be a lever to change until we are called upon to use them. Denny came in to see me because his wife (and best friend) had just been diagnosed with cancer, and he needed a place to talk and strategize as she went through treatment.

It does not have to be a cataclysmic event to begin the journey toward our social and emotional potential. Simply deciding we want more can be the first step forward on the journey.

Finding what works for each person is the key. I have administered the competency feedback sessions involving the EQ-i 2.0 to thousands of people. Not everyone embraces how a measurement of emotional intelligence can be an opportunity for change or feels a desire to liberate themselves from what is holding them back.

The assessment tool does provide a road map when readiness (or desire) and opportunity intersect. If either element is absent, the process of change usually is deferred. If an opportunity and a desire to be as socially and emotionally intelligent do come into confluence, new possibilities for social and emotional growth can take root and grow. And the EQ-i 2.0 can show paths to make it happen.

Finding the Right Note: Leslie

A woman named Leslie was working in a celebrated local orchestra. She is an example of what is possible when someone no longer allows fear to guide their life. Leslie had developed the habit of overanalyzing everything she encountered and staying largely in her own head at the expense of engaging her emotions and the world they live within.

Her childhood set her on this path. In sessions, Leslie compared it to a prison that lacked any sort of personal privacy. Seeing a documentary on prison in seventh grade confirmed the feeling.

"I can't say there was a point where things went wrong," Leslie told me. "They always just felt wrong. . . . I knew what was happening at home was wrong since before I can remember."

Leslie placed her father's behavior at the root of the issue. "My dad had this issue with privacy," she recalled, "you know, not wanting us to have any. So he took all the doors off the hinges and no one could go anywhere to really be alone. Yes, I know what you're thinking. Even the bathroom. But he didn't take his door off on his bathroom, and you couldn't go in his room. You'd be beaten if you did."

Leslie's father had custody of her and her brother because of her mother's drug addiction. "She was a mess and lived mostly on the streets or in jail, like so many of the shadow figures that populate [the African American] landscape."

Her father's control was overwhelming and tyrannical. "I couldn't listen to music because it would bother him," she remembered. "And I couldn't use earphones because he thought I'd be listening to the wrong music. I never had anyone over because he was unpredictable. That is the best word to describe him. My brother never talked at all. It was weird. He played all these sports, worked on the school paper. He did everything possible not to come home, because it sucked, right? So, we didn't talk. I didn't have anyone to really turn to at home. It made me feel kinda crazy. I had friends at school but the problem is they would go do things and I couldn't go. Unless I played a sport or had a job, I couldn't go out."

Music eventually provided Leslie—who was becoming an accomplished flute player—with an escape. "I could only play at school because my father couldn't stand the noise," she told me. "I played in the school orchestra. Luckily, my dad liked church, and he said I could join the youth group. That is what saved me. There was a woman who ran the group. Her uncle was the pastor. I came in one day, and she came over to me, real gentle, and put my face in her hands and said, 'It won't be like this forever. You are so talented and smart. It is time to believe in what you can do.' I felt real embarrassed, and then she said, 'Don't be. Don't be embarrassed.' She didn't know what was happening at home, but she could see that whatever it was, it was emotionally eviscerating me."

The church group leader arranged an audition for Leslie at NYU's Steinhardt School of Music. She was accepted on a full fellowship. She says that the church group leader "did rescue me from what would have been who knows what? I . . . get sick to my stomach when I think what would have become of me had I stayed in the home with no doors."

Professionally successful, Leslie could not bring herself to shed her past. She remained aloof, especially with men. It was a lingering issue deeply related to her experience with her father.

"There is a guy who comes to almost all of our concerts during the season and sits in the third row; these tickets are not cheap, but he is always there," Leslie told me. "Handsome, seems to be a professional, and brings me flowers at the end of the performance. I hear myself screaming inside. I want to reach out, and I can't. I just can't. I say thanks and walk away. He tries to engage me in conversation, but I just walk shyly and quickly away."

How did her EQ-i 2.0 in figure 3.6 suggest a path forward for Leslie? It confirmed that she had very little confidence emotionally, and to a degree, socially. Her Assertiveness and Emotional Independence scores were the lowest of all. Even her Emotional Self-Awareness was accompanied by a low capacity for Reality-Testing, which meant that she spent a lot of time daydreaming about what could be—rather than actively creating it based on understanding what she felt and needed.

The assessment offered other key information. She had low Stress Tolerance and did everything she could to avoid things that would enhance her stress, such as dating. She was quick to anger, very impulsive, and managed her close friendships by editing everything she wanted to say. "My spontaneity took a major hit," she said. "I was more robotic and stilted." The effort exhausted her, because white knuckling can be sustained only for so long.

When Leslie looked at her results, her head kept nodding in agreement: "Yes, this is me—strikingly me." The first area she wanted to concentrate upon and improve was her assertiveness.

"I know these other areas need my attention," she observed. "But I am not going anywhere unless I know what it means to fully understand

and get my needs met. I get so angry because I don't know how to get what I want in virtually all areas of my life except music."

She was right. She was professionally assertive. She had even told me a story about standing up to a conductor. "Often the skills we need

Figure 3.6.

to utilize most are being utilized in discrete ways in different parts of our life, though more inconsistently in all parts of our life," I stated. "Let's take what you do naturally in your professional setting and begin bending it toward the other areas of your life!"

Leslie started to do so. And a month after discussing the assessment, she came in looking radiant. It was so striking that I mentioned it the moment I saw her.

She was eager to tell me a story. The man in the third row attended their last concert of the season. Bearing flowers again, he handed them this time to a stagehand and asked they be given to Leslie. When she ran to the lobby to catch him, he was gone!

It was only when she picked up the flowers and breathed in the wonderful fragrance of white and pink lilies that she noticed his business card was tied to one of the stems, with a note on the back: "If you ever want to grab a cup of coffee, my info is on the front."

Her heart pounding, Leslie immediately picked up the phone and called his cell. He had just gotten to his car and was getting ready to leave. He came back, and they went to have a late dinner. Tears welled up as she told me, "I would pay any amount of money to preserve this feeling for the rest of my life. He is beyond wonderful. I really have a vision of what it means to be my own person!"

As Leslie's assertiveness strengthened, so did her other competencies, as we predicted. And she has been happily married now for several years.

Finding the Levers

A given competency in our emotional intelligence has the power to leverage change in other areas. After reading these stories, how does it work? We can identify four key components: awareness; emotional regulation or management; awareness of others; and how we utilize our social skills.

Awareness

How well do you understand the rhythm of your emotions? Can you pinpoint your emotional strengths and weaknesses and make good decisions in your life based on them? Remember, Chas realized his unexplored anger was infecting his life. Once he became aware of it and devised a plan to reduce it, change began to occur at a consistent and broad level. He could begin planning different and more emotionally intelligent responses.

The first step to managing emotions is to have an accurate system of identifying what a person is feeling. I often ask clients to rate their response to emotional awareness from 1 to 10. One signifies very little immediate awareness of what they are experiencing. On the other end of the spectrum, 10 is an absolute identification of what is happening emotionally.

There are times people come into my office and don't know what they feel. Often, abuse that occurred in childhood or emotional and physical pain spanning a long period of time explains this. If someone is not sure of what they feel or is not aware of their feelings, there is a protective reason that must be acknowledged and explored. I have had to show people pictures of faces expressing different states of feeling so the client could begin recognizing them.

Then I send them home with three-by-five cards showing emotionally expressive faces. I ask them to glue these in their journal throughout the week, accompanied with the feeling word and a brief description of a situation that occurred, how they felt, and what the outcome was. This often stimulates a new level of awareness that had been inaccessible or outside their peripheral vision. Some of you reading this may be thinking, "Wait, he is interacting with these adults like preschoolers." Not preschoolers—individuals who were robbed of their natural ability to feel and recognize feelings. What some people have had to manage to survive in this world is mind-numbing. And that is why I am a clinician; these individuals make me a better man, a better husband, a better father, and a more compassionate person.

Emotional Regulation or Management

Once someone recognizes and is aware of their varied feeling states, learning how to balance emotions is essential. Before encountering the concept of emotional intelligence, if I didn't acknowledge my anger or appropriately express my disappointment or pain to someone based on what they said or did, they probably would not know the extent to which their actions were hurtful.

Remember, pain fuels anger. We are hurt when someone acts a particular way or says a certain thing or doesn't follow through. That hurt is converted to anger. Even if we struggle to identify a feeling such as anger or sadness, leaving it unaddressed eventually or inevitably manifests itself in things we do or say. This is frequently referred to as "passive-aggressive" behavior.

The term "passive-aggressive" has become well-known. For instance, a mother will forget to give her son or daughter an important message from someone because the kids did something hurtful. Not identifying the catalyst for anger and dealing with it appropriately sets the stage for it manifesting inappropriately.

I had a client whose wife would forget to pick him up from the train station every time he took the bus to the train station in the morning rather than ride with her. He took the bus when he had to leave earlier because of an appointment. She never would say anything about being disappointed. She simply would forget—like clockwork—to pick him up.

On the other end of the spectrum is learning to manage feelings at a particularly deep level. Let's look at two cases of clients with low Assertiveness, Emotional Independence, and Emotional Expression.

Thom came to see me about managing his anger more appropriately. He would let things build up over time and often quite unexpectedly and inappropriately go off on his wife or children.

Thom learned to talk about things that were happening in his environment as they occurred, rather than pretending it didn't bother him. As he learned to be assertive and share his feelings, he found that two things happened. First, traditional annoyances began having less and less impact. Second, he did not become explosive with those he loved.

It was a major shift, allowing Thom to feel a sense of personal control and emotional competency, which also was a huge relief to his family who no longer walked on egg shells wondering if he would explode should they say or do the wrong thing.

Or take another client named Ellie. She would withdraw when she was angry. She wouldn't say anything to the person whose words or behavior were hurtful. She would simply stop talking to them, avoid them, and make the relationship extremely uncomfortable. Often, the person she was acting out toward wasn't sure precisely what the problem was.

Once Ellie learned to identify when she was angry or hurt, she role-played being appropriately direct and to the point with the person. Initially, it was very difficult and even painful for her. But when Ellie saw the pattern, she could choose to manage her reactions differently.

Rehearsal allows us to minimize the fear associated with being more assertive and to become more vocal in what we need, allaying our natural worries about what the other person might say or do. As Ellie noted, "It is liberating acting like a grown up, holding people accountable for what I perceive as a slight, or just meeting my needs around what is happening and letting it go once I assert myself by sharing how it made me feel. I always would feel like this bratty little kid who wasn't getting her way. It was an awful feeling. I also felt entitled to have people magically figure out what they were doing to upset me, which was unrealistic."

Awareness of Others
Being aware of and reacting to the needs of others relates to empathy and social responsibility. This provides us with an honest sense of what others are going through and connects us with others in a meaningful way.

Being able to check in with someone regarding what you are seeing is vital to building any relationship. We don't always know what is happening with someone. As noted above, being empathic doesn't suggest you are a mind-reader, but it indicates an awareness that something is happening to another and you want to find out if you can help. This all exists on the foundation of Emotional Expression.

Sylvia was aware that her sister had become quiet and withdrawn. It didn't seem like something she was going to snap out of. She sat down with her sister—who according to Sylvia was not very touchy-feely—and gently touched her, saying, "I am not sure what is happening with you right now. All I know is that something seems really heavy for you. You have not been yourself and I would like to offer any support I can."

As it turns out, her sister believed that she might be pregnant and didn't know what to do or who to talk with. She opened up to Sylvia, who offered support that proved to be extremely helpful. Had Sylvia not said anything, it is likely her sister would have continued to suffer in silence, because she did not feel prepared to have a child. Sylvia's sister was not married and had not even considered the implications of being pregnant. She was able to talk through her concerns and gain the perspective she needed if in fact she was pregnant. As it turns out, she was not.

Social Skills
Whether you are introverted or extroverted, a social animal or socially shy, we all need relationships to flourish. How well do you get along with others? How well do you react to the emotions of others and read the proper interpersonal signals to gauge the most appropriate response? How well do you solve problems in relationships, excite people to action and to be their best, or generate a cooperative spirit in groups, relationships, and the workplace?

Some people are naturally gifted at motivating those around them, creating a wonderful team atmosphere and reading interpersonal signals flawlessly. Most of us, however, have to learn these skills. And learn them we can.

Communicating honestly requires us to be Assertive and Self-Expressive. Hearing what others say in person or in a group calls upon our Social Responsibility. Impulse Control means being considerate of others before acting or speaking. Believing that what you have to offer is compelling and unique is a signal of Self-Regard. Feeling that what you have to offer will make a difference in the outcome of the event or situation is a hallmark of Optimism. Self-Actualization is a belief that our goals will be achieved through thoughtfulness, hard work, and dedication.

As we see, these competencies are integral to getting what we want in life. The learning curve follows a natural progression: Being aware of what we want to strengthen, regulating our emotions to invite people toward us rather than push them away, keeping the needs of others in our awareness, and knowing how we want to react, while realizing social skills can be sculpted to represent precisely what we want in relationships.

Being emotionally intelligent is a process, not an event. It is something we continuously work on and move toward. Learning to communicate our feelings while valuing the feedback of others is essential to living an emotionally balanced life.

CHAPTER FOUR

EQ-i Map

When Strength Is a Weakness

Invisible at Home: Rene

As a clinician, I have witnessed an important and particular pattern in clients' emotional intelligence profiles, an aspect of their emotional intelligence that is so pronounced—Assertiveness, for instance—that it overpowers other competencies and throws them out of balance. We refer to this occurrence as an overused strength. Overused optimism places the person in the crosshairs of not seeing reality for what it is at the moment. A wife finds lipstick on her husband's shirt; he is now traveling more than ever, yet nothing has changed in his job; she stumbles upon receipts to fancy restaurants; she could not fathom that her husband would have an affair. After all, they are married and made vows to one another. Overused optimism blinds us to the realities, at times harsh, of what is happening in life.

Rene is a partner in a law firm. She also has a passion for writing song lyrics and poetry and playing the piano, but she rarely shared these talents with others. After some time in therapy, she shared one of her poems with me:

> Loss approaches for which there is no bullet proof vest
> A rumble in the nether world forecasts the impending tsunami

I grieve, I miss, I want, I long for the impossible;
More time to get it right, to cradle your tender face, stroke your cheek
For you to know at the depth of your being that I gave my best
I didn't though. I am consumed with what wasn't rather than what was.
Busy life, yes, a busy wife, consumed with consumption.
And you would say, 'Let's slow it down babe.'

Rene was alive to a creativity that was deeply and personally meaningful to her. But her husband rarely appreciated her for who she was or what she brought to the world. He never once asked to hear one of her poems or requested that she serenade him with an original song on the piano.

This emptiness penetrated other parts of her marriage. Rene's husband often made her feel like a parent, not a spouse. When she would speak of what she wanted and needed from him, her words fell on deaf ears. He was very good at what he did professionally, but as a couple, they rarely occupied the same emotional or physical space.

Rene's children were a treasure, but she did not want another child. What she wanted was a lover, a spouse, and a partner with whom she could parent their children and take on the world. She did not have that, and she felt very much alone.

I asked Rene what other options were available.

"Short of kicking him out or me leaving, what else is there?" she replied. "This is the father of my children—and the kids do enjoy him for the most part. He tends to be moody, and the kids have learned to be cautious around him. However, he does love them and enjoys spending time with them. He is not a bad guy, just always distracted and not in the moment."

When it comes to relationships, we often learn to exist in the space where the partnership is "good enough." People who feel stretched by a situation—or feel unappreciated—often fail to put their own needs first. They learn at some level it doesn't matter. They must put their children's needs, those of the larger family, and even their spouse's needs ahead of their own. Yet the flaw in this imperative is that we each have a finite emotional reservoir. Every moment we put the vast needs of others ahead of our own, the emotional reservoir is depleted that much more. While Ayn Rand is a controversial figure, what she espouses is fighting for yourself and your needs. Always putting the needs of others before yours (altruism) is flawed and emotionally deadly.

> "My happiness is not the means to any end. It is the end. It is its own goal. It is its own purpose."
>
> –Ayn Rand, *Anthem*

As Rand indicates, the caretaker reasoning that others' needs must come first at all times is flawed, because taking care of one's own needs keeps the reservoir full. The caretaker who fulfills their own needs has more to go around and can hold other people accountable for their behavior.

I wondered if Rene could imagine putting her needs first. What would that look like?

"It would feel selfish and self-serving," she said. "As a parent, you can't put your needs first. Right? If the parent doesn't focus on the child, then who does?"

I offered Rene this picture: She is getting ready for work, or going over a brief that is due the next day, or taking a phone call from a friend. Suddenly, one of her kids or her husband wants something. What usually happens? She drops what she is doing to help them. But what if she took care of her task, and taught her family to wait until she was finished? No one is on fire or falling out of the window. It is possible—even reasonable—for them to wait.

She remarked that this scenario felt counterintuitive. So, I tried a different tack: "What are the things your husband does on a daily basis that make it seem as if he is another child, and not a consistent life partner?"

Rene recited a litany: Leaving his clothes everywhere, forgetting to bring home a requested item, unreliable timekeeping in comings and goings, abandoning projects.

And when I asked what might happen to him if he behaved that way at work, she laughed.

"Oh, my," she observed. "He'd be fired."

So why didn't he bring the same approach to life at home?

"That is a great question," she replied.

I agreed, "It would be a great question to ask him."

We devised a plan of what she would say to him—and how. It wasn't a new question in their relationship. But I pointed out that how she said it might be a key element. "My sense is generally when you say something, you are frustrated at that point," I advised. "And that frustration shows."

Rene began processing what type of behaviors were problematic, and exactly what she needed to see to feel more support. The point was that she had to let him know she would not encourage behavior she found frustrating. "What if you didn't pick up after him? What if you let him know that, from this point forward, he is responsible for his life in your home just as he is at work? Either the home will start to look like hoarders have moved in, or he'll begin doing what is necessary to be your partner, and the children's father. It is all aimed at reducing stress in your life and having him more engaged."

I also invited Rene to take the EQ-i 2.0. Her results in figure 4.1 conveyed not only why she has felt so stuck in her marriage, but also the immense impact someone else's behavior can have on critical aspects of our own emotional life. In Rene's assessment, the notion of overused strengths was readily apparent.

Rene is intensely Emotionally Self-Aware, as well as very adept at expressing herself emotionally (Emotional Expression). Key connections with friends and family are also a strong part of her life, as reflected in a high Interpersonal Relationship score.

Rene doesn't often mention the difficulties in her existence. "It just makes me sad," she said, "so why talk about it?" By and large, her pain and disappointment are funneled into her creative outlets, as opposed to speaking directly with the source of her pain and disappointment. Rene's husband has skillfully taught her that talking to him is of little consequence. This is clear from her low scores in Assertiveness and Independence.

So where do overused strengths come into play? Look at Rene's scores in Empathy (her highest) and Flexibility. As is the case with many musicians and poets, she feels things at an intense level. So her sense of being disregarded and disrespected by her husband was particularly wounding. Her strong Flexibility underscores the suppression of her own needs and desires that we explored in therapeutic sessions.

EQ-i Map: When Strength Is a Weakness ~ 107

So how did Rene finally have that long-needed discussion with her husband—one in which he actually listened? She told me that a visit from her parents gave them a chance to go to lunch while the kids had a day with their grandparents.

Figure 4.1.

Rene started the conversation by telling her husband how impressed she was with his professional career. She asked how he did it. Her husband warmed to the conversation, because demonstrating reliability and responsibility while growing up was hard. He said his childhood inability to focus on tasks was actually painful. It was only when he began taking martial arts in his junior year of high school that he explored meditative practices and gained inner focus. His grades improved, as well as his ability to listen.

Rene wondered if his parents had noticed the difference. He said they had. But he admitted that his successes were mostly outside the home, and that his mother still nagged him about being a slob. "It is hard," he observed, "to break bad habits at home." He saw it as a place where he could relax and not have to prove himself. A place where he could recover from his professional exertions. He said that doing consistently well at work required every ounce of time, attention, and emotion. At the end of the day, he is whipped from yet another day of white knuckling it. Rene responded with:

> I really appreciate what you are saying, and I can only imagine what it must take for you to stay on point at work. I want you to know (as she stroked his fingers) that I feel like your mom. You do such a remarkable job outside the home. However, you get home, and you want to turn off and tune out. Based on what you are saying, I get it. It requires huge energy on your part to be as successful as you are. What I need, though, is to be your wife, not your mother or some type of parent figure. To the degree it is stressful for you to remain on point throughout your professional day, it is just as stressful for me to feel you are not engaged in my life—or that of the kids—at an emotional level. I know it takes energy. And I also know it is an energy you have worked hard to harness and utilize.

Rene told me that tears welled up in her husband's eyes. What he was hearing resonated with him. He was able to hear her pain, and, more importantly, her desire to have an emotional relationship with the man she fell in love with. Eventually, she was able to share a book with him: *Driven to Distraction*, by Ned Hallowell. It was written for people living with and trying to manage ADHD, and while Rene's husband may not have lived with the challenge of managing ADHD, he was often internally distracted and manifested many of the characteristics of someone living with attentional issues.

The conversation created a tipping point for her husband; he vowed to achieve a place of balance in all aspects of his life. He also decided to see a physician and discuss the options (including medication) that exist for a person living with ADHD. He went to the website ADHDonline.com where he received the diagnosis of ADHD Combined Type (this is where the big "H" resides). As he said to Rene, "Taking this medication feels almost like a miracle. I am far more efficient at work and when I get home, I have energy coupled with an enormous sense of gratitude. After reading Dr. Hallowell's book I am ashamed about how this has impacted you and the kids. Particularly you, though. I am just so sorry and committed to being the man you want and deserve."

Rene's husband initiated setting boundaries with their kids (because in a lot of ways he was the "Disney Dad" who swooped in to play with the kids while Rene did all the heavy lifting around the house). She now had the partner who had existed only in her imagination. They celebrated their 10th wedding anniversary by attending a nearby coffee shop that featured local talent every Saturday evening. Rene played the piano and sang as he watched, mesmerized by her ability. As he later told Rene, he was filled with so much pride and love for her it felt difficult to contain.

Way Too Much: Grant

When Grant came in to see me, he told me he wanted to "bridge my awareness with behavioral change." He already had been on a very long journey to try and do so.

When he was 16 years old, Grant had been diagnosed by his pediatrician with both ADHD and BPD (Borderline Personality Disorder). When he walked through my door, he was 25. Grant was motivated to change and anxious to find some form of lasting change.

But nine years had passed since the initial diagnosis, and Grant was not much closer to reaching his potential. He had grown weary of the mounting existential pain of his choices.

"I am not sure even where to begin," he told me. "Do you have any idea what it is like to be an impulsive person living with Borderline Personality Disorder?"

I said no, but then shared with him what I imagined might have been the contours of his personal narrative. Being told he was bright and capable, and yet never reaching his potential. Cutting people off that try to hold him accountable for his behavior. This was particularly true of his family. Moving forward and back again, without any real work or relationship progress. Friends and family cutting off all contact, usually after one of his angry outbursts or insulting emails. And work? That never seems to work out. Settling for low-paying or minimum wage jobs, which he resented. No real commitment or stability. Relationships, too, are unfulfilling. Often, in desperation, he resorted to manipulation to keep his partners from leaving.

Grant looked down at his crossed hands. He was sullen and silent. I inched my chair a bit closer to his chair.

"In my experience, when someone willingly comes through my door seeking guidance and a better way to live their life, they get it," I told him. "You chose to meet with me. This is a choice you'll make every time we meet. If you continue to come back, each time you do, you will be that much closer to living the life you want. Your brain and heart are swimming in pain which generally shows up as anger. This is what you can change in your life—who you are right now and who you want to continue to be over time. You can create new memories with your family. This will take time, discipline and starting with the end in mind."

I asked what, if anything, he found deep joy in doing. He quickly said it was soccer. "I have some health issues, which kind of get in the way," he continued. "But when I am healthy, I play."

Grant told me that he didn't really know what he wanted. "It's all confused and in pieces."

I replied that he knew what he *didn't* want. "You don't want to remain on this path," I said. "Reading the same map directing you down to the same dead end, and rendering the same gut-wrenching results."

I asked him what the opposite of his current experience might look like. Grant described his desire for a balanced relationship with his family. He wanted them to trust him, rather than thinking he was running some sort of scam. They often thought this, and they were generally correct. He was a master of ulterior motives, and his family had known him in this particular way for a very long time.

What might be a path to get there? "They are not going to believe what you say," I told him. "They will pay attention to your behavior, something they always have done. This time, however, they will see a very different person. A person whose words and behavior match."

Grant needed to show his family that the ridiculous behavior of the past remains there—in the past. I asked him to begin imagining, as clearly as possible, how his family might react to consistently respectful interactions with no strings attached. I wondered if there was something about him that no one else in the family knew, something that would surprise them.

"My senior year in high school," he told me, "I had a teacher who opened up this amazing world of philosophy to me. I got into Descartes, who battled with the scholastics of his time, challenging them in their belief that all knowledge came from sensation. He believed our senses could deceive us, so they were not a completely reliable source of knowledge."

While he was speaking, Grant had an epiphany. "Wow, as I am saying this, I realize [Descartes] also stressed it was not prudent to trust someone (or something) that has deceived us even once. So, what do I do with this knowledge as I prepare to be different with my family?"

I offered my thoughts. "Yes, you have deceived them, lied to them, and caused them heartache. You also are, right now, preparing to stop the bleeding and bandage the wound. If they experience a change in you as real, they will learn to move toward you rather than away. Members of your family trusting you is up to you; they have learned through the course of your development to avoid you and doubt everything you say or do. You trained them. Consistency will teach your family to trust what they are seeing, hearing, and sensing. And as your teacher taught you about philosophy . . . so you too can teach your family that the depth of their ability to forgive is aligned with your ability to change."

"I know what I have done to them," Grant admitted. "And still, up to this point, I have done nothing to reverse . . . this disaster."

Grant began to bushwhack through his own emotional forest to find a plan for change that made sense. He told me that he thought about one particular metaphysical principle a lot: "What is done cannot be undone."

I countered with some philosophic concepts of my own. "Immanuel Kant said, 'Ought implies can.' If you really want this, and do the heavy lifting necessary, ought will become can!" He smiled and said,

> I remember Spinoza said something like: If you live with and are guided by reason, as much as humanly possible, and you meet hatred, frustration, and inappropriate demand with love and nobleness, the good will prevail. I want this. My mind has been a crowded, busy, and frenetic traffic jam. Jammed with people waiting for me to snap out of my bad behavior. Yeah, I am just done subjecting people in my life to emotional torture.

As we worked together, Grant connected with the notion that we all have choices. But I was reminded of the saying: "The world would be a better place if everyone else would change." Reality dictates that change must start with us. When we realize we are not happy and want things to be different, that is what we seek control over. Limiting beliefs, longstanding negative patterns of behavior, and blame are often the smokescreens sabotaging us from taking that control. Grant and I began using the therapeutic model of growth and change developed by psychologist Marsha Linehan called Dialectical Behavior Therapy. DBT serves to anchor the most essential aspects of personal change deep within a person's psyche. This is particularly true of those trying to manage DBT.

A month into our therapy, I asked Grant if he wanted to take the EQ-i 2.0. I also gave him some articles on emotional intelligence. Looking at his results in figure 4.2, perhaps you will see what Grant saw. As he examined his scores, Grant said,

> It's just so odd how accurate this is. It is like someone secretly took a video of my life, and then sat me down and showed it to me in a written report. I don't want my results to look like someone's EKG during a heart attack. Is it possible to achieve some kind of balance with these competencies? . . . I do have to admit that I am surprised at my Assertiveness and Independence scores. I thought they would be much lower.

I told him something readers will already know: The fact that those two scores were his highest was not necessarily a positive thing. Grant was intrigued, but a bit thrown off as well. "Higher must be better, right?"

I told him about overused strengths, and that their impact is generally negative. His Assertiveness was more like aggression, and it played

Figure 4.2.

out in many areas of his life. Already in our sessions he had described an incident when he took a date to the movies. Someone seated in front of them was reading on his phone and creating a distraction. But instead of asking the patron to turn off the phone, he unleashed a series of expletives that resulted in a fist fight. Not only was Grant thrown out of the theater, but he never heard from the woman again.

Emotional Independence—as an overused strength—was also an issue. It meant that Grant couldn't care less what other people thought about him or his actions. His conversational manner was aggressive enough to shut them down. There was also something false in that sense of independence. Grant would abandon it when it suited him, adjusting his attitude or opinions if he felt it was advantageous.

Grant's low scores also made sense. Take Empathy. The relational stress and emotional pounding that he endured over time with his family and others eradicated his empathy. Indeed, Grant's low Empathy—in concert with low Flexibility and low Impulse Control—was a recipe for disappointment.

One thing we worked on was enhancing Grant's Flexibility. In many ways, it was the gateway to opening up and strengthening other competencies. Inflexibility circumvents being open-minded and more adaptable to changing circumstances, and deficits in this area are most noticeable in how one copes with variable task demands. By reinforcing Flexibility through repetition, consistency, and stability, Grant was able to move closer to achieving the type of relationships he desired. It also had other salutary effects: increased feelings of appropriate Emotional Independence, augmented Emotional Self-Awareness, and a bolstered ability to express his emotions positively—all in accordance with his emotional awareness (Emotional Expression). All of these competencies working together also lead to a stronger sense of Self-Regard.

One strength did help Grant along the path: Self-Actualization. We have seen his deep interest in philosophy, which sprang from a desire to learn through voracious reading, watching documentaries, and taking classes. He had not earned a college degree, largely because he preferred to dive deeply into subject matter that interested him, rather than engage with the broader general requirements.

Grant's high Social Responsibility score was also of interest. Much of it was related to North Korea. As a senior in high school, Grant was introduced to a North Korean defector, and he learned firsthand what life was like in that nation. He became active in local efforts to help those who had defected and involved himself in other service opportunities for the people of North Korea. By his own account, the people with whom he worked on North Korean issues with saw him as bright, hardworking, creative, and dedicated. The person that his colleagues saw when he worked on North Korea issues became an avatar for Grant. He planned to create a new way of living with those qualities in mind.

Together, we used the Simple Strategies for Development, and utilized George Doran's S.M.A.R.T. action plan. S.M.A.R.T. calls for a plan that is *Specific* in scope and concentration and *Measurable* in order to know that it is actually working. Such plans are *Achievable* and call for detailed activities to achieve the desired increase in competency. They are also *Realistic* plans. Can these goals be achieved with requisite motivation to push through discomfort? Can they be supported via Grant's thoughts, behaviors, and available resources? Such plans are *Time-bound*. They achieve results within a specific timeframe, and at a moment that makes sense in the context of a person's entire life. I have found utilizing the S.M.A.R.T. paradigm (which is located toward the end of the EQ-i 2.0 Comprehensive Feedback Report) with the EQ-i 2.0 competencies is an exceedingly effective way to help a person discern their overall level of commitment to a specific area of personal growth.

So how did it work with Grant? As we've seen, one key goal was to increase Grant's Flexibility. Our goal was to emphasize activities and tasks that required reliability and consistency. We placed a specific focus on interactions with his family, as well as other close relationships that had been strained.

The plan required us to harvest ideas to handle the dynamics of change. How could Grant manage the shifting demands of others as he met his own behavioral and emotional goals? It required us to brainstorm looking at all the potential outcomes. What we settled on was that Grant would possess a set of go-to responses when he felt pushed emotionally. Preparation was key. If you are unprepared, then old attitudes and emotional responses can take over. Grant had to know that his family would initially meet him with resentment and anger. They'll question his motives and essentially wait for the other shoe to drop.

When a person is properly prepared for it, change can be a powerful opportunity to learn and develop appropriate social and emotional responses. It allowed Grant to be aware of how people in his environment managed behavioral and emotional flexibility. Being flexible does not mean muffling your feelings or needs. It means learning to announce those needs and feelings in a way people can hear them—this is the essence of respect. This takes practice, as well as close observation of others who demonstrate strong flexibility skills.

Sufficient time to prepare was also essential. If change were easy, Grant would have done it long before he sought therapy. A realistic plan with specific, action-oriented, and achievable steps made a transition more tolerable. Time was also required to shift the response from his family and friends. Suspicions take time to be overcome. Knowing this helps.

Much of the practical work for Grant centered on time management. Strong development of this skill positively influences our Flexibility. Others become disappointed when we don't honor commitments. This induces stress that defeats any effort to change. But strong time management skills can support Flexibility. Grant's family will meet him with the expectation that his presence will end as it always has—in disappointment and heartache.

We started at the foundation. Prioritizing was critical, especially for a "fly by the seat of your pants" person such as Grant. Understanding the demands and commitments others made on him was also key. How do we finish tasks when they are imperative but offer little or no reward for completing them? We wrote things out and divided large tasks into manageable chunks. Grant had never done that before, but he quickly saw the value of this exercise—and the rewards it produced.

Creating a proper balance between his work and life demands was also a priority. Change is labor-intensive. You can't perform a complete, 180-degree turnaround alone. We had to build rest and relaxation in between his exertions. We also addressed how he would ask for help, another necessity. When possible, we set up ways for Grant to delegate, defer, or get assistance with some of the demands on him. In the past when Grant encountered task-related stress, he would dig in with resistance, creating even more anxiety and relational fracture for everyone in his life. We talked at length about what success in this area would look like. We also story boarded this on a large white board. Using a white board, chalkboard, or newsprint is visually the best way for people to see the impact of specific behaviors and specific responses to that behavior. Grant's family will be skeptical of anything he does or says that has a prosocial aspect to it.

Change along these lines had the potential to be transformative. Previously, Grant saw himself as countercultural, with built-in laziness. However, when he interviewed for two sales positions with multinational companies, he realized that his life and his time commitments must change to succeed in such a job. He needed clarity about the actual impact of this work on his days. How would he manage low-reward tasks that he didn't like? What would achievement on this job look like for him in real terms? I asked him to write this out in paragraph form.

In part due to this clarity, Grant interviewed well and landed both jobs. He took the one that seemed the most challenging but also offered the most rewards.

A year after he first took the EQ-i 2.0 and he began the job, he agreed to take it again. Examining these comparative results, I could see dramatic changes. It is processes like this that make me feel so honored to know a young man such as Grant. He is a poster child for what's possible when we are committed to changing the trajectory of our life.

Reflecting on the challenges of Grant's journey makes his triumph all the more impressive. He lived with, struggled with, and tried to navigate an unpredictable world with Borderline Personality Disorder and ADHD. Even when he was in kindergarten, his end-of-year report said:

> Grant is not an easy child. His demanding nature, challenging style, and disrespect for rules will make his school experience wrought with difficulties. It is recommended you consider a special school placement for him. This school does not have the resources to help meet his demanding needs.

Imagine being five years old and already feeling like a lost cause. Then imagine overcoming it.

His mother wrote me this note after Grant took his second EQ-i 2.0 and had been on his new job for seven months. Our therapeutic journey had lasted for two years. He had achieved his goals and no longer needed my support:

I am Grant's mother, and while we haven't met, I feel I know you through Grant's stories of your talks. It's still hard for me to believe that when I see him across from me at the dinner table—often in a suit after work—that it is my son Grant. I honestly never imagined, after a while, that this would be possible. I believed we lost him to the world of mental illness. A cruel world that is . . . But, there he sits, laughing, telling stories; it's as if he was raised from the dead. I want to thank you for believing in my son, especially when everyone else, including me, had given up on this ever occurring.

As a therapist, I have the great luxury of entering the play of anyone's life after the battle scene has occurred. I never see precisely how the carnage was created, so I'm not traumatized. This made me able to accommodate where Grant was emotionally, offering support and guidance to help him get where he wanted to go.

No one can remain objective if they actually live through what his family endured regarding Grant's borderline behaviors. Objectivity is what therapy can offer. Repair through living and behaving consistently differently was the only way for family members and friends to reopen their hearts to Grant. His story was a happy one, but in chapter 6, we'll meet Jean and see how, with the same set of challenges, she struggled more and did not ultimately prevail.

The EQ-i 2.0 and the therapeutic process offered structure and momentum. But Grant wanted things to be different and was willing to do the required heavy lifting. Things changed for the better because opportunity and desire intersected at the right moment.

Frozen in Time: Diane

Even strengths in essential areas—when overpronounced—can cause significant problems. Take Diane, for example. She worked as a lawyer for a nonprofit in Washington, D.C. According to her, it was a dream job. But she came to see me a year after her brother Peter, a graduate student, committed suicide. After our fourth therapy session, I invited Diane to take the EQ-i 2.0, so we could use the results in our upcoming meetings.

As you can see in figure 4.3, Diane's Impulse Control and Independence were strong. But her Problem-Solving, Self-Regard, Self-

Actualization, and Emotional Expression competencies were in dire need of enrichment. How did this all play out in the context of why she sought therapy?

Much of our conversation focused on her brother Peter and her family.

> I grew up in a pretty stable environment, with loving parents and an awesome brother. . . . Peter inspired me on almost every level. He was kind, strong, sometimes headstrong, never shied away from speaking his mind when he felt injustice was occurring and had this incredible way of connecting with almost everyone he spoke to.

Diane told me Peter's friends called him "Billy," after Bill Clinton. She said that Peter and Bill Clinton shared a way of making you feel like the most important person on the planet by completely focusing on you when speaking. One morning, we were on a bus, and Peter was talking with a woman. All of a sudden, she looked up, and said, "Oh my, I should have gotten off the bus six stops ago." People would get lost in a conversation with him as he would with them. No matter who it was, he felt he could learn something from that person. Every day, whether they were together or apart, he would ask Diane the same question: "So, what happened today that challenged the way you think?" He would also share his experience from the day.

Fear was an enemy that Peter longed to conquer. He once told Diane about his investigation into how some Americans spoke about radical Islam and said, "It was shocking to see how fear, hate, and intolerance was invading the American psyche, so that every practicing Muslim would be seen as a potential terrorist. This is exactly the kind of stuff that breeds racism, suspiciousness, incivility, impulsiveness, and exclusiveness."

Diane took Peter's attitude toward fear—and his encouragement to get beyond it—to heart.

> He would challenge me to look beyond my fears and see how those fears are keeping me from truly living and learning. I wrote a paper in college on the role of fear in our life and how often it serves to suffocate our potential. The professor thought it was one of the most original and reflective pieces he had seen from an undergraduate. He gave me the

name of a person he believed could help me in taking my writing talent to the next level. And while I did write the paper, Peter actually edited it quite a bit, and added his own touches. I can honestly say his input [improved] my writing.

Peter's intellectual and emotional support was essential. "I was conscious of the importance of the relationship in my life," said Diane. Yet she revealed that she was not able to help Peter with his great challenge: depression. He refused her pleas to get medication and therapy to help.

"I felt like a broken record," Diane told me. "I kept saying, 'Listen, you can't pull out of this alone, because you haven't been able to up to now.' He would hang onto the 'up to now.' He said: 'I'll get my arms around this eventually.' He didn't. . . . Ever since he was in middle school, depression was, as he would say, 'a constant and unwelcomed companion on my journey.'"

Eventually, Peter was hospitalized for a week. He took medication and saw a therapist. But Diane saw, in retrospect, that her brother "was a fly caught in a web from which he never felt he could fully escape."

I asked if Peter had made direct or indirect references to suicide. "He would make veiled references to letting go," she replied. "The night before he died, he said, 'Checking out of this torment feels pretty inviting. I honestly wouldn't mind if a tree branch fell on me.' He had said things like this before, so alarms weren't going off."

The tragedy had a profound effect on Diane. It also called some strengths that may have been overused into play. "It almost feels like Peter left me with both incredible memories and his depression," she told me. "I haven't been able to get out of bed many days. Eating is a chore. I have lost 20 pounds since he died. I have no interest in seeing friends, especially friends whom Peter and I shared in common. I don't want to be bothered. I don't want to be a bother. And most especially, I don't want to talk about Peter. I think about him constantly. . . . I just don't want to talk about him."

Diane had kept a journal since Peter died, reflecting on her life without him. "It feels like living each day with this insatiable thirst you can't quench," she observed.

"Or an itch you can't scratch," I added.

"Uh huh. Exactly. It is life, right? I mean people go through this every minute of every day. Losing someone they love long before they are ready to let go and say goodbye. Once we breathe our first breath, we don't know how we will breathe our last; well, at least the vast majority of us."

I pointed out that Peter did know when he would take his last breath. It was a means of taking control of an unknown. A way of ending a pain on his terms no one could understand.

"He did," Diane replied. She sobbed and looked at me. "He was in such pain, wasn't he?"

"He was, Diane," I told her. "And with the little bit I have heard in terms of how he loved you and you loved him and how he lived his life, the pain must have been excruciating. I am not justifying Peter taking his life. I am putting into perspective what must have been happening for him to leave something he so loved."

Diane told me that Peter read constantly, everything he could get his hands on. He loved David Foster Wallace, the author of *Infinite Jest*, and read everything he could find that he written. Wallace, too, took his own life. He was regarded as a brilliant writer by many, but also had demons that medication, loving friends and family, and a stunning intellect could not exorcise.

The void of meaning around suicide, and the inaccessibility that those left behind have to deal with, were things that Diane grappled with ferociously: "What do you say about suicide? It is one of those things no one can wrap their minds around. Someone takes their life and there is always the living left behind. Sometimes people can somewhat understand; most of the time they can't."

Yet Diane's love for her brother closed off some avenues of anger in the anguish.

> I have been involved with an online support group, and I hear many people talk about their loved one being profoundly selfish. Their suicide was the ultimate act of selfishness. Their feelings, and the loss they would suffer at the hands of someone suiciding, was never taken into account by the person they loved. I feel some of that too, but I also have to believe that for Peter to take his life, things have to have been so unbearable. As he said shortly before he died: "The threads in the knitting are fraying." I did say that taking his own life made no sense because he

had to see how the story ended. He laughed. What he was saying though was he was threadbare and worn out. It was just too hard.

I asked whether it had gotten too hard for Diane. Not from the standpoint of taking her life, but rather in seeing little on the horizon that feels inviting. "Life has lost it shine, its color," she admitted.

> What is the point, I suppose? I want the color to return. Damn! . . . With it, my energy and creativity have crumpled. I don't want to keep swimming in a pool of sadness and regret. As you say, it doesn't serve me and distances me from my potential. As Wordsworth says, I want to be that "discontented sojourner: now free." The only way to make sense out of life is to turn toward it. Rather than run from what is out there, making excuses why things are happening and blaming everything that can be blamed. No one is going to make it better for me. I am the only one who can accomplish that task.

I turned the conversation toward the future we would plot with her EQ-i 2.0 results. She mentioned that even taking the assessment felt like a move out of a "stagnant" life. What would it look like to begin getting what she wanted on a daily basis—and in a lasting way?

> It starts with just not being afraid any more. Releasing the reins of doubt and pain. Our talks have allowed me to see that I make so many damn excuses for not embracing the life I want. I originally talked about having the perfect job, which, to be perfectly honest is not the truth. I feel like a monkey could do what I do. I accepted the position believing I would be able to use my skills and challenge myself in a way I haven't up to that point. The first thing I must do, even in a shitty economy, is look for the job I want. I have an excellent education, some top academic honors, and I am crafting a vision of what I want. Now is the time to begin acting on it.

Diane's EQ-i 2.0 results reflected much of what she had told me in our sessions. She was not in a place where she felt good about herself (Self-Regard) or was aware of what she was feeling (Emotional Self-Awareness). Low Self-Actualization made it challenging to achieve her goals.

The strengths were equally telling—and seemed to be straining with overuse. High scores in Impulse Control and Stress Tolerance indicate that Diane was holding back the best of who she was. But even more concerning and unhealthy was that these two strengths indicated a propensity to allow the stress to stack to the point of collapse. Independence demonstrated that she had been cocooning and leaning on self-reliance, rather than sharing her thoughts, worries, and pain with others.

While Diane seemed to maintain requisite Emotional Self-Awareness, she was not talking about what she was feeling or experiencing (Emotional Expression). Once Peter died, a profound expressive outlet died with him, albeit temporarily. Diane realized she was at her best when she shared what was happening in her life, but it was something she had not done in a year.

The appearance of Independence as a strength is of particular importance, because Diane may have placed too much importance on her brother's opinion, as related to her own decision-making. We later verified my supposition in our meetings. She had to change tack to find her own voice and learn to rely more on herself. Not relying on others at all, however, meant that she would not receive helpful opinions and support. My challenge as a therapist was clear. Could we explore what it would look like for Diane to truly find her voice, while still interacting with others?

As I dug deeper into the assessment, I saw more roadblocks. While Diane has been plodding through life with the weight of the world on her shoulders—eliciting a high score on Stress Tolerance—she actually didn't deal that well with stress. Stress caused her to shut down emotionally and socially. Peter's death also put Diane under extraordinary stress as she managed the grieving process.

Flexibility also became an issue. Peter and Diane had developed a dance together where Diane relied on what Peter said, and she expected his input and guidance. With that support gone, Diane showed no interest in meeting people halfway in order to gain new support. Breaking out of a painful and overly self-reflective state can be grueling.

Solutions are even more difficult when a person underutilizes the Problem-Solving competency. In Diane's case, this challenge was directly related to her low Self-Expression, high Independence, and low

Self-Actualization. She recognized that she carried immense anger at Peter's death that she has not wanted to address.

Diane's strength in Emotional Self-Awareness did give her an ability to frame the issue.

> The problem is that I never got out of the problem-solving loop to actually make a decision and attempt to truly solve the problem. It used to be [that] Peter would show up like a superhero and save the day by telling me the best way to go. Now I just brood and think, which creates additional stress, and makes me feel that making a decision is far off. Since I have not learned to rely on anyone the way I did on Peter, I just spin my tires going over things intractably. I didn't want to admit how much I relied on Peter's opinion, and how quickly I would abandon my ideas to embrace and follow his. I have been too flexible and didn't want to continue that with friends, so I shut down.

I often look up what a client finds important or interesting to see if I can refer to it in our discussions. Diane was fond of William Wordsworth, and early in our sessions, she quoted a line from Wordsworth's poem, *The Prelude*. During the session where we examined her EQ-i 2.0 results, I quoted Wordsworth to her, saying, "'The heavy weight of many a weary day' is rapidly becoming a thing of the past."

Diane was consciously doing everything possible, each and every day, celebrating Peter's life and the life she was capable of living. As we started to talk about her assessment, she replied, "I also believe the weary days are being left behind. And I feel a true sense of optimism."

Examining her scores, Diane surveyed the challenges ahead of her. "I have not been very happy nor optimistic," she said.

> My sadness and reticence [reluctance] about exploring ways out of my quagmire is illustrated in my being far too Flexible. Not wanting to see or hear from friends simply kept me stuck and a victim of my own devices, which has become deadening. Through it all, however, I am feeling better in my own skin, and I believe in who I am. This was not reflected in the Self-Regard score, because it is just now bubbling to the surface. My brother's death left me doubting many things; including who I am—to myself and others. I feel like I am beginning to recapture a sense of contentment or happiness in the world.

Peter took much of her Self-Regard with him when he died. A score of 85 indicates that a person is on the cusp between okay functioning and dipping into a place of self-doubt. Diane's competency was 72.

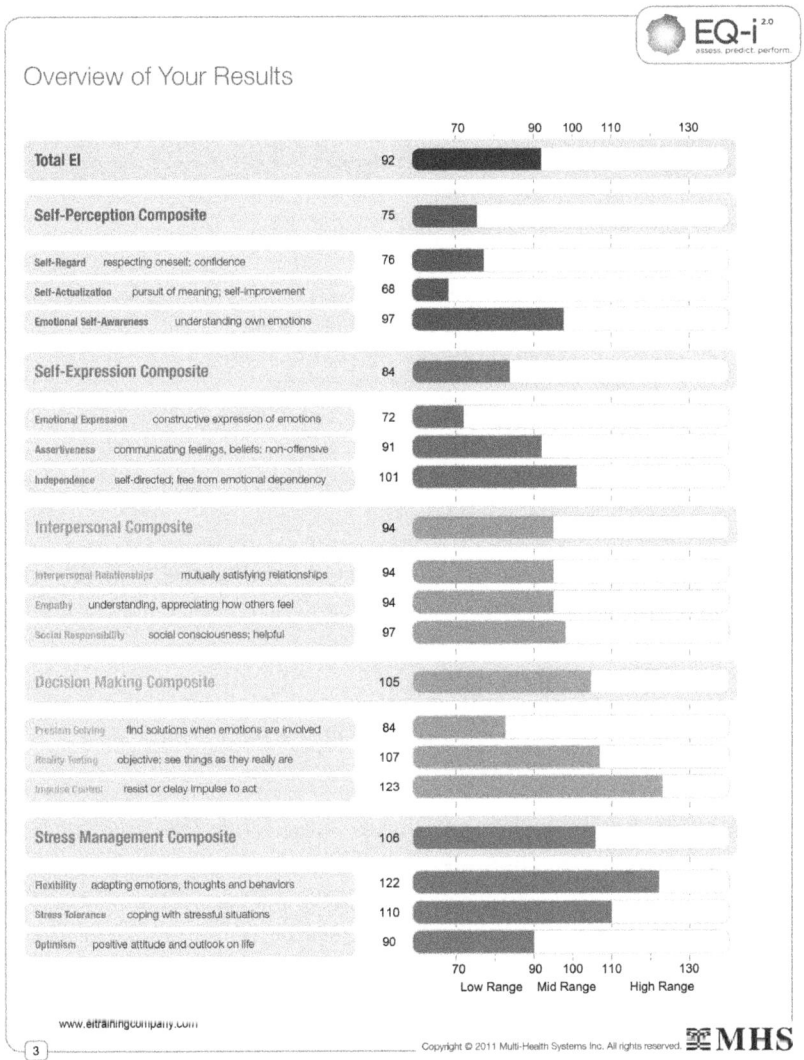

Figure 4.3.

Diane's EQ-i 2.0 assessment was a snapshot of where she was at that moment, and the positive subsequent shifts in her demeanor were noticeable. In one session, I shared with her some relevant lines from *The Prelude* that spoke to her personal movement and growth during this breakout time in her life—and her embrace of a newfound awareness and desire to maximize her talents:

> A discontented sojourner: now free,
> Free as a bird to settle where I will.
> What dwelling shall receive me? in what vale
> Shall be my harbor? underneath what grove
> Shall I take up my home? and what clear stream
> Shall with its murmur lull me into rest?
> The earth is all before me. With a heart
> Joyous, nor scared at its own liberty,
> I look about; and should the chosen guide
> Be nothing better than a wandering cloud,
> I cannot miss my way. I breathe again!
> Trances of thought and mountings of the mind
> Come fast upon me: it is shaken off,
> That burthen of my own unnatural self,
> The heavy weight of many a weary day
> Not mine, and such as were not made for me.
> Long months of peace (if such bold word accord
> With any promises of human life),
> Long months of ease and undisturbed delight
> Are mine in prospect; whither shall I turn,
> By road or pathway, or through trackless field,
> Uphill or down, or shall some floating thing
> Upon the river point me out my course?

Diane wiped some tears from her eyes as I reminded her that she had wanted to become "the discontented sojourner, now free."

"*The Prelude* is so beautiful and so true," she said. "Thank you for this. This is the type of thing Peter would often do for me. Hear something I was interested in and get it for me."

I observed that I was able to do so because she allowed it to happen and that many more things would start coming her way now:

The touch of a friend, the consolation of someone who has missed you, the ability for you to give, as Peter so often did. And, to begin believing more fully in your abilities. Allowing your friends to reinforce, or not, as the case may be, the direction you want to go in your life. It means inviting them in, not asking them to make a decision for you. Peter was a wonderful friend and companion on this journey through life who, in many ways, did not want to see you uncomfortable, or struggle with an issue. He therefore taught you to let the decision rest with him. If you really did not believe what he was saying, my sense is you would not have followed this direction.

Diane's ability to begin living a life uninterrupted emerged from both awareness that was gained from the EQ-i 2.0 and our sessions, as well as from her own actions.

Diane easily could have blamed her life woes on her brother's death. His suicide stripped her of his love and consistent presence, and she could have used this as an excuse not to shoulder the responsibilities of her life. Instead, she chose to take her brother's memories, as well as her talents and desires, and begin building a meaningful life in an unpredictable world.

"We don't know what tomorrow brings," Diane told me. "So, I must invest the best I can in each and every moment I encounter. And that is life. Life is this constant stacking of memories and desires on top of one another."

Why is finding that peace so evasive for some? I honestly don't have an answer. Some people find their answer in God's will, or acknowledging the plight of the human condition, or glimpsing the randomness in the universe.

What I do know is that the guardian angels in our life are sent in the form of family, friends, and the multitude of other resources we encounter. For some, faith in a higher power plays a pivotal role in making sense out of life's nonsense. Accompanying faith is an enduring sense of connection to others and finding solace in their touch, their words, and, at times, their silence.

I have seen through my own lens that those who find comfort in faith find an equal amount of comfort in others. And faith does not mean embracing a particular religion or spirituality. It means finding something of enduring meaning outside of ourselves and relying on that to move us through life's turbulence and accompanying calmer moments.

This, too, is part of being an emotionally intelligent person. Knowing our ship has a rudder makes the expedition far more predictable and less stressful. It keeps the balance between strengths and weakness as we steer. How we use the rudder makes all the difference and clearly informs the direction we go.

CHAPTER FIVE

~

The EQ-i Map
Finding the Pattern

Willy, a former Marine special operator who served in both Operation Enduring Freedom-Afghanistan and Operation Iraqi Freedom, talked about liberation from pain.

> You know, it is not like my brokenness comes from the wars. Some of it does . . . but it was there long before. I was a hard ass, with this bug-repellent-type stare that kept people away. I thought that was what it meant to be a man. All steely eyed and like Teflon when it came to feelings or emotions. That is not at all what it means to be a man, and I have wasted so much damn time playing this character that did more than keep people from entering into my world; it kept me from really feeling and knowing myself. Changing that has felt so foreign, but so amazing at the same time.
>
> I was at a hockey game the other night with a couple of friends, really having fun. This woman in front of me kept turning around and staring at me. She eventually said, "May I tell you something? You have such a kind face." I wanted to, like, hug her. No one would ever have said that to me a year ago. You know my Emotional Independence feels so much more balanced, and my anger passes by like the wind, where it used to get hung up like a kite in a tree . . . I also feel tons more optimistic about what I can do to direct the course of my life. It feels like getting a second chance. I feel lighter.

I am using our time together as this kind of incubator to practice, explore, try things out, and then bring it to my day-to-day world. I used to drink a lot. My friend and I were at the hockey game when he commented, "Is everything okay? You seem really different lately. You drink very little, smile more than I have ever seen you. It's like you have this secret that no one else knows." I suppose he was right!

Willy's relief from pain came from our mutual understanding of his EQ-i 2.0 map. It's one thing to take the assessment, and even to observe the competencies and weaknesses. But how do you get from there to true freedom?

The assessment poses a common conundrum, one wrapped around interpretation of the results. What does it mean? I introduce the client to what seems like a complex tangle of competencies that need to make therapeutic sense. When you picture this, instead of a knot, you can try thinking of a ballet, where each character moves with purpose, affecting other characters. How do these competencies interact to reinforce, either negatively or positively, their strengths? Understanding the intricacies of the tool allows us to use it in alignment with its potential to inspire personal change. Like examining a spider web, the client begins to see how the competencies are connected, with some closer or more distant than others. The competencies are also like a mobile hanging from the ceiling; touch one piece and they all move.

Mastery means learning what these competencies tell us. To the untrained eye, someone low in emotional Problem-Solving, yet high in Emotional Independence, may simply appear self-assured. Where in reality, Independence may well be an overused strength, and when his/her vision/opinion is tested, the low Problem-Solving is represented as anger. The world sees nothing beyond the competency. I don't expect my clients, or anyone, to immediately understand the relationships among the competencies. We understand first our clients and then the competencies, and we invite clients to explore the interplay between the two.

What happens when one of the 15 competencies is enhanced, or, in the case of the mobile, touched? What happens to the ones near it? The tool can detect if and when, for instance, we juxtapose competencies such as high Empathy and Emotional Expression against low emotional Independence, low Problem-Solving capacity, and low Assertiveness.

What is the dance among these competencies, and how does it place a client at an advantage or disadvantage in the effort to forge a better life?

For example, consider this relationship: High Empathy and Emotional Expression means a person often wears their heart on their sleeve. Not standing up for what they need (low Assertiveness) and tending to react emotionally rather than reflecting (low Problem-Solving) both become evident in low emotional Independence. We get a person who does not express their opinion if it differs from the larger group. Their feelings are muffled at best and jammed into the nether world of emotion at worst. The low emotional Problem-Solving would suggest there is a great deal of anger both above and below the surface.

That is the excitement of learning the language of the competencies. While the Comprehensive Feedback Report does a brilliant job of talking about how the competencies impact and influence one another, the therapist, counselor, coach, or whoever the professional may be takes the client on a much deeper dive, to see things you simply cannot see on the surface. The difference between this and other interventions is like watching a caving expedition on the National Geographic channel, versus going spelunking with a guide. After reading this book, you'll have the knowledge of the competencies to begin your own treasure hunting.

Monochromatic to Color: Gabi

Initially, I considered writing this book for those of us who hold ourselves out as healers in a turbulent world: therapists, counselors, psychologists, psychiatrists, coaches, mentors, and mental health clinicians. But as it unfolded, I felt it is also for those who have carried a satchel packed with life's pain, disappointment, and false beliefs, far too long. This personal suffering must be unpacked, sorted out, and much of it discarded. Then, we can begin truly feeling free to explore and create the life we want, a life that has felt elusive. This process is different for each of us. I recently provided a student, Gabi, with her EQ-i 2.0 Feedback Report. She was extremely low in Self-Regard, Assertiveness, and Optimism. She was almost off the charts in Stress Tolerance and Social Responsibility, suggesting her needs were almost always subservient to the needs of others.

Imagine this young woman, shouldering remarkable amounts of stress while putting everyone else before her own needs. She felt essentially worthless. And, as she noted, "feeling like a worn-out welcome mat, where people walk over you without even noticing you are there. I don't want this to be melodramatic. I cannot remember when a friend or family member truly asked about how I am doing." Yet, to look at her, no one would immediately notice the burdens this woman carried. She has tried countless things to feel better and enjoy life more. In reality, there really is nothing outside of us that can create healing. This invariably resulted in her experiencing life as a weary endeavor.

What patterns do we currently engage in that are healthy versus damaging? Knowing that there are very real and sustained patterns of thinking and behaving in the world can move us toward social and emotional liberation. As a client said about this freedom, "I see glimmers of it, but it feels more like something I eventually wake up from; something I have only briefly experienced." No one deserves to see themselves as less than, or that the sum and substance of their life is an endurance race where they never slow down, never rest, and are never really at peace.

Brotherly Love—Not! Jon

Jon resisted talking to anyone about the abuse he suffered at the hands of his brother while growing up.

> I walked around with my heart feeling like it was going to pop out of my chest. It was way more than anxiety—it was pure fear. It often kept me from eating or feeling anything other than pain. I learned to lose myself in work and outperform everyone, simply because all I did was work. School was an essential outlet for me, which later converted to my professional life. It does seem I couldn't let anyone outdo me. Winning was the only thing that made me feel somewhat okay. This type of thinking . . . has been exhausting.
>
> One day a VP of my firm came up and put his hand on my shoulder to congratulate me. I turned pale as all the blood rushed out of my head, looking absolutely terrified. My brother would often come up behind me, grab both shoulders and buckle my knees so I would fall flat on my back. No matter what I was carrying, he did this incessantly, among

other equally shitty things. Just remembering it, my heart is pounding. . . . Anyway, my boss asked if I was okay, and I said I was coming down with something. Later, he came to my office where he shared his own struggle with people touching him, because of what his mother used to do to him. It really caught me by surprise, and I wasn't sure what to say. This was the beginning of my healing. It is hard to describe what that experience was like. I must sound like a puss. I am telling you though; it was unrelenting bullying.

Listening to my VP tell his story, I began to loosen a bit. I was fighting back tears with everything in me. While I didn't say much, I did thank him for talking with me. It was surprising what he said: "The risk is in not talking. For me, not telling my story continued to give my mother power over virtually everything in my life. The space she occupied in my brain was overwhelming." That moment of terror where my VP innocently touched my shoulder, and him coming back to talk with me, remains one of the most significant moments in my life. Can you believe it? I am learning to talk, especially here, and share it with other people in my life. Romantic relationships having consistently been difficult . . . because I just don't share anything of real substance about my life. I now understand through our work together that I am at a crossroads; either I use the strategies for personal growth we have talked about or I remain in this emotional prison. This is one of those binary moments in life where the switch is either on, or off. This is scary as crap!

Jon's parents knew his brother was abusive, but they felt incapable of protecting him. They did, however, see Jon's great promise and ability and tried to reinforce the fact he could do anything he wanted in the world—once he got out of the house. Jon did not come out with his sexual identity until he was in college, so he didn't think the abuse had anything to do with his being gay. His brother was simply a mean, self-obsessed person, openly jealous of Jon's intellectual talent and ability to have solid friendships.

As you can see from Jon's strengths on the EQ-i 2.0 in figure 5.1, he felt good about who he is and what he contributes.

> I have had good friends, who I know care and are reliable. They know virtually nothing about how I grew up. I also get positive feedback from my colleagues at work. I learned early on that my brother's abusiveness wasn't really about me, though it affected me deeply. My parents would

say, "You know Jon, he is just troubled." I generally feel pretty good about who I am, because so much of it has been based on what I can accomplish, which has been a lot. In looking at my EQ-i results, in order to survive, I powered down my Emotional Self-Awareness and Expression. It has been like shooting a rubber band at the wall. It bounces off and falls lifeless to the ground. That is exactly what I would do with my Emotional Self-Awareness. I have had people describe me as the "silent, brooding type." While guys I dated initially find this intriguing, they grow tired of me being so closed off. Simply put, I checked out emotionally (low Empathy).

I have also been called "the professor" because I take such emotional distance from things. It is not that I don't feel things; I do. I just don't really let them stay very long. I also do not give much weight to what people say or the advice they may offer me (Emotional Independence). When decisions have to be made, big or small, I lock onto what needs to be done and by when. I seek out very little assurance or reinforcement from others. I do not toe the party line or say things I think people want to hear. My brother did this as we got older, and I find it spineless (Jon has no contact with his brother and has not since he was in college). If you believe something, let it be known. I never understood how someone could believe in something they are not proud of. Being proud of it is having no qualms about mentioning it to others. Like Ann Coulter! I don't agree with her positions on most things, though I admire her willingness to publicly say and argue what she believes.

Jon's three low competencies have served to sabotage romantic relationships. His romantic partners felt shut out and unable to read where Jon was emotionally. Since he didn't express himself, they were left to try and guess what was going on, with very little success. This frustrated them and Jon, because,

> You know, I really just checked out when someone needed something emotionally from me. I was dating this one guy who was being bullied at work. An adult being bullied. Like, come on! I literally said nothing as he told me what was going on. I was an emotional flatline. I had this Post Traumatic Stress response to what he was saying. I remember feeling bad for him; I just couldn't figure out how to express it. I didn't blame him for telling me to go plant myself in the forest where I can be surrounded by other trees as we all sit in silence. Intellectually, I knew I was out of step with everyone else. I just didn't know how to keep it from happening.

The EQ-i Map: Finding the Pattern ~ 135

Jon began paying close attention to his emotions, writing the words down in a book designed specifically to capture those feelings. What color were they? How long did they last? What generated them? Jon worked hard to become more emotionally aware. He leveraged his

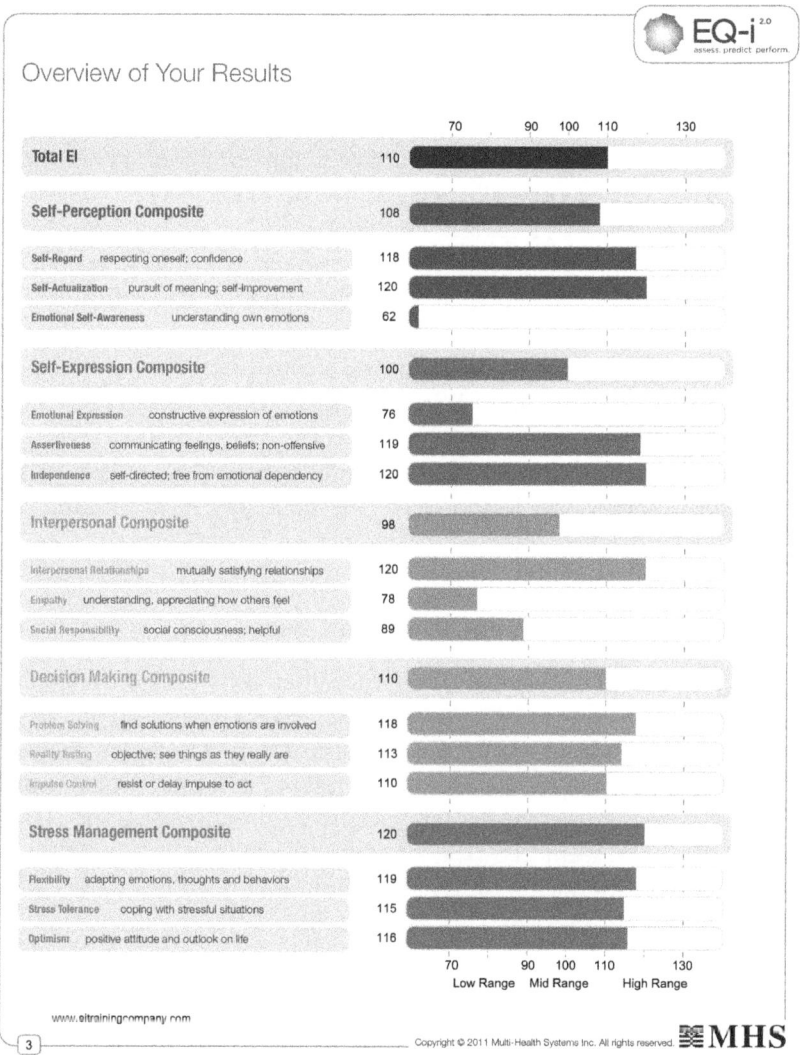

Figure 5.1.

strong Self-Actualization competency and Optimism to make this happen. Jon is very goal-driven, and when tasked with something important, he dedicates himself to it. His strong Optimism stemmed from the fact that if you work hard, you receive some sort of positive reward. He believed that whatever he put his mind to, he could achieve. He got this from his parents who reminded him often that if he wants something, and is willing to work for it, he will achieve it.

The more Jon recognized his feelings, the more connection he had with those around him. He fell in love with someone with whom he could talk about his work in therapy and what he was trying to accomplish emotionally. His partner actively supported Jon's growth and desire to be more Emotionally Self-Aware and Emotionally Expressive. The competency most impacted by this was his increase in Empathy.

You would think that someone who is so emotionally Independent would be far less Flexible, but Jon was the opposite. He was intensely Flexible, which served him well in business. Those around him did not persuade or dissuade him from following a course he believed in. He is overly Self-Actualized, and his business success was the only real success he cared about. It occupied all of his thinking. He was extremely Optimistic when imagining what he could accomplish professionally, but before therapy, he did not have the same ability to imagine his personal life. Now he does.

What We Don't See

When people walk through my door, they often do not show their pain. They have learned to cloak it from others' perceptive eyes. Some seem to have what it takes to make things work, and in many ways, they do work. They are often productive, with a refined skill set for success and all their energies directed toward specific and attainable goals. They survive and even seem to thrive despite feeling broken, misunderstood, emotionally abandoned, unloved, unheard, unnoticed, unappreciated, and unbelievably stressed. This then can lead to feeling unmotivated, depressed, anxious, as if one can't catch a break, uncertain about what talents they have, and uncertain which direction to move in. As one very jittery and overactive woman noted not too long ago,

When I slow down, I begin to think, and when I begin to think, I begin to remember, and when I begin to remember, I begin to fall apart. I see a collage of all the crap in my life. I see the many hues of pain, not the colors of the rainbow. This is my life.

Her life has been a path of deep pain and sorrow, with moments of joy sprinkled on it. You can't see it, however, because she works so hard to cover up her unhealed wounds. Her life has consisted of staying busy and constantly moving, as if being tracked by a sniper. She has achieved a variety of professional accolades, but most days she feels as though any moment it will all simply fall apart. Considering this, she concluded, "This isn't living; it is holding on. It is a clawing toward something, but definitely not living."

When someone sits with me and begins feeling safe enough to tell their story, it is often a mixture of regret and pain. They recount things they have done wrong or mismanaged, outrageous expectations foisted on them, loss and choices gone bad, or opportunities not seized. At some point, I gently steer the conversation toward their particular triumphs. Honoring the pain is critical. However, I also want to hear when things have gone right, even if they seemed fleeting at the time. Seeking out therapy requires courage. Initially in therapy it is difficult for people to see beyond the pain and disappointment. The objective of therapy is for the client to break free of invisible chains, like Prometheus unbound. Pain and fear are the invisible shackles. Getting someone to truly see the pain and the role fear plays in their life is what entering into therapy is all about. It is an investment in finding personal liberation.

I often ask someone who struggles with substance abuse issues, "Tell me of a time you were sober. How did it feel? Was there a time in sobriety you felt good? What was that like? Bring me to that place with you. I want to feel it. I want to share that moment with you." There is such a reluctance on the part of those in pain to acknowledge their strength. It feels almost like a betrayal. I honor their struggle, with an eye on their strength, those personal victories that exist for all of us. We all deserve to embrace our past victories and move toward the victories yet discovered.

The Time Bomb: Jeb

Jeb grew up in a breeding ground for anxiety and interpersonal tension. His parents strictly adhered to a religious tradition preaching simplicity, and they imposed poverty on the family. They did not celebrate holidays, there were never any gifts, and individuals were not celebrated, especially not Jeb. The first time he experienced a traditional academic setting was at college. It was completely overwhelming because, though homeschooled, "I was home, and somewhere there was school going on, just not with me." He was at least four grade levels behind his peers. Passing the GED was monumental for him. While attending college, he majored in the sciences with great success, because he had a brain like a racecar that had only been idling up until college. College and graduate school allowed him to intellectually take off.

The message he got from his parents, however, was clear: You are not smart, so quit trying to pretend you are something you are not. We are not trying to be mean, but we don't want you to have false hope about what you can accomplish. Two graduate degrees later, he still feels like an imposter. He has learned through the years to doubt what he sees and feels, instead relying on others to make choices on his behalf. This belief structure has been costly in romantic relationships and in the workplace.

His internal self-doubt, layered on top of very real social and neurological disabilities, continually threatens a disaster that has not occurred. He keeps waiting for the tectonic plates to shift and destroy everything he has worked so hard to create. He describes it like a bomb buried in his brain, one that will go off, but he just doesn't know when.

Countering this belief took a yeoman's effort on his part and a reshuffling of his basic beliefs. He wasn't the one who set this bomb. He contributed nothing to its placement. His parents, siblings, and religious community members built it and set it. Once constructed and placed in his mind, it was only a matter of time. The bomb parts consisted of, "You are fooling yourself to believe you can do anything academically." "Dummies get by and are grateful for what they get." "There is no one who would want to be with you. If someone is with you, it is because they are using you." "It's okay to accept that you are limited. I don't want to see you get hurt by tilting at windmills and believing you are something you are not. That just leads to disappointment."

It is hard for me to imagine parents, siblings, religious leaders, and close family friends saying this to him, but say it they did. In spite of this, Jeb achieved academic success. Their parting gift to him, even though he saw them eat crow, was this time bomb. Getting the ticking time bomb out of his head was critical.

The bomb generates, perpetuates, and instigates self-doubt; that is its purpose. It erodes and washes away confidence as if a five-day rain fell hard on a dusty, dirt-covered hillside. It anticipates things fundamentally not working out. Instead of his parents finding resources for Jeb's neuro-physical and learning-based problems, they reinforced his swelling negative internal feelings. Those feelings steadily grew, eventually making him feel like an Outlander. It is mind-boggling to consider the display of strength necessary to earn three academic degrees and have enviable professional influence. At work, however, he distrusts what he does, what others say, and the impact he is making. He swims in doubt, and others sense it like a dog sensing fear. "If you ever walked through the woods, off the beaten trail, where you are now fighting through brambles, bushes, interconnected vines and the like, that is what it feels like for me to deal with social interactions," he said. He often did not really know where he stood and how to challenge people if they did not follow through on what they said to him.

This has also been true in his romantic relationships. For example, a woman invited him to Richmond on a business trip, to spend time with her after meeting a client. The day before they were supposed to leave, she said, "Oh no, I didn't say you'd come to Richmond with me. I said I am going down there for work. You are putting way too much pressure on me, and I feel claustrophobic." This is the definition of gaslighting someone. He felt so emotionally dismantled by this that he questioned everything, somehow believing that he heard her wrong. When pressed, he was clear in what he heard, but he also admitted that this happens quite a bit. Someone he is dating will say how much she likes him and that he is exactly what she has been looking for. Then, she'll drop him like yesterday's news once he holds her accountable for what she has said. This was the nexus between living with the time bomb or finally getting the bomb squad in to remove the damn thing. He chose the latter.

After our fourth session, Jeb took the EQ-i 2.0. His results are in figure 5.2. Considering the boulder he has had to repeatedly push up a hill, day after day, week after week, his Comprehensive Feedback Report is not terribly surprising. My sense is that because Jeb grew up with devastating and repeated negative messages, his stress endurance has been drained (Stress Tolerance). He has a near-constant sensation that he is failing at work or in personal relationships. There is nowhere for him to seek refuge, away from a rain that is constant and drenching. Considering what we know about him and the remarkable odds he overcame to achieve academic success, you would think he'd have more Optimism. Suppressing his optimism is a constant fear of failure. Also, at any moment that hidden time bomb could explode, laying waste to everything he has achieved.

He also has a low Interpersonal Relations composite exacerbated by his low Stress Tolerance and Optimism. We see this when he has a hard time connecting with people and maintaining relationships. Things start out well, because in friendships or romantic encounters he is always honest about his struggles. This seems inviting at first, until the others tire of it. I guided him to say less about what he has been through initially and to practice just being in the moment with them. Considering the remarkable fund of knowledge Jeb has, it is unlikely he would be sentenced to sitting in silence with a partner or a date.

When he feels things deeply, as noted in his Emotional Self-Awareness, he becomes too Emotionally Expressive. Jeb simply does not have a good barometer when it comes to understanding how his expressions affects others. In what he described as an unhealthily religious family, his siblings did not like him, and it seemed his parents did not either. They discussed empathy as it appeared in scripture, but they didn't demonstrate much toward him. I believe this is also related to his low Social Responsibility, since it requires empathy to put the needs of others appropriately before your own.

One of Jeb's college professors thought he may be on the autism spectrum, and Jeb could see how that made sense. He said in our initial meetings that he struggled to understand both verbal and especially nonverbal cues. This also could explain why he was chosen as the family's sacrificial lamb. As a young child, he was out-of-step with members of the family and the community. The Christian principles his parents espoused and based their life on were not directed toward Jeb. Quite the opposite, actually.

This woman I was dating said she was excited about going to a concert on Saturday. Starting Thursday, I sent her texts working out the logistics.

Figure 5.2.

On Saturday morning, she texted me to leave her alone and stop bothering her. I didn't get it. I wasn't bothering her. I just wanted to make sure we were on the same page. I missed something along the way. You know, this is always what happens.

Fortunately, Jeb kept the texts he had sent to the woman. When he showed them to me, I thought the notes he sent were absolutely appropriate and also spaced far enough apart to seem understandable in waiting for a response. Also, just as he said, her response text was terse and to the point, "Stop bothering me."

At first, I thought there must have been a prior misread, and something in their communication he missed. But there wasn't! Before the exchange he showed me, he texted on Tuesday saying what a great time he had and how he was looking forward to Saturday. He said, "I'll drop a line Thursday-ish to hammer out the details." She responded, "Awesome." The next text from her was the negative one, but it did not track what she said previously. This happened frequently to Jeb, and he invariably blamed being "on the spectrum" for not being able to read the tea leaves correctly.

Jeb began to accept that some people are not fully upfront. They make it seem they are all in until they are not, at which point they end things. Jeb saw more clearly that this pattern had been present in his dating life for a while. "Yeah, okay but how do I know if someone is genuine?" The reality is that you don't. Dating or developing a friendship is a process that follows its own current. You don't know what is around the bend until you get there and can see a bit further ahead. Learning to see pink flags turning red became the barometer he followed to determine someone's investment in a relationship. He began detailing the flags he noticed and challenging these observations with assertiveness.

This was a huge turning point for Jeb. He no longer saw himself as the carrier of a virus. And just as important, he changed his expectations of how things might end up when first meeting new people. This visibly relaxed him over time, allowing a greater sense of ease to guide each interaction.

At work, Jeb felt people made fun of him, and that he didn't get the joke until it was too late. He thought he was having a positive social interaction, only to later realize someone was actually "setting him up to fall," to use his term. We focused on the moment someone says something in his presence that takes advantage of him. He did know something felt wrong, but the ambiguity left him uncertain how to respond, so he'd ignore it. His inability to stop when something felt off is partly because he spent his tender and formative years being made fun of by those who mattered most. He may have dealt with his pain by pretending not to understand. This playing-dumb behavior is similar to when a child with a learning disability or ADHD acts like the clown in school in order to seem disruptive instead of stupid.

Drawing on his competencies such as Emotional Self-Awareness, Expression, and Assertiveness, and combining them with his strong Self-Actualization (a desire to keep learning and growing), we developed a plan. Certainly, the risk was exposing himself to more hurt and pain when recognizing a slight and confronting it. However, the upside was demonstrating his resolve and interpersonal strength with others.

This quickly took shape at work when a colleague said, "I am talking about those of us who understand the complexity of the case." Jeb looked her dead in the eye and said, "If you are referring to me, let's both lay out how we understand the intricacies of this case and see which one is 'far' more accurate." The colleague verbally stumbled and said she was not at all referring to him. Just other people. After this, he walked taller and felt more competent, which became his new normal.

He also did the same thing with dates. If someone new seemed to distance him the way the woman going to the concert did, he would ask her to "Please tell me exactly what you mean or want." Although people may have seen him as a doormat before, Jeb convincingly dissuaded them of such opinions going forward. It took a lot of work and resolve for him to be his own best ally.

A year after beginning therapy, Jeb took the EQ-i 2.0 again. Figure 5.3 shows his results. He improved in every area. This includes being less Assertive, which to some degree was an overused strength that could distance people. Even though his competencies gained noticeable strength, he had to pay close attention to his Emotional Self-Awareness and Empathy so that they didn't become overused competencies. As stated in the Comprehensive Feedback Report regarding his Emotional Self-Awareness:

Being aware of what you are feeling, and why you are feeling this way, can help guide your actions and even avoid self-defeating behavior.

Your result suggests that you are well attuned with the way you feel and know the true reasons behind your emotions. This helps you pay attention to your feelings, so that you appear reliable and well-tempered

Figure 5.3.

[in your social interactions] at school and/or at work. The ability to perceive why you are feeling a certain way, and especially the ability to perceive others' reactions to your emotions, can be extremely helpful for success in relationships, academically, and in your career.

Jeb's Empathy score of 123 jumped over 50 points, or three standard deviations from his original score of 72. Although this sounds good, he was committed to understanding how Empathy could combine with overly high Emotional Self-Awareness to become problematic. He did not want to feel like or be seen as this obsequious underling that people used to their own advantage, without regard for his needs. A significant part of his therapeutic goal was to become more open-minded, less judgmental, and more empathic. I would say he nailed it! Jeb reshaped his entire experience of others in the world.

He examined how he opened his heart, learning to question his perspective on what was really happening to him in interactions with others. This was like irrigating dusty, dry land. All of this required developing a new set of interactions with his emotions and attending behaviors. Being empathic means truly connecting to what someone else is going through. It does not mean adopting those feelings merely as a way to become the person's ally.

His Comprehensive Feedback Report defines true Empathy as "the ability to understand another person's perspective; it nurtures the strong relationships required for leading a successful life (personally, academically, and professionally)."

Jeb is undoubtedly doing this. I have never seen someone on the spectrum create a complete emotional makeover. Instead of some variant of autism, the emotional abuse he encountered growing up temporarily robbed him of emotional stability—a stability he reclaimed.

White Knuckling: Deidre

Life is just tough and sometimes feels like it can break even the strongest of us. I see the brokenness when people bring it to therapy. They have a deep desire to make things better, to somehow transcend all the crap they have experienced and cultivate a more desirable piece of emotional real estate. As Deidre put it,

We carry around other people's baggage that was foisted on us. We feel bad because bad things were said to us, done to us, or we saw bad things done to others and felt unable to help . . . or we were the victim of ever so subtle messages like from my mother, "Oh, sweetie, it's okay you were not born pretty. You probably have other strengths that people will eventually notice."

Her mother's jarring comment, delivered in such a nonchalant, almost instructive manner, left a wound, stacked upon countless other wounds that haven't fully healed. Deidre's mother leveraged her own physical beauty to get what she wanted. She did not work until later in life, when she could no longer rely on her looks, or the supplemented payouts from social services. She intermixed her wretched feelings about beauty and success with other behaviors and strengths that Deirdre reluctantly admired, so it was difficult to sort out.

This mix of virtues and being simply awful, terrorist-type behavior is a typical mix that narcissistic or self-absorbed parents routinely use to keep their children off balance, while deterring them from fully breaking away. Such parents have strengths, but those better moments really only serve the desires and needs of the parent. As an adult, Deidre has struggled mightily, trying to figure out what type of relationship she should have with her mother. Her tender and forgiving heart has been stretched beyond its limits.

Interestingly, Deirdre is highly intelligent with striking good looks, but, of course, after all of her mother's comments, she doubts both. Fortunately, she found friends and caring adults to strengthen her resolve, giving her courage to challenge the outrageous behavior by her mother. Even with such strong support, however, Deirdre has lingering doubts. Under the right light, her scars become visible.

There is great value in telling our stories. As the student in the first chapter taught us, sometimes we have to tell them a lot to achieve the desired distance from trauma to heal. One route directed toward healing is talking about the moments or situations when Deidre did not doubt herself.

Deirdre's insecurity about her intellect and beauty was apparent in both therapy and with friends and love interests. One day she came to therapy apologizing for not wearing makeup. "I know I look gross without it, but I have been running since the moment I got up." She looked great, but she was playing a kind of duck-and-cover, trying to hide her un-made-up face so no one would see her. As you can anticipate, in her teens, her mother warned her never to go out without makeup, because she required it "to look a little bit attractive."

Recalibrating how she thinks about herself takes work. She has to override a plethora of her mother's agonizing injunctions. This means continually reformatting her understanding of how others view her and, of course, how she views herself. When she came to see me, she had a graduate degree from a top university, she was in a long-term but unfulfilling relationship, and she had a promising job. Using my perceptions and encouragement as a starting point, an external grounding if you will, gave her a sense of how to focus on her strengths. She had lived her life up to this point as if she was an actress playing roles, rather than a woman with an innately strong identity.

When individuals take the EQ-i 2.0, they are often surprised to see the accuracy of their emotional competencies, and they generally agree with what they see. However, Deirdre's response was unusual. We looked at her results (figure 5.4) in my private practice office, where I gave her time to determine whether the competency scores mirrored her understanding of self. As she went over the competencies and their scores, she started sobbing to the point of shaking. Even when talking about some of the worst things her mother had said to her, she never cried, which I found surprising. When I brought this up to her in our sessions, she said, "I have cried so much, it feels like there are no more tears. I am numb to it now." After the tears subsided, I asked her what they were about.

> This is me, right? I have cut off my feelings, so I don't talk about what I feel, because I don't [feel]. I am as emotionally flexible as a tire iron and don't have a strong grip on reality. I always blow shit out of proportion! Which just makes it all worse. Yeah, I'd say that is me?

We talked about where all this came from, concluding it evolved as a survival strategy. She learned to power down her Emotional Self-Awareness to minimize the inevitable pain from her mother. This carried over into what she would feel—or not feel—in relationships. Her distance from her emotions made it hard to talk about them. She mimicked what she saw others do or say, while simply not feeling anything.

This is where Reality-Testing comes in. What was real for her? She never was fully sure if she understood what was going on, how to respond, and what the outcome would be. It was painful for her to

Figure 5.4.

be with a friend who was struggling with something, while not really knowing what to say. By default, she learned to sit quietly, after saying, "Just know I am here." She felt alien, like she was on another planet interacting with the local species.

We discussed at length her strengths, which were surprising to her. As noted earlier, she was very driven (Self-Actualization), in spite of what she encountered growing up. It came from a spirit of proving her mother wrong. Her mother never really acknowledged the impressive things she accomplished, offering classic taglines such as, "Don't mess it up," "Enjoy it now because it won't last," and "Everyone gets lucky sometimes." Deirdre learned to move away from proving things to someone else. Instead, she focused on what she truly needed in order to feel a consistent sense of well-being. Her mother would not be there to celebrate her daughter's triumphs, so Deirdre learned the difficult task of letting others celebrate these things and celebrating them herself. She previously downplayed any compliments people gave her, especially women. These kind words made her uncomfortable precisely because they went against the grain of what she grew up with. Learning to accept compliments by looking someone in the eye and saying, "Thank you," was the beginning.

Once she left home, one of her goals was to craft an independent life. As a countermeasure to what her mother used to say, Deirdre developed her own thoughts and beliefs about things (Emotional Independence), and she stood by them. She would listen to other people's ideas, and then appropriately compare them with her own opinions. Strong Assertiveness also allowed Deirdre to bolster what she wanted in terms of Emotional Independence. She demonstrated high Stress Tolerance, which could be a positive thing. However, when robust Stress Tolerance showed up alongside high Social Responsibility and low Reality-Testing, then an accurate analysis of what is happening around her required drilling deeper.

As we discussed in chapter 2 with the story of Jennifer the military veteran, high Stress Tolerance and Social Responsibility were causing Deirdre to put the needs of others before her own. She carried the weight of not having her own needs met in kind. When this is fortified through low Reality-Testing, it creates a relational loop capable of bringing Deirdre to her knees emotionally. She rarely talked about her feelings, articulated her needs, or made clear how friends could support her. At the same time, she consistently put others before herself, resulting in her feeling angry and unappreciated.

The anger and lack of appreciation would be appropriate responses had Deirdre shared her feeling with those in her relational orbit. Up until entering therapy, she did not. To have truly strong Social Responsibility, we appropriately meet others' needs without depleting our own. Although Deirdre's friends were likely quite willing to support her, she projected an image of having it together and needing very little emotional or social support. This connected to another one of her mother's expectations, that Deirdre should give and expect little in return. Friends had learned to treat her as a solid resource who needed very little. As you can imagine, this lowered her Interpersonal Relationships competency, which in turn left her feeling a lot of unspoken resentment toward her friends. Finding balance in terms of equality in her relationships received our immediate attention.

Feeling life was a stage and she was an actress, she had to control everything she could. There was no deviation from her script. She overused her Impulse Control, an asset at times that now strangled her intellectually, creatively, and socially. She learned to take the risk of infusing more of her personal needs into relationships. This took the shape of announcing more clearly what she needed. This meant she would need less control, because being more emotionally authentic, she could loosen the reins and realize the outcome will be acceptable.

Once she left home for college, she very much embraced an adult status; however, she embraced it too much, resulting in her never really having fun. She couldn't remember having fun in childhood. Even when she did, there was so much anxiety woven into the moment that truly enjoying the experience was impossible. Everything felt heavy. What was predictable was the unpredictable behaviors of her mother. She was always on guard, anticipating an enemy attack, making the need for control unambiguous. Learning what it might mean to reclaim her child and have fun was probably her biggest challenge. She began considering what it meant to have fun and be a child by going to a park and watching what the kids did. It was eye-opening, and not because she started climbing on the jungle gym or going down the slide, which she did, but because she learned how to let go, release stress, and laugh.

Our last session was on the heels of Deirdre accepting a new job overseas, a coveted position that, while it would be a stretch, was what she had hoped for. This was just over a year after our first visit. She had exorcised her mother's critical and negative voice, and now she felt far more real in friendships. She even found a new love interest, which was dynamite for her. He was living in the country where she was going at the time. He was also a scuba diver who parachuted and did many adventurous things that he invited Deirdre to try. She fell in love with all of it. "He is very ambitious, motivated, and curious about the world. He also is a big kid in an appropriate way." He valued talking about what was happening emotionally, encouraging her to continue being aware of and talking about her feelings. This became wonderfully reinforcing for her. He was one of the fortunate kids growing up that had loving, encouraging, and disciplined parents. The boundaries they erected were appropriate, with an enormous emotional expanse to experiment with life.

Living an emotionally intelligent life means we can be firm yet kind; considered in our responses, yet open to spontaneity; optimistic, yet not seeing the world through rose-colored glasses. We can put others first, but not at our own expense; be emotionally self-aware, yet not oversensitive; and we can learn how to have fun in all sorts of constructive ways. Building an emotionally intelligent life occurs over time, with an eye toward relational honesty. We are so often a culture of what I call have-to-haves: I have to have this or that, or else I am not complete. We are often defined by achieving, not by being a good person, an excellent listener, a compassionate colleague, or a devoted partner. A client once said something very compelling, "I don't know anybody who is emotionally intelligent the way we talk about it. They drink too much, use drugs on a regular basis to decompress, cheat on their partners, and the like. They are definitely not living within the lane of well-being, and I don't know if they would want to."

This is an important point, because being as emotionally intelligent as we can is mostly for ourselves. We can model for others the benefits of living a balanced life, but some won't care, will be resentful for a host of reasons, and will distance themselves from us. Some will actively try to disrupt our lives. Achieving social and emotional balance may mean leaving a group of friends to develop a healthier one, or letting people know what you will and won't accept in terms of their behavior toward you. Changing our approach to life often requires switching the pieces on the game board. Deirdre let her mother know what she was doing to heal and that their past interactions represented a toxic part of her life. When her mother didn't respond to the limits and boundaries Deirdre set, she chose not to speak to her with any regularity. She did what was needed to achieve more balance in her day-to-day life. Understanding the patterns of interaction among the competencies allowed her to plot a course toward emotional change and, in many ways, emotional liberation.

The Value of the EQ-i 2.0

There is a debate in the field of emotional intelligence about how to best identify the degree to which EI is manifesting in what we are doing. For instance, will subjective tests like the EQ-i 2.0 accurately capture what someone is actually doing with regard to EI? Or are performance-based measures, like Salovey's MSCEIT, more accurate objective measures of an individual's ability to perform on socioemotional-related tasks? The tension between these two models of understanding the strength of EI is an outgrowth of a controversy, when Daniel Goleman made some astounding claims in 1995 about a direct relationship between EI and success. EI is not an object we can eventually see through the murky waters of what constitutes a person. It is an amalgamation of specific traits, mental abilities, emotional awareness, the strength of relationships, the amount of distance we have from historical wounds, the ability to tolerate stress, and our degree of optimism. The EQ-i 2.0 is a subjective test that creates an opportunity for an authentic discussion about where the person is with respect to EI, where they are going, and what is possible based on their abilities, desires, motivation, and personal vision.

Personally, I believe there is room for both the subjective and objective measurement of EI, for both tell us something about the individual's emotional and relational constellation. In this book, I'm sharing how the EQ-i 2.0 allowed individuals in a clinical setting to see their potential anew. With it, they had context to examine alternate possibilities about how they emotionally respond to those around them, learning how relationship choice is intimately wedded to our emotional responsiveness. The EQ-i 2.0 is what I know and the instrument I have used for years in both my clinical practice with college students, my private practice in the community, and my research at Georgetown University. I know how to take a 133-question assessment and analyze it as a three-dimensional avatar, complete with rich possibilities of what to do with the information it represents. As I have said, I see the EQ-i 2.0 as a socioemotional MRI of how we are regarding emotional intelligence at this moment in time.

But this is also possible via Marc Brackett and Peter Salovey at Yale with the objective abilities-based MSCEIT. The existing assessments related to measuring EI tell essential stories of where people are in relation to their emotional abilities and potential. My focus is on individual, relational, and emotional potential, and I empower the voices and visions of people who count and who are unabashedly on a journey with me and themselves toward personal balance as evidenced by uncompromising emotional and relationship stability.

Awareness and Change: Mara

In our supportive roles as therapists and coaches, we are like air traffic controllers monitoring the progress of our clients' flight paths. It is particularly important for those in therapy to feel a sense of partnering and attentiveness during the occasional turbulence, lightning, and overall bad weather that they typically experience at different times during the therapeutic process.

Mara exemplifies this well. Life had dealt her a shitty hand. Even so, she was not about to fold or give up. Her belief was that life is an endurance race, pacing yourself through the disappointment.

> These are just words that will not change my reality. The fact is I am branded. I belong to the world of what I get, not—as you say—what I deserve. These words are not going to change my circumstances. They are not going to take away what has happened. . . .They are not going to unburden my soul or whitewash my canvas to somehow start over!

And yes, she was accurate. Regardless of what we say in therapy, there has to be an element of internal and external change that allows us to begin living a different life. Creating that change often requires a great deal. Leaving an unhealthy relationship for some is fraught with difficulty, because the relational void that would be created is surrounded by the unknown. "You know, she really wasn't that bad. I mean, I am not that easy to live with. What if she is the best I can do? Ending the relationship will just set me up for more heartache down the road." The process of change is akin to careful tailoring, and it takes time and skill. If our patience wanes, we can easily revert to our old, comfortable clothes, which may be threadbare, but they are familiar. There are times in our life that feel like a frightening leap of faith. Shifting toward what we want is by no means immediate, and the route is never linear. Our movements tend to meander, though hopefully we keep moving in the direction we want. All this happens despite our very normal fear that what is good in our life won't last. Staying the course and believing in what we want will give birth to opportunities that once felt out of reach. This process is not magic but rather a practical and consistent challenge to those existing thoughts and perceptions that previously conspired to spiral us downward or keep us stuck in an unfulfilling life.

This captures a common complaint I hear about self-help books. They place before you a tantalizing recipe without some of the most essential ingredients required to cook the meal. Having all the ingredients for sustained change is one thing, but knowing how to put them together to create what you want in a lasting manner is like a culinary art. That is why I believe that exploring these 15 competencies (the ingredients of living a balanced life) with a trained therapist or coach can move us that much more quickly into lasting change and emotional freedom.

Mara initially resisted any belief that things could change. In our sessions, she was able to discuss what she wanted out of life, but then she turned on the cynicism, as if I were trying to convert her from one way of thinking to another. Whenever she began believing in herself, in others, or in a better life, she soon felt like she was walking a well-worn plank leading to certain disappointment. She saw herself as Humpty Dumpty, who could never be put back together. As she put it, "I cannot bear anymore disappointment. That's why I live a very simple and isolated life. I manage the variables . . . the points of connection. I decide who and what comes in. Yeah, it's lonely, but I know what to expect."

Although she finished college, she considered it a failure, filled with relationship torment. She now faced bleak post-graduation job prospects. Her outcomes tracked the old adage: "If we believe it, it is true." Whether our beliefs are positive or not, they still guide our thinking, feelings, and behaviors. I said to her, "If this is what you believe, this is what you will see. Your aim is not to forget the trauma you had to endure; it is to live a life not defined by it." Mara fought hard to distance herself from the emotional pain of losing her mother to a violent crime when she was a child. Around the same time, a friend's father began to abuse her sexually. To make things worse, if that was possible, she had a bipolar sister who physically assaulted her, and she had difficulties with learning in school.

When I examined Mara's EQ-i 2.0 results in figure 5.5, the areas that have held her back seemed evident. When she looked at the results, she became furious at how much had been taken from her, shrouding her emotional growth for so many years. Although I wanted to start with her strengths, she initially resisted. Instead, her eyes immediately went to the lowest competencies on her feedback report.

I gently brought her back, saying, "Did you realize the strength of your Emotional Self-Awareness and Emotional Expressiveness? Also, the depth of your Empathy, considering what you have been through, is very impressive."

She then mentioned something she hadn't previously. She had been taking an improvisation class through the local community center for several years. She had even become good enough to fill in for the main instructor from time to time.

This was intriguing, and I asked how it worked.

"Well, you are given a word, a scenario, a character or whatever, and you must play that out as much as possible. It is often while interacting with someone else who has been given their own character, which often is not related to what you are doing at all. It can be hysterical." She became very animated describing this.

I asked if we could do an improvisation, and she agreed. She said I was a wounded squirrel, and I said she was Little Red Riding Hood. I limped around, looking quite pathetic. She tried everything she could to make me better. Nothing worked. She eventually said, "Squirrel, you don't want help, and I can only help if you let me."

She then stopped and looked at me, astonished. "I haven't asked for help, have I?"

"By coming in here, you did. The next part of the journey is believing you can heal."

Figure 5.5.

Someone like Mara who has experienced physical, sexual, and emotional trauma may find it challenging to connect with what she has had to endure. Mara's trauma proved to be an unrelenting adversary. What she wanted most, she felt least capable of achieving. She showed me a picture of herself shortly before her mother's death and the advent of sexual abuse. She was sitting on a couch with her big golden retriever's paw on her head as she laughed. I saw this beautiful little girl whose heart and spirit were about to be broken and tears just flowed down my cheeks. Many months later, as Mara was finishing therapy, I asked her if there was anything particularly meaningful or specific that she found helpful in therapy. "A turning point for me was watching your reaction to the picture I showed you of me and my dog Snuffles. Your eyes were filled with tears as you gently rubbed your thumb over my face . . . I knew at that moment I had found a place to begin healing."

She also said talking in depth about her experience with improvisation was incredibly healing. She began designing a very different life from that point on. We never know what may make a difference in someone's life, what becomes the fulcrum leveraging a new way of perceiving and living life. Understanding an individual's story is critical if change is to occur.

Mara's early childhood and adolescent experiences weakened her Stress Tolerance. In our last session, she shared with me a quote that became her mantra: "It is not the future you are afraid of; it is repeating the past that makes you anxious." She realized how she spent so much of her energy trying to avoid the pain of the past, even though it always inevitably found her. When so much of our thinking is devoted to avoiding something, we lose any sense of contentment. As Mara put it, "Focusing on my future as something distinct from my past gives me a sense of hope."

She initially balked at the notion that things could be different. "Life is a caste system, and this is my caste: the dented and imperfect." Slowly, however, things began to shift in a direction she felt was "completely improbable." These good changes began when she found work in a field she really liked, at a company that felt like a reach. She introduced visualization and meditation into her daily life, along with the ingredients she needed to feel her strength and power on a daily basis.

"Life is difficult." When M. Scott Peck stated this now-famous opening line to his multigenerational bestseller *The Road Less Traveled*, he brought us together under the umbrella of, "This is going to be a tough one, just know that." It was a brilliant start to a classic book, but it also has the potential of keeping all of us mired in the mud of life. As Mara could attest, life can sometimes feel like nothing but crap. So how would it alter our emotional constellations if we were to read, instead of, "Life is difficult," a different phrase, "Life is challenging"? Would this work better for someone like Mara, who already knows such difficulty?

There are ways, every day, we can decide to move toward our emotional potential, casting off poisonous relationships, even if they happen to share our DNA. When people like Mara commit to modifying counterproductive patterned behavior and thinking, while embracing the fact that "life is challenging," they learn to manage it better. Understanding where the river divides between what we can control and what we can't allows us to consistently funnel our energies into a space of personal well-being. It is shocking how many of us repeatedly direct our attention and time toward things outside our control. Like believing we can minimize the negative impact of alcoholism by rescuing the person from negative consequences stemming from their addiction. What we can control is our response to inappropriate or disrespectful behavior. Mara was not in a position to control the abuse heaped upon her. As she grew older and challenged the long-held perceptions she had of herself, she learned to believe that life was more than just a series of interrelated disasters. While she could not control what was done to her, she definitely could control being kind to herself while holding people in her life both responsible and accountable for how they treat her.

Recognizing specific events as challenges instead of problems allows us to find out what is most important regarding the strengths and resources we possess. This requires acknowledging who supports our emotional stability and growth, and asking, "Does this allow me to live more authentically?" Knowing this provides us with the strength to withstand those moments in life where negative forces push against us. Mara shared this realization: "Can I influence people? Yes. But can I control what they will or won't do? Certainly not. Will they control me? No longer."

Outside Looking In: Karla

What if we believed everything in our life was predetermined? That the die were cast early on, delimiting our own choices? What do we do if, at our core, we feel we just don't matter, and "it is what it is"? Karla describes living much of her life on the fringes of society, held captive by the belief that she was less than. She felt her life was predetermined and that, as the idiom goes, she drew the short straw.

> I grew up with parents who directed their devotion toward my twin brothers [who] were handsome and athletic and personable. They were basically what I was not. I was bookish, generally opinionated, and frequently dismissed or overlooked. It is not that I *felt* my brothers and I were treated differently. It was blatant. When I was 10 and my brothers were 12, we were going to the circus for a wonderful night. Before the circus, we were all going out to dinner. My mother's sister was in town, and as we were preparing to leave it was evident there was not enough room in the car. My father gave me 10 dollars and called for a pizza. I was staying home so my aunt could go. I still feel the jarring pain of that moment. The feeling that I was disposable and if I disappeared or something happened to me who really would have cared?
>
> How do you get by that feeling of being excess baggage weighing other people down? When my father told me I was staying home, my brothers gave each other some weird high-five-type thing saying, "Woohoo, she's been dissed." I was a disposable afterthought that no one considered, unless of course they were considering how to generate more pain in my life. My aunt never even blinked an eye, like, "Oh, no way, Karla is going, and I'll stay home and relax." That type of consideration that seems natural for most people was completely absent in my life. It literally never happened. So, this spawned my internal operating system: If people spend time with me, it is because they are being polite, though they would probably rather not, and I look for signs and signals that suggest precisely that. That's why I chose a profession that required very little human interaction. It minimized the degree to which I could be overlooked.

The pain of this I cannot imagine, truly. Professionally, she chose a path that guaranteed as much as possible that interacting with others would be limited, thus controlling both the pain and the human contact she craved. She continued with the story of how this affected her now.

Just two days ago, pretty much my only friend and I went to lunch, and she seemed totally disinterested. I started feeling nervous and almost out of control. Like a combat soldier in a firefight, I was looking furtively all around with my head in this [hung low] position.

As we were leaving lunch she said, "I am sorry I have not been very attentive today. I am on my period, and Jim thinks we should see other people. I am really just so sad."

So, it really wasn't me, but had she not said something, I fully would have blamed me as the central problem. I am tired of feeling so bad and always like I am on the outside looking in.

The evening I was left at home alone and everyone went to the circus, I went upstairs and packed a bag with clothes and stuff. I remember sitting on my bed, sobbing so hard I wanted to throw up, being aware that my absence would bring rejoicing, not worry or panic. [But] leaving abruptly would swap out one pile of shit for another.

Karla had a keen intellect, and she was what most people would probably call an intellectual. She soaked up the classics and read many of the contemporary books you might imagine on the must-read lists of the Nobel laureates. However, she came from a family that did not prize this deep level of thinking and intellectual endeavor. They were not interested in challenging the way they saw the world. Although her parents were college graduates, the college experience for them was about networking and unearthing social opportunity rather than an academic and intellectual proving ground. Even though Karla did feel college had been a rich academic experience, she was so emotionally bruised and battered that she took very little if any risk and actively avoided socializing. She remembers her father saying, "You know, you are just like your uncle Steve (his brother) and my dad; lost in books, living in some alternate universe. Read the tea leaves Karla. You continue this way of living, and you will become invisible."

She did manage to be vocal in class, sharing her opinions and ideas freely, largely because her professors encouraged it. She went to a large university, but her major was a bit on the boutique side, and the number of students around her was small. Software engineering was very male dominated, consistently reminding her of her brothers' insensitivity. Outside of class, she went out of her way to avoid interacting with classmates. She wanted her college experience to be far different from her parents' stories about partying, the Greek system, and those all-important contacts you were supposed to make to guarantee career success. For them, what mattered wasn't what you know, but who you know.

After Karla received her EQ-i 2.0 results pictured in figure 5.6, she held them as if she were reading her own obituary. Her eyes were teary, and her hands trembled. "I see failure, miserable failure as a human being." Her results indicated low Self-Regard, Optimism, Assertiveness, Problem-Solving, and Stress Tolerance. However, her other competencies were solidly in the healthy range. She had strong Empathy (maybe too much), Social Responsibility, Emotional Self-Awareness (also perhaps too much), and Impulse Control (again, a bit too much). Her Independence score was high, which makes sense considering she felt very much on her own from an early age and frequently did things on her own.

> I rarely share what I am thinking or doing with others. This can be troubling for people at work, where their ideas are important, I mean I am a software engineer who doesn't have all the answers, yet I avoid reaching out. I know people can feel I radiate this danger alert! I just can't take hearing one more person say that I haven't done enough, which I hear as, "I am not enough."

Actually, no one at work has ever said that to her. If they mention something can be tighter or offer a coding strategy to move things along quicker, she hears it in a critical voice, not a constructive one. So, people have learned to give her a pretty wide berth.

"If you were to begin involving more people in your projects, your thoughts, your life, how would you begin going about it in a way that didn't feel overly threatening?" I asked.

"Just hearing it feels threatening. I feel the blood rush out of my head."

"Asking for someone's guidance or opinion is far different than being slammed any time your family felt you were an inconvenience," I responded. "I truly cannot imagine being treated like that, and you spent your formative years being picked apart. Now, though, you are the gate keeper, not your family or other people. Giving people a chance to add value to your life, through work or anything else, can create a different way of seeing self and other."

We then spent a lot of time discussing how she would invite her colleagues' ideas and opinions into her work life, which would enhance the deliverables for the clients. For example, she realized that:

Figure 5.6.

> Asking someone to share their thoughts is different than growing up and having people go out of their way to criticize everything about me. They wanted to brutalize me, and they did. Asking for people to be involved would be different, yes. I have spent so much time in a defensive position, like survival mode . . . that stepping out from behind the shield would feel terrible.

At this moment she was only just beginning to consider stepping out from behind a protective place that has served her well. "You are sketching this out on paper," I said.

> You are imagining what it would feel like to genuinely connect with people you want to connect with. This honors your high Empathy and Emotional Self-Awareness. You feel so deeply and have kept your feelings on a very short and predictable leash. Karla, you are no longer at the mercy of cruel family members taking full advantage of your age and innocence. You decide who you allow in. Like anything else worth achieving, this will take practice. Stepping out and feeling exposed does not happen in one fell swoop. It unfolds and strengthens in accordance with the social risk you take.

This was the avenue Karla traveled down to make substantive changes in the way she thought and behaved with others. She became more inclusive, less defensive, and far more solicitous.

As noted, Karla's emotional self-awareness was very high. Based on her narrative, this level of awareness magnified the pain instead of reducing it. She did not express how she felt; she simply had no avenue within to do so. Her lack of Assertiveness clearly indicates this. Her negative feelings and self-loathing were continually present, crashing against an emotional wall resembling Fort Knox. Karla learned to see things too clearly in Reality-Testing. Her overused impulse control kept her foot squarely on the brakes with regard to interacting with others. Spontaneity was avoided at all costs. As you can imagine, she was not flexible at all and was extremely independent, which she had to be considering how she was treated. Her emotional Problem-Solving suggested she kept everything inside and managed what she was feeling like an ER doctor dealing with a seriously injured patient. Based on her family's brutal actions, these unhealed feelings continually circulated in her mind as if in a washing machine cycle that never ended.

In order for healing to occur, Karla had to see herself acting out of a new script while replacing the old. Her Emotional Expression was far lower because she had trained herself not to express feelings, as evidenced in the encounter with her friend. Her low emotional Problem-Solving meant she needed to learn how to engage difficult emotional feelings and resolve them. She was used to a constant cycle of internal triggering that kept her in an emotional loop, resembling the pain she endured growing up. She feels deeply (high Empathy), but rarely investigates it, because she has grown to expect the outcome will result in yet another helping of pain. Ever since she was young, she has had the discipline to write in a journal regularly, and it became a repository for her feelings. Her journaling suggests how often she has been trapped in an unforgiving negative feedback loop.

She allowed me to read some of her entries from her early teen years. They were very well written, capturing the devastating emotional pain she endured at the hands of family members. A child should be able to look to their family for love and affirmation. However, there was an entry from her freshman year in high school when the brothers got a Doberman pinscher for Hanukah. The mother and father thought it was funny when the boys taught the dog to growl at Karla whenever it saw her. She was afraid of dogs after having been bitten by one when she was small. Dogs terrified her, and they knew it, so this made her feel perpetually afraid around the new pet. She wrote in her journal, "This is my life . . . not even a dog can love me." There were small smudges on the page from her tears.

As Karla became more expressive, she developed more inclusive habits and fewer dismissive ones. With this came a desire to be less emotionally Independent and separate from others. She discovered a formula for inviting people into her life that was invitational rather than oppositional or distancing. As she saw people respond positively, her Self-Regard increased, along with being less controlling. She enjoyed more spontaneity and less social rigidity (Flexibility). This retrained how she entered into and moved through life. She felt consistently more Optimistic about her future. Importantly, she began to manage her stress much more efficiently (Stress Tolerance). She stopped fearing that everything would cave in around her, and she enjoyed feeling a heightened sense of inner calm.

Because of her history, it was no wonder that her Stress Tolerance competency was the lowest of all. Years of emotional pounding and neglect, failed attempts at self-soothing, and her adopted belief that she was both not enough and broken left her life perilously close to imploding. The sustained abuse smothered her internal flame for much of her life. Her life had been spent socially surviving by dashing from one tree to the next for cover and safety as if running from a predator and doing all she could to avoid being devoured.

All of us are the product of what our senses absorbed while growing up. If you could not use your dominant writing hand for six months, you would begin using your other hand to compensate. Karla began using her emotional equivalent of the nondominant hand. While it initially felt so alien to her, she realized what was at stake if she stopped. Each of us can choose thoughts, attitudes, and behaviors that challenge us to stretch toward being a better version of ourselves. We should all use our nondominant sides more!

Karla learned to take more social risks and accept more responsibility at work, particularly in group settings. She took the time to establish a blueprint for connecting with others that made sense based on her experiences, many of which had been excruciatingly painful. She felt many things growing up but love was not one of them. She wanted to challenge existing patterns that denied her the one thing she wanted, human relationships. She had to begin by honoring her painful experiences, while developing more of what she wanted socially. We began by having her imagine each interaction before actually trying it out.

We can imagine our own lives. We can picture how our experiences while growing up have shaped our current approach toward living our life. In terms of the competencies, we can assess what has been missing and ask how its presence could make us feel more balanced, more engaged, and less afraid, all of which means being more alive. If we believe we are stuck, afraid, not enough, an imposter, or insignificant, then we will be correct!

CHAPTER SIX

Struggles on the Journey Forward

Two questions naturally arise: 1. Does the EQ-i 2.0 work with every client? 2. If not, why not? Although this book is filled with positive stories, and I could tell hundreds more, in this chapter we'll consider some of the times that didn't work out as well. Change occurs only when desire and readiness meet opportunity. When all elements are present, then the EQ-i 2.0 is a great tool, but without them it is unlikely to move the dial.

It can be difficult when the coach or therapist is the only one who gets it. Sometimes it is so clear how the client could benefit from embracing the type of change implicit in the competencies. We can give them all the necessary guidance to fly, allowing them to feel as safe as possible, but in the end, it is their journey. They must land the plane. The feedback from the EQ-i 2.0 can forge new social and emotional strengths. The competencies can reveal things that we in the helping profession don't always see on the surface. It can feel like such a great power, as if we are providing our clients with a secret weapon. However, each individual must come to believe at a foundational level that they are capable of achieving and maintaining the type of change that would benefit them most.

Many will, but some will not.

Ignoring the Wakeup Call: Pete

Pete came into therapy after a particularly harrowing drinking experience. He was working in the financial field, doing intricate math modeling. He described his undergraduate social experience as enjoyable. "I'll admit I drank a huge amount," he said, "which caused problems for me and a lot of tension with my parents."

He believed his frat-boy behavior would somehow morph into more reasonable habits after graduation, and he expected to exhibit greater maturity and achieve a more normative adult status. While this is what he hoped and expected, he actually took no steps to ensure that the adult Pete would show up. Pete was like a person who talks about getting into shape and considers in their mind what it would take, but then doesn't do what is necessary to see results.

Pete had never actually considered what a more balanced social-personal life would look like. "I didn't want to completely get rid of the drinking," he said, "because it was fun and relaxing. I just figured with work and all, you know all the responsibility, normal drinking would bubble up."

It was evident from the beginning that Pete had a high-octane brain but very little emotional Self-Awareness, Social Responsibility, or Empathy. If he felt an action would serve him, or if it seemed to be a good idea at the moment, he would do it. He engaged in only very limited internal dialogue to make a cost/benefit analysis of his actions. After the fact, he would rationalize his behavior, which created a perpetual cycle.

Whenever he had an especially bad drinking experience, with problematic consequences, he would sober up and then draw a line in the sand. For a week or so, he would act responsibly and feel better about himself, only to start the cycle again. This went on throughout college, during the start of his career, and into the first couple of months of therapy. Then, one day, Pete was arrested for assault. This put his job in jeopardy, because he was in the process of obtaining a security clearance that was required to rise in his field.

Even though Pete took challenging academic subjects in college and did very well, he never really had to apply himself. His grades were competitive even with minimal effort. When it came time to secure post-graduation employment, he was creative and determined in finding one of the best positions in his field. However, as he told it:

> The night before this big phone interview I went out and got hammered. I was so drunk the next morning that I slept through the alarm, missing the initial interview. Scrambling, I woke up with a wrenching hangover, and called the company to say I was in a car accident and could we talk later that afternoon. They agreed and were worried about me, even offering another day. Considering how competitive this was, I thanked them and sounded like a martyr on the phone for insisting we do it later that day.

As it turns out, and probably to no real surprise, Pete lied a lot to protect his drinking. I noticed in our discussions that he lied even when he didn't need to. He graduated from an excellent university, landed a great job, and was smart and likable. Yet when he met new people, usually in bars, he pretended to be what he was not.

> I became everything from an attorney to a fighter pilot to a Navy SEAL. I slung so much BS that I almost began to believe it. Of course, I couldn't follow up on any of these relationships because it was a lie.
>
> I remember meeting one girl in particular who was great, and I was very attracted to her. I woke up the next morning so pissed because she thought I was working complicated ciphers for the NSA.

While many people seemed to like Pete, very few really knew him or considered him a very close friend. His entertainment value increased as he drank, and people liked hanging out with him, though only to a point. After that, the more he drank, the more consistently they wanted to get away from him. Often Pete blacked out, with no memory of his behavior. People would tell him about what he did, which he would file in some distant recess of his brain instead of analyzing the information. This feedback never led to any substantive behavior change.

Several people in Pete's life thought he was a narcissist, obsessive-compulsive, or bipolar, and, while all or some of this may be true, there was no way to know with any certainty until the drinking stops. He may well have some of the mental health challenges just listed. In reality, the drinking creates a dense emotional and social fog that must lift in order to see the surroundings. The drinking had stunted his ability to grow emotionally, interpersonally, psychologically, and spiritually. His behaviors were not the type one would typically expect in a person of Pete's ability and at his age.

Wake-up calls occur for all of us in a host of different ways. What constitutes a wake-up call depends on our personality, life experiences, and what may be at stake. It could be realizing that if things don't change, we will lose something of value and an important part of our self. Even so, it amazes me what some people are willing to risk because the thought of stopping a particular behavior is incomprehensible. And this is the power of addiction. I've seen many people like Pete barter and rationalize to continue the addictive behavior.

Damaging behavior can continue when the person receives external reinforcement. Parents who don't want to see their children suffer because of youthful behavior often rescue them from the natural consequences of poor decisions. No one should want to see a husband, wife, child, friend, or colleague suffer. But if the behavior continues, with a promise to stop, and then continues to recur, what then? People like Pete and their families and close friends can find themselves in a dance where both the rescuer and the rescued reinforce one another. This gets worse the longer the dance has gone on. Even though help feels like the right thing to do, the addictive behavior has a greater chance of ending when we stop the rescuing dance.

Pete's parents protected him at every turn. Though they fought about it and disagreed each time about whether or not to save him, they always cast a net beneath him to catch his fall. In reality, though, this didn't keep him from hitting the ground. It was not a matter of if he would hit; it was a matter of when.

One day, Pete confided to me that he had completely changed his drinking habits. "No more hard liquor. Just beer . . . and light beer at that. It is the hard liquor that seems to wreak havoc with me." For two weeks he maintained this discipline. If I mentioned any inconsistencies in his thinking or tried to offer some facts, his skewed logic would reject it all. He couldn't see how even light drinking was his gateway to drinking more, including hard alcohol. He simply would not make the connection.

Pete has no memory of how much he drank that fateful night, or how or why he tried to grab the officer's service revolver. All he knows is that it ended with two days in jail, stitches in his head, and a two-count felony. He sat in my office, supporting his head with his hands, wondering aloud how something like this could have happened.

The results of Pete's EQ-i 2.0 in figure 6.1 revealed details he didn't want anyone else to see. Even I was surprised by what it showed. Though he was an academic standout who received a coveted position right out of college, he felt particularly bad about who he was (Self-Regard) and had very little notion of where he was going (Self-Actualization). I thought there was something else occurring at the mental health level, but as we discussed, unless he stopped drinking, I had no way to determine what it might be. The competencies unambiguously revealed the negative things we knew were happening. Lying suggested not being comfortable in his own skin, with no real sense of what he was living for.

Things up until this point had just fallen in his lap because of his talent, but he always stopped short of full realization. For example, in college he had been up for several prestigious awards. The highest, and one for which people felt he was a shoo-in, slipped through his fingers because he missed the interview. He had a drunken blackout the night before and didn't set the alarm. Again. Pete just shrugged it off.

Pete's low competencies that did not surprise me were Reality-Testing, Empathy, Social Responsibility, Emotional Self-Awareness, and Emotional Expression. He was consistently closed off to examining his feelings, and he did not know how to emotionally express himself. This was, unsurprisingly, directly proportional to the drinking.

The vast majority of us know someone with a substance abuse problem. We may also know someone in recovery. Entering recovery is painful because anonymous programs have designed their 12 steps carefully. They make sure you examine how your drinking has hurt yourself and those around you, and to what degree. Anyone who chooses recovery and remains there can tell you the challenges embedded in the recovery process. Pete did not want to deal with what drinking cost him. His remarkable talents, at some level, were also a big problem. They enabled him to continue drinking without serious enough consequences.

Any time those consequences began to escalate, his parents or roommates rescued him. Pete's low Reality-Testing revealed his gap between fact and fiction. It also explains why he spun stories routinely to make himself seem like someone he was not. Without drinking and lying, he felt that his life was mundane. Ordinary. Boring. By day, he was a

Figure 6.1.

financial professional, but at night he transformed into a CIA operative. He wanted a relationship, but it is impossible to find and sustain one built on lies.

Pete's high Emotional Independence meant he couldn't care less about what others thought or did. He had his personal vision, and damn the torpedoes, he was going full speed ahead. This intensified the more he drank, which is why friends hit the eject button, distancing from him as quickly as possible. Even worse, Pete knew it. He said with a smile, "It's really like a ritual where I start the evening with people and end up alone." He met my attempts to challenge this with ambiguity and deflection.

Oddly enough, his next highest competency was Flexibility, and it became an overused strength. While he was not inclusive and did not care what others thought about him, he nevertheless had a gift for saying what people wanted to hear. He cast himself in another role, this time as an appealing colleague and the quintessential team player. This meant people were drawn to him but almost as quickly turned away. The more they got to know him, the less they wanted to be near him.

When Pete looked at his EQ-i 2.0 results, he said, "Come on, that caught me on a day where I was seriously hung over." Pete could have accepted the EQ-i's roadmap and set sail for change. He did not. Before the arrest, I asked, "Where do you think this is going to wind up if you continue to drink like this?" "It hasn't been a problem so far, right?"

The next day, a lawyer called him at the request of his parents to strategize about the impending court hearing. Although Pete and his parents could have used this opportunity to elevate their relationship to a new level, they never opened the door on that opportunity. A former client once told me that when she called her parents after running up a $3,000 bar tab in college, her mother said, "Giving birth to you was excruciatingly painful, though worth it. Not bailing you out is also painful, and worth it for us both." That was the last time she was irresponsible with money. Again, parents don't want to see their children fail/suffer, spouses don't want to see their partners lose jobs for substance-related behavior, and friends often feel they are being good friends by being there every time the person has a negative drinking experience, even when they shouldn't. As the saying goes, "Fool me once, shame on you. Fool me twice, shame on me."

A good friend who is in recovery wrote this, and it seems appropriate at this point:

> The man in the mirror
> He keeps getting nearer but I am not moving
> The man in the back street is holding a track meet
> But I will not run
> Someplace inside you a seed has been born
> You've got to watch it grow
> Someplace inside you a river is waiting to flow
> Will you let it go
> Those voices you're hearing are never worth fearing
> They're only inside you
> They'll tempt you and taunt you
> They'll help you and haunt you but don't try to hide
> Sometimes the sun will be right at your shoulder
> Helping you keep your stride
> Sometimes you might have to give up a piece of your pride
> Have you even tried

When Family Comes Second: Peg

Peg, a CEO of a burgeoning company, came to therapy just as her husband was preparing to leave her. She really didn't understand why, claiming she provided him with an enviable life where he could devote time to his writing and other artistic endeavors. However, their emotional connection and intimacy had become a desert. He wanted more, and she was stumped on how to give it to him. She did not hear that what he was asking for could not be bought. It wasn't a gift to be wrapped. She couldn't secure happiness by giving him more space. Quite the opposite, he wanted less time alone and more time with her. He felt the relationship had atrophied from a lack of connection and touch. It took him moving out of the house to get her attention. His love for her was undeniable, but their differences became intolerable.

Peg's EQ-i 2.0 results showed she was extremely Emotionally Independent and highly Assertive. She had low Empathy and Social Responsibility, but she was high in Self-Regard and Self-Actualization. Her Emotional Self-Awareness was extremely low, and Self-Expression was even lower, as evidenced by her not comprehending her husband's pleas for connection. When she saw her results and understood more clearly what they meant, she decided that was not how she wanted to live. Though it was difficult for Peg, she tried turning toward her husband rather than away. She learned what it meant not to block the empty space between them with material things. Her husband and children all enjoyed this change. But the surprise beneficiaries were people who worked in her company.

By the time some of us realize change is necessary, we have exhausted the goodwill of the relationships around us. People typically check out emotionally or move on. They seldom return, regardless of what shifts or insights we claim. Sometimes it takes such losses to finally make us willing and able to conceptualize the lives we want and ask for the support we will need. This is particularly true for those who have suffered with addiction or who have mental health problems. Often left in their wake are the remnants of irreparably damaged relationships. In spite of such loss, pushing forward in recovery is possible if the individual really wants to develop better social and emotional intelligence.

Peg came by her emotional distance honestly. She grew up with a father who was brilliant, though mentally ill. Her mother seemed emotionally fragile, incapable of making up for what her father couldn't provide. In order not to make her brother's mistake and reside in a codependent relationship with her father, she powered down her emotional side and ramped up her intellectual abilities. This was the only route she could see out of the family chaos. She stayed away from home as much as possible and wisely distanced herself from all that family drama.

When we meet clients with this type of developmental history, the path forward for these individuals can follow two divergent paths: like Peg, who seemed to outrun the pain and trauma by employing her talents, or like those whose life seems disjointed, broken and emotionally vanquished. Understanding what people have battled through in the arc of their development, where family interaction was chaotic, painful, and destabilizing can enhance our empathic perspective. As individuals begin to see the power of the 15 competencies in leveraging personal change, they begin actively authoring their life from this moment forward.

Peg's strengths were astounding! However, her weaknesses were striking. She had very low Empathy, Emotional Self-Awareness, and Emotional Self-Expression, as seen in figure 6.2. She was not in touch with her feelings and was limited in her communication of empathic understanding of employee needs and her family needs. She felt great in her own skin (Self-Regard), she saw the sky as the limit in terms of the profit her company could generate (Optimism), and she knew exactly what she wanted to do and where she wanted to go (Self-Actualization). She was profoundly Independent and Assertive, which served her well in industry. As an excellent emotional Problem-Solver, she could shoulder a large amount of stress while simultaneously remaining productive. She would adroitly adjust to whatever the market demanded with the efficiency of a F-35 Raptor Fighter jet.

On the more challenging side, however, she highly overutilized her Independence and Self-Actualization, which makes sense when you think about how she described the circumstances of her youth. This meant she ran into some problems as a boss. She was fluid and agreeable and also knew how to hire extremely skilled employees. But she didn't give enough guidance to her direct reports, nor did she know how to solicit their feedback. She tended to be overly accommodating/flexible, letting people blaze their own trail with their respective talents.

Besides work, this pattern also affected her marriage. She did not ask how her husband was feeling in their relationship. In both arenas, when people gave her constructive feedback, either criticism or praise, she bulldozed right through it. Her belief was that the more she did, and the more money she made, the happier everyone would be, including her husband and children.

The kids did not see her often and grew quite accustomed to not having her around. As her husband put it,

> Yeah, it is a very nontraditional family where I am home working on what interests me while Peg is out foraging in the world of industry to largely provide for our living and maintain our lifestyle. I feel I have had to double down and provide the emotional support that Peg doesn't bring to the table. I am the soft disciplinarian, and she is the hammer. The kids often say they prefer when she is at work!

While Peg has heard variations of this theme over time, instead of thinking about it, she typically storms off, telling people they are simply acting spoiled. She expects gratitude for her hard work and what it provides. Meanwhile, her husband and children see her as a phantom who flits in and out of their lives.

Figure 6.2.

Though Peg recognized the need for change, she largely paid lip service to it. Her life was akin to Zeno's Paradox. The closer she came to the goal of being more present and involved, the farther away it moved, because she didn't sustain her efforts. Every time the clouds parted and the sun broke through, new storm clouds quickly gathered. This was primarily because Peg was not making these changes for herself, to enhance her own journey. Instead, she was trying to adapt for those around her. As she emotionally and physically tried turning more toward her family, she had to initially endure difficult feedback. They were understandably skeptical that she was different now, which unfortunately proved to be true, because knowing doesn't mean doing.

Peg treated her family as an afterthought. The real challenge she leaned into was parenting her business, not her children. The growth of sales was her priority, not her marriage. Her husband eventually moved out and got on with his life. He took physical custody of the children, so Peg saw even less of them. Even armed with the information that can keep us tethered to what is important, there are those of us who won't or can't do it. Sometimes shifting our mind set and behavior is simply too hard—or too emotionally costly.

This next situation focuses on an emotionally independent person in a relationship with a partner who consistently lies. Remaining in such a toxic environment is not only suffocating, but it also fails to honor the independent person's core beliefs. We can see this imbalance in the example of Carl.

Wishful Drinking: Carl

Carl and his wife came to see me for couples counseling about a month after their second son was born. She had a demanding job, which she had put on hold during maternity leave. The situation felt unforgiving. They needed the money, and she liked working. However, the thought of going back while caring for a newborn—especially leaving early and coming home late every day—created a great deal of anxiety.

Carl was in business himself and had launched a second start-up company. Unscrupulous partners ran his first business into the ground, he told me.

Just greedy MFers who only cared about a paycheck and not the product. I guess I was lucky it fell short of the runway. I now can concentrate on what I wanted to do for a long time. I am working my butt off to care for this family to create the life we want, and, well, she is on my ass all the time. If she would just leave me the F . . . alone, things would be fine, and we wouldn't have to be here.

Carl's wife had a very different perspective:

> He drinks whiskey like there is a run on it. He is hammered by 10:00 p.m. and up to that point, when he starts drinking in the evening, he is of no use or help with the kids. He just checks out. When drinking, he is brutal with people: yelling at them, cursing, just plain mean. This is with friends, not strangers. My friends that I grew up with are afraid for him and for me.

Carl played down the concerns around his drinking, saying that his wife's friends thought he was great. He added that his drinking habits were no different now than when the couple first met. Carl's complaint was that his wife changed from being a dream to a dud. "I haven't changed one bit," he insisted. "She has. This isn't the woman I married."

What Carl could not see was how having children had changed his wife's priorities. Her top concern now was their children. Not so for Carl. Whenever she tried to point something out to him, he would dismiss it. He thought she did not understand the stress he was under. He accused her of constantly riding him and calling him names. Looking at his own behavior holistically was simply too much for him.

During one of our sessions, Carl screamed at his wife. Then, he looked at me, assuming I had seen her behavior and would agree with his reaction. Instead, I was rather stunned. The only thing I had witnessed, I told him, was him losing control after she quietly pointed things out that were true. "Yeah," he replied, "but there's all sorts of meaning behind it."

A close look at Carl's EQ-i 2.0 results was revealing. His competency results lined up closely with what we saw in the relationship. Open disdain for a partner is the most dangerous development in a relationship, but just after it, and almost as important, is a lack of willingness to examine our personal behavior and emotions. Clinicians must be vigilant when one or both partners subscribe to, "Hear no evil. See no evil. Speak no evil." When self-examination and personal responsibility are absent in a relationship, disdain becomes the natural byproduct. We don't hear the other person, we don't see how our actions are contributing to relational problems, and we don't talk about the issues creating relational strain. When this exists, a relationship is in a death spiral. It is heartbreaking to see. Personal responsibility and accountability in a relationship are essential for emotional well-being and relational balance.

Carl heard his wife's complaints. But then he would laugh and roll his eyes with disdain, insisting that their problems were her fault. Though Carl did admit he was an alcoholic, he still did not see his drinking as a problem. After all, he said, his friends drank just like he did. But was that really true? As it turned out, most of his friends did *not* drink like him. Yet without fail, when Carl was challenged on his perception that everyone drank like he did, he only dug in further.

It would have been devastating for Carl to admit that he was failing as a partner to his wife and as a businessman. He would have to rethink everything he thought he knew about the life he had created. He was great at talking about getting deals done or how the money would roll in, but it never seemed to happen with any consistency.

"I am walking the razor's edge," said his wife. "I have two children now. I get it, so why doesn't he?" It reminded me of the scene where Aldonza begs Don Quixote to see her as she really is. Quixote, however, cannot do so. He only sees her as his dream, his Dulcinea.

The chart for Carl's emotional intelligence competencies in figure 6.3 confirmed this. His Self-Regard was not great. Whatever contributing factors led to this belief, Carl felt small, the victim of a blood-sucking world. Though he led a start-up, he also possessed very little Self-Actualization. Did unscrupulous business partners really crash his first business after all? Examining Carl's role in its demise would be important. Indeed, his wife said this quite directly.

Carl's Emotional Self-Awareness was also very low, and his Emotional Expression was only slightly better. Possessing more expression than awareness may also have accounted for his explosiveness while drinking. His sub-par Reality-Testing helped to explain his disconnect

Struggles on the Journey Forward ~ 181

with many of the issues occurring in his personal and professional life. He thought other people in his life generated his problems, not him, and so he operated within a gigantic blind spot.

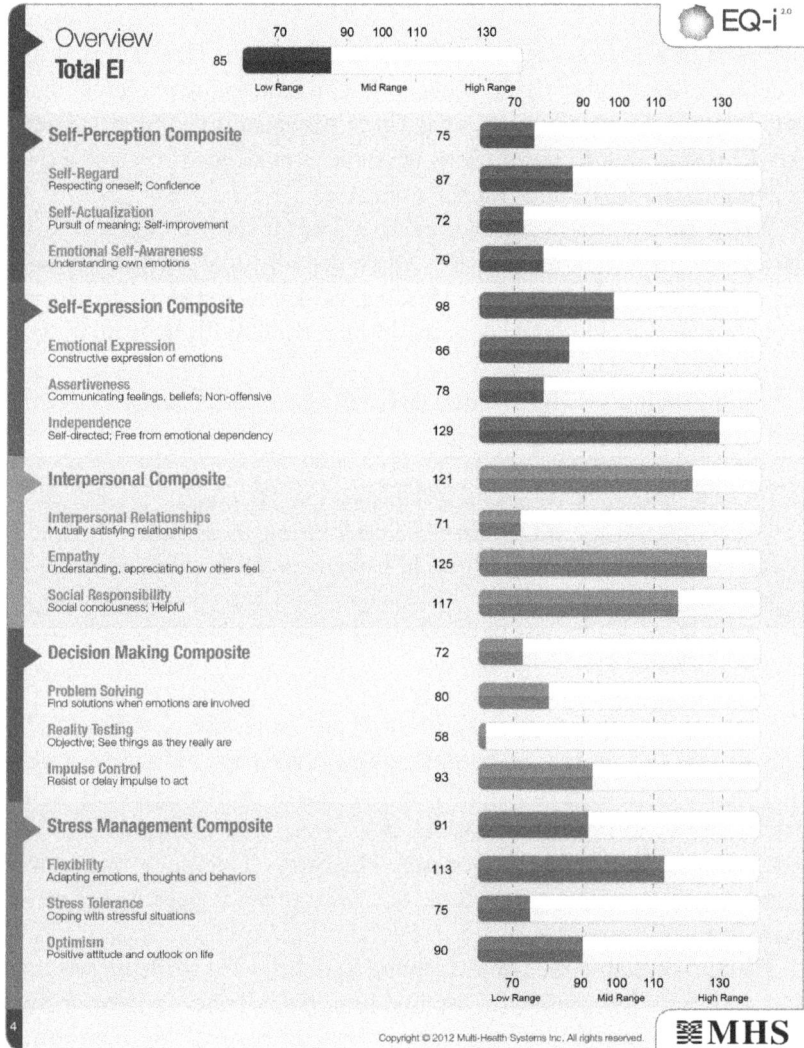

Figure 6.3.

Independence was Carl's highest score and was strikingly higher than the majority of his other EI scores. In this case, it presented itself as an overutilized strength. If other people's actions did not line up with Carl's worldview, then he dismissed them out of hand. This was a recurring theme for him, running through all of his thinking and interactions.

So, what are we to make of Carl's high score in Flexibility? It appears contrary to all of the lower scores. As a tech industry professional, where meeting clients' needs is the tip of the spear, Flexibility is essential. Carl was able to morph into whatever was needed to close a deal or bring in the best talent for the company.

When we dug deeper, however, there was a fresh revelation. Carl may have played along, but he didn't actually like working closely with colleagues, sharing ideas, finding workable solutions to thorny problems, and seeking out mentors. In fact, these skills were anathema to him.

Carl's problems with his wife and his interactions at home also testified to this. His wife said it best:

> He really is more of a chameleon than a person. He would stop to move a squirrel across the street rather than risk hitting it. But when the car stopped at its destination, he would have no problem telling someone to their face to go [expletive] off. He does have empathy for those he doesn't know. With those he does know, his expectations are completely unrealistic and upside down.

Carl would consistently ask his wife for more space, saying, "The only thing I need is for you to stop talking." We tried to figure out how that would work with two small kids dependent on their parents. Children require nonstop negotiation, discussion, and compromise. Carl was not able to provide any of this. His Stress Tolerance was so low that every new request, problem, or uncertainty dragged him farther away from his center.

He held on to his excessive drinking so tightly. Yet while he saw it as an antidote to his stress, it consumed him like a flame. In light of this, his Social Responsibility competency was interesting. He mentioned running his college's Big Brother program, where he did a wonderful job. He had gotten the most people involved in the history of the school. He would frequently mention to his wife that he wanted to get back into volunteering, though it never happened. Alcohol abuse has a way of severely narrowing what we can do in our world.

Over time, Carl clung even tighter to his drinking, drifting farther away from the family and his responsibilities. His wife left, moved into an apartment, and luckily found a solid job much closer geographically than her old position.

Carl's emotional abuse escalated, finally ending in a stay away order from the court. He moved in with his sister, and much of his money goes to care for daughters he cannot see. When someone is unwilling to acknowledge they are walking farther out onto fractured ice, without a desire to turn back, the most we can do is back away and care for ourselves and those who depend on us.

The Ties That Bind: Jean

While Jean's story was not a success, it is one that can teach us a lot about the power of personal defense mechanisms and their role in supporting a life lived on the margins. When asked to take the EQ-i 2.0, she said, "You know it is like all these new flavor-of-the-day assessments that really go nowhere." She privately took an online assessment of emotional intelligence, which concluded she had robust emotional intelligence and extraordinary leadership ability. Instead of sharing the results with me, however, she simply said, "I know you don't think I have very strong emotional intelligence and the extremely valid and reliable test I took online discredits your opinion."

Of course, I never said she lacked emotional intelligence. In fact, I never even spoke with her about it except to offer her the assessment, along with an article written by its creator, Reuven Bar-On. When she told me this, I cautioned her to be wary of online, free tests. Finally, begrudgingly, she took the full test.

Although Jean is exceedingly bright, she didn't finish college. She struggles to hold onto anything of value in either work or relationships and makes wildly exaggerated excuses. Now and then she has moments of true awareness about how her behavior influences the people in her life. Unfortunately, this dissipates like dropping an ice cube in a hot cup of tea, and soon she returns to her pattern of irrational beliefs, broken relationships, and unfulfilled talent.

Jean lives with both ADHD and Borderline Personality Disorder. BPD is kind of like the fibromyalgia of the mental health field, because although it describes something that truly exists, it is quite hard to pin down. It is difficult to accurately diagnose and even more challenging to address. Successful treatment depends on the person's willingness to recognize its negative impact. This is far easier said than done. There is something about BPD that blocks those it inhabits from seeing how negatively the disorder affects their lives. These individuals are not delusional, but to the outside world it may seem as if they are.

People living with BPD are often very smart, sometimes having enough brain power to rule their worlds if only they could. They can't, only because, in their opinion, everyone else blocks them from demonstrating their true potential and ability. Claiming that nothing is their fault, they often justify their outrageously negative responses. A typical BPD system of emotional defenses would make Bruce Lee look like an amateur. Mix into this particular world ADHD's classic inability to focus, impetuous behavior, and executive functioning difficulties, and you have someone stuck on the steep side of a mountain. Jean never tried looking for an exit strategy or a shelter from the storm. Instead, she blamed everyone around her for choices she was very obviously making herself.

The therapeutic process didn't fail Jean, in my opinion, because therapy never really occurred. She came in to see me initially to create the appearance of making changes in her life for her family's benefit. As we saw before with Peg, we can't change because someone else wants us to. All of Jean's relationships occurred online in a virtual world, and she had no real friends. Her family believed she desperately needed therapy, so here she was. She wasn't coming in order to examine her life or seek greater emotional freedom, stronger relationships, and the fulfillment of heretofore unfulfilled potential. That would be too painful. And I agree, therapy may initially seem overwhelming, temporarily leaving someone feeling scared, naked, and vulnerable. But this is only temporary. Soon, if she had let it, the process would have strengthened her social safety net and assuaged some of her fears. She could have learned how to be the brick and mortar in her relationships instead of the wrecking ball. She could have used true friendships to find genuine comfort and shelter from the emotional rain.

To help Jean, I offered Marsha Linehan's dialectical behavior therapy, which has proven so effective with BPD. However, we didn't get far because she was so fixated on how others in her life hurt her. She would also artfully mix fact with fiction, making it difficult to steer her toward identifying and deconstructing the fictional aspects of her halting and circuitous narrative.

Jean did not act lovingly at all. She resembled a porcupine with its quills up, backing away and then furtively zigzagging through life. Her brother remembers a time when she could have been or done anything she wanted. She could read people well, but she was also far too emotionally independent. She never hesitated to say what she thought or felt. Although she was precocious, she had an unconventional personality, and people tended to dismiss her as idiosyncratic. In high school she became strikingly troublesome.

She always had a temper, and her argumentative streak now became the rule rather than the exception. She complained that her mother never gave her the love she wanted, while her father was aloof and dedicated to the world of finance. Jean began making up stories designed to hurt her parents deeply. They struggled to talk her down from the frequent emotional precipices she consistently climbed onto. Although her family cared for her, sent her to excellent schools, and gave her access to resources aligned with her talent, it wasn't enough to produce a loving and balanced child. Her mother felt the relationship was broken, and both parents finally bowed to unworkable familial and genetic predispositions. It was understandable. When you feel your family consistently being emotionally and physically fractured by one member, then it's likely the problem isn't you, and there is little you can do other than set clear and immovable boundaries, much like what Grant's family did with him. There comes a point where it is emotional survival.

After Jean begrudgingly agreed to take the EQ-i 2.0, we examined the results in figure 6.4.

The range of her emotional and social struggles is glaringly visible. Her Emotional Expression competency is way overutilized and presents itself as anger, hostility, and even vitriol toward others. As you can probably imagine, her Emotional Self-Awareness is low. She rarely, if ever, directs this explosiveness toward herself, which is why she has no friends outside of chatrooms (Interpersonal Relationships). She doesn't do anything within the community to pay it forward or give back (Social Responsibility), and she shows little Empathy. Her low

Figure 6.4.

Reality-Testing makes sense with respect to weaponized behaviors and low EI competencies.

Remember, she thinks others manufacture her trials and tribulations and then foist them upon her. She fails to see how her own choices affect her life. She has very little Stress Tolerance, emotional Problem-Solving ability, or Flexibility. She views life solely through one lens. She also doesn't feel too bad about herself, because she is sure she is a victim. The low Self-Actualization explains why she hops from one low-paying job to another, has no interest in school, and has no interest in pursuing a job that could intellectually challenge her. She can't see what is beyond this moment or relate her present experience to the past. Her low Impulse Control is the angry spark that sets everything ablaze.

It is interesting that Jean could not answer the call to bridge awareness with behavioral change, but Grant—who we met in chapter 4—was able to do it while also living with ADHD and BPD. It was heart-wrenching to see such a talented woman refusing to get out of her own way. Her life was this constant and predictable turbulence joined with unrest, sorrow, pain, and an overarching lack of joy. My hope is that someday, a desire for change (stemming from Emotional Self-Awareness) will positively impact her socioemotional trajectory.

What Keeps Us Stuck? Darren

Awareness or insight into our behavior does not necessarily equate with change, as we have seen before. Darren, though living a seemingly charmed life, battled a number of demons. These demons, with incredible precision, sucked the life force out of the marital relationship. Darren felt his wife was becoming his mother, and for good reason; he didn't follow through on what she asked and needed, and she worried he was in the throes of a psychological break. There were a number of exits he could have taken on his journey to save his marriage. The marriage was in a death spiral, manufactured by very specific choices, habits of thinking, and relived historical wounds. Like Jean and Paul, Darren had intellectual gifts, and he didn't have to assert much effort to achieve academically and/or professionally. He had used drugs and alcohol consistently and seemingly without consequences since he was a teenager. Darren married a remarkable woman, but over time as a couple they replicated the same pattern he had grown to resent with his mother. He would refuse to do anything she asked, even when the requests were typical for a partner in a committed relationship. There is an inevitable progression in strained relationships where asking transmutes into nagging. Over time, people can tolerate only so much. Darren's mother and wife hit their limit, and their responses made them seem angry and controlling. They learned to stay on him as if he were a wandering three-year-old, always worried about what he was getting into, and trying everything possible to control his erratic behavior and get him to do even the basics.

As the marriage progressed, so did Darren's refusal to follow through on the simplest requests regarding the children or doing his part around the house. In therapy, he shared with his wife what she could do to "inspire" him to be more of a partner—which essentially was to stop nagging him. His wife also shared what would permit her to be more accommodating to his needs. It sounded good in my office, but regardless of what she asked for and what he agreed to, he consistently failed to deliver. Consequently, she had no incentive to treat him the way he requested. To do so would cast her firmly as an enabler, and she knew better than to play that role.

Emotionally, she felt it almost impossible to honor his requests and needs considering how much he let his responsibilities fall through the cracks. She worked, cared for the children, and had a series of side gigs, which brought in more money. The gigs orbited around what she really enjoyed doing, which also paid fairly well. What was consistent for his wife was knowing how consistently Darren neglected his husband/father duties. Darren never really saw what was needed to run a house, have a good marriage, and make other relationships run smoothly. His wife summed it up when she said, "My children are far more responsive and helpful than their father."

Darren began hanging around people who pulled him further into the murky world of illicit substance abuse, until he discovered methamphetamine (and quite possibly some form of crack cocaine). He used this for months, coupled with stimulants, resulting in both a physical and psychological break. His body revolted against the toxins, making him believe that various microbes were attacking him. He responded by mutilating his skin (it is hard to imagine what someone can do to their body during a drug-induced psychotic episode). His wife and family tried everything to figure out what was wrong. At the time, they had no idea what was causing this flight from reality. Physician after physician told him he needed therapy and nothing else. He considered them quacks engaging in malpractice, neither of which was true. His wife and family made a series of interventions, including an inpatient treatment program with an intensive outpatient component.

Darren lost one job, and then another. Meanwhile, he continued to lie to himself and those around him. Because he was so intelligent, he used his knowledge and sharp analytic skills to discount the value of anything that could possibly help him. Because of his substance use, he is now, and for the foreseeable future, dependent on an antipsychotic medication to fend off delusions.

Though Darren took the EQ-i 2.0, he placed little stock in the results, chalking up the information embedded in his personal feedback report to be an extension of pop culture fads that come and go. The EQ-i has been around for a quarter century and is far from a fad. The 15 competencies generated by the EQ-i 2.0 permit us to see up close and personal what works in our life and what does not. Darren refused to take the time to go over the results with me.

From another client's perspective, the feedback report offered, "A bittersweet experience of seeing where I am right now but knowing where I absolutely can be if I put in the effort to make it happen. No one else is going to do it for me. No one else can." Darren was not remotely interested in the information embedded in the Comprehensive Feedback Report. He was like that person who is driving on empty and keeps believing they can make it one more exit before pulling off, only to become stranded on the side of the road in an unfamiliar place, often at the mercy of strangers.

As his avoidance behavior predicted, Darren's EQ-i 2.0 results in figure 6.5 were fairly low. Based on what I knew about Darren up to that point, I can't say there were any surprises. He didn't feel great about himself, and he knew he was letting his wife and family down. Nevertheless, he grew even more distant, piling up further resentments.

Although Darren was capable of deep thought and analysis, he did not have insight into his feelings (Emotional Self-Awareness) and therefore did not articulate them to others (Emotional Expression). His wife never even knew about the meth use until a friend tipped her off.

Darren's low Self-Actualization means he has limited awareness about what he wants out of life. Substance abuse can confuse and clutter what would have been a seemingly unencumbered path forward. If you don't know where you are going, how will you get there? He was not very Assertive or Emotionally Independent, and considering how

Figure 6.5.

he acted more like a child than an adult, both of these make sense. His lack of Emotional Self-Awareness is intimately connected to his unwillingness to stand on his own or make informed decisions regarding varied information. He was fairly Impulsive and did not have a solid grasp on Reality-Testing even before his psychological break. This was largely because he couldn't see that his behavior was fragmenting his relationships at home, professionally, and with his parents.

His Interpersonal Relationships were his lowest competency, reinforcing his movement away from healthy friends toward those who rallied around substances. He was not very flexible, so when his wife, bosses, or parents demanded he make changes and meet his responsibilities head on, he resisted in order to continue the self-serving behavior.

It is interesting to see that Optimism was his highest competency. This could be related to his low Emotional Self-Awareness, Reality-Testing, and Social Responsibility. He just did not see or pay attention to the ground crumbling beneath his feet. He believed that no matter what, he would survive. Even though we discussed at length in therapy the fact that he was destroying a promising life and relationship, these concerns simply ricocheted off his mind into oblivion. Darren did not have, nor was he interested in developing, self-reflection. Self-reflection is the cornerstone leading to self-correction and the basic rewiring of his choices. I felt as though I was watching a car careening out of control in slow motion, knowing the outcome was going to be devastating.

What We Can Learn by Weaving the Competencies into Therapy or Coaching

I created this list to help us think about when work with the EQ-i 2.0 is effective and when it isn't. The EQ-i 2.0 model of personal discovery and growth is guided by specific outcomes that both the therapist and client want to see occur in the clinical relationship. These are:

- The focus throughout the therapeutic relationship is on the resiliency and strength of each individual in overcoming a myriad of obstacles.

- We develop a common language in the therapeutic relationship that is directed toward what the client wants and how they can achieve it.
- While someone may not initially feel resilient because of life circumstances, it is possible to help that person or couple redefine their map while using resilience-based language, which challenges the inner critic. For example, "The fact that you are here, telling your story and striving to reframe your narrative, suggests remarkable strength."
- Clients learn to sculpt their own strategies to bring about desired change. Through questions, respect, compassion, and support, we help clients move from the shallow end of the pool into the deep end, recognizing that they can now swim.
- With initial support, clients have the capacity to live the life they want and deserve. Situations and environments lead us to feeling stuck and disheartened at the possibility of change. The process of change is dynamic, allowing successes in life by scaffolding one on top of another.
- The therapeutic relationship confirms in the client an ability to both heal and grow, with an emphasis on strengths over deficits and solutions over problems.
- The client feels prized and valued for who they are and what they want to accomplish. This creates feelings of optimism and confidence, consistently reassuring that change is both possible and sustainable.
- Together, we can redefine how they use their maps of the past, present, and future to begin creating and remaining on the path they want.
- We can successfully determine what is realistic for them based on their specific goals, the environment they emerged from, and the vision they have for what they want to achieve.
- The client is able to build lasting coping strategies that consistently move them toward their specific goals and desires.

Regardless of any client's perceived constraints, they can create and implement the strategies necessary to acquire the level of emotional and relational support that has been wanting. From an emotional intelligence perspective, they learn to appropriately manage their emotions, which in turn produces the quality of interpersonal relationships they want and need.

At the end of the day, each person comes to understand what they can and cannot control. Essentially, the only thing we can truly control is our desires and the choices surrounding them. Desires encompass thoughts and perspectives. While we can certainly influence people, we cannot control anyone.

Getting to Know the Client's Main Obstacles for Moving Forward

I wondered for many years if there was something that could improve the therapeutic process or complement my approaches to the clinical session. I had an ever-increasing stream of people seeking therapy whose stories of abuse, loss, and despair challenged what I alone could do with them. Some clients' boats were taking on water faster than they or I could bail them out. The process entailed unpacking their narratives and examining all the different pieces that brought them to this moment, often accompanied by enormous emotional angst. At times, it seemed the pain was so constant and omnipresent that it forced its way over their resolve like the roiling ocean over a hurricane wall. They had been battered for so long that this was all they knew, even though the storm surge would occasionally subside. They believed that wall would give way to the ocean's power soon enough.

The majority of my clients through the years have come from what is perceived as opportunity and privilege. Most have middle-class backgrounds. Some struggle financially, but the majority are more affluent. All were born into situations that positioned them to take advantage of life's opportunities. If they had wanted to, these were people who could have learned to reach out and help those caught in an ongoing cycle of poverty, despair, and socioeconomic stagnation.

Introducing the EQ-i 2.0 into the clinical environment proved to pierce the ever-familiar angst, showing them what might actually be achievable. Our work validated who they are now and what they traveled through, all with the intent of preparing them for a new journey. A client once aptly stated, "This has been like mowing a big-ass lawn.

It seems overwhelming. You have to know you will get it done and begin someplace with a sense of where you'll end up." The strength of an individual's current emotional intelligence might explain the degree to which they have already experienced an array of successes. The higher the emotional intelligence, the greater probability of emotional, interpersonal, and professional positive outcomes. But where do they get stuck? The results of this instrument allow anyone who is willing and eager to leverage their specific strengths and improve the areas that need enrichment.

Little Bird

Song with music, written fall 2012, Dylan Mulcahy

> Sleepy little bird,
> lying broken on the bough
> This is not where you belong,
> among the creatures of the ground
> I see your feathers are still fine;
> you haven't flown these skies too long
> still your colors keep their light
> here in the shadows of the dark and down
> So how did you get here?
> It must have been a mighty thing
> to take the flight out of a bird
> to clip your mighty little wing
> Only if I could
> I would fix your bones
> save you trouble from the hurt
> and fending off the beasts alone
> I know if you take care
> find some shelter in these trees
> these wounds will make you strong
> it's a matter of belief
> I'm asking you trust
> that you will fly again
> out among the upper reaches.

CHAPTER SEVEN

The End and the Beginning of This Journey

By now, after all these extraordinary stories about the strength of ordinary people, I trust that the 15 competencies of the EQ-i 2.0 have taken root in your emotional garden. The trimming and care of your competencies are fully up to you. And it is essential to realize that just as in a real garden, the weeding never stops. If we consistently want beautiful dahlias, apples, and peppers we must diligently calculate:

What are we feeling?
Where is it being directed? To whom?
What is the potential outcome if we remain on this emotional course?
Are we directing our feelings appropriately?
Are our actions, based on what we are feeling, either emptying or filling our emotional buckets along with those around us?

In many ways, assessing the 15 competencies is similar to playing a card game. Do you have a strong hand? Are you bluffing? The journey we have been on in reading this book has pointed to the kind of hand we want to play to get the most out of the game of life. As adults, we have incredible choices. If we pay attention to and honor what our competencies are saying to us, we won't need to bluff or act, because we will have an exceptionally strong hand.

For example, I know I have the capacity to become too high-strung and intense when someone pushes my emotional buttons. I learned while raising my children how just one wrong word can wound them. Anger is often not a choice. It is a feeling related to what immediately is happening in our lives. It grows from blocked expectations, unfulfilled needs, painful disappointment, or myriad forces that can splash red all over our canvas. Anger happens to all of us. How we manage it and other intense feelings is one of the essential keys to living an emotionally intelligent life.

Now It's Your Turn: Analyze Craig's Story

You should now have all the information you need to evaluate Craig's competencies. You will see his EQ-i 2.0, you will be able to compare it with his backstory, and I invite you to consider what you would do or say to help create shifts in his socioemotional intelligence. Then, I will share my thoughts and how I managed what was happening after seeing his five composites and 15 competencies. Every one of us who has an intuitive understanding of the 15 competencies will approach this case differently, but this is as it should be. We are all a product of our own perceptions, experiences, and belief systems regarding how the world works. So, consider what his competencies say to you, and how you would use your insight, intuition, and intelligence to support this young man's forward movement.

Craig was 28 when he came to see me. He had a college degree, worked as a paralegal, and repaired motorcycle engines as a side gig. He was an old soul and remarkably well read. His life was mechanical and solitary, to hear him tell it. "I live a fairly dull existence. It takes a lot of effort to keep things this predictable," he said with a slight smile.

During our first session he came in carrying the book, *The Wild God of the World: An Anthology of Robinson Jeffers*. I asked him to tell me about it.

> In Charlie Brown, Linus carried around a security blanket. My security blanket comes from reading books. Jeffers is incredible, and, in a nut-

shell, it is about how we are all connected in the world. Therefore, what we do matters and how we treat one another and nature ripples its way through the world, affecting all sentient beings. I draw great comfort from thinking in a more far-reaching way. I am deeply cynical and have very little faith in the human condition. I mean, it takes a child to wake us up, or try to! Greta Thunberg represents this duality in my life: One is a belief we can keep this ship from hitting an iceberg and the other is that we are asleep at the switch and we are all going down. My heart spends very little time in the former. Can you imagine running a sword through your mother's heart . . . ? That is what we are singularly and collectively doing to our Mother Earth.

This young man in front of me was engagingly bright, but he used his intelligence and love of learning to blot out as much of the sun as possible. He preferred being unnoticed. It was within the world of shadows that he felt most at peace. I shared this observation with him.

"It seems books create a refuge for you. From what though?"

"I have to share with you that I think therapy feels very unnatural. You know, talking to someone you don't know about the things most disruptive in your life."

"Okay, I happen to agree, it can feel really unbalancing at first," I said. I have always believed that going to therapy requires courage. At that moment, I knew very little about Craig and his story to know what type of support I could offer. So, I asked, "How can I, hopefully, be of support?"

"Support," he repeated. "That is an interesting word, one I have thought a lot about through these past years. You know, like, what would really have helped during my most formative years? Thinking about this does and has always left me monumentally disappointed."

Craig's life up until the age of 14 was pretty much idyllic. His father was an accountant with a big firm on Wall Street, while his mother was a consultant with an expertise in Mergers and Acquisitions. He liked sports, and his dad would show up to his games regularly. Because of her more demanding job, his mother was usually unavailable. This wasn't a big problem, because he knew his dad would be there.

His brother Timmy had Down syndrome and was four years older than Craig. Their nanny often brought Timmy to watch Craig's games. Timmy loved Craig, who in turn found comfort in Timmy's optimistic attitude about life. Timmy would scream out to Craig at these games, "I can't do it, but you can."

It was hard for Craig to express the amount of love he had for Timmy.

After the games, they'd often go to Coney Island for hotdogs. Describing those times, he considered himself a very lucky kid.

When Craig was 12, his father left Wall Street and entered the police academy for the NYPD. He had talked about doing this for a long time, but with his wife's income it finally seemed to work. Both Craig and Timmy thought this was pretty cool. Dad would come home from work, regaling both sons with all the crime-fighting he did that day. Timmy was so into it. He would wear his dad's police hat and bulletproof vest while their dad told all these hair-raising stories. Some might have been true. Many probably weren't, but it was fun for both boys.

The only downside to Craig's dad being a cop was that he rarely had weekends off anymore to watch Craig's games. As a new officer, he got all the shifts that older officers didn't want. But his dad was into it, and the boys felt that excitement.

Now Craig's life was mostly spent in school and with their nanny, Tia, who became their most constant figure. Because of her, Craig learned how to speak both Portuguese and Spanish.

Craig often stared at the floor for a long time when discussing aspects of his life he wished he could recapture.

I asked, "When you are talking about something you miss, you stare off in the distance and become silent. Where do you go during those moments?"

> I really miss parts of growing up. I miss the safety of it. I miss the predictability of it. I miss being a kid with no responsibilities. When I become distant or quiet, I just drift away . . . and reclaim that feeling and those moments . . . It is more powerful than nostalgia for me. Talking about all this brings up just so much crap! So, on one hand, it is pleasant and warm and on the other it is just red-hot pain.

The wounded part, that part of our developmental history we would rather sidestep or pretend is in the past continued to invade his emotional life. I asked him what images come up for him during those times where he would "drift" (this is what he called it when he would remember his past).

> [I feel all of it], every bit of what did or didn't happen in the past. I am always trying to figure it out. Going over it and over it and over it. And it always brings me back to where I started—Why?

"Why?" can be an unforgiving question. We want to believe it is possible to find a satisfying answer, and, in doing so, let go and move on. But pursuing the "why" of situations and moments in our life often serves to keep us stuck. We rarely come to a satisfying conclusion. As we discussed in an earlier chapter, it can take us in circles, so I moved Craig from "why" to "what." What has happened in his life up until now, how has he responded, and in what ways has it been emotionally helpful or hurtful?

Here's the "what." Craig was 14 and Timmy was 18. They were eating dinner as usual without their dad, when there was a knock at the door. It was the watch commander and the precinct chaplain. There had been a shooting. After pulling over a car in lower Manhattan, the driver got out of his car as the boys' father was approaching. The driver shot their dad five times. His bulletproof vest stopped three of the bullets. A fourth bullet tore into his shoulder. The fifth entered his groin area, severing a major artery, and he began to bleed out. Meanwhile, his partner exchanged gunfire with the shooter and killed him.

The ambulance got there fairly quickly, and the EMTs did all they could to slow the bleeding on the way to the hospital. He arrived in a coma due to massive blood loss. They also discovered that he had cancer in his testicles.

Craig and Timmy's dad remained in a coma for 10 days. He lost a lot of blood, which deprived his brain of oxygen. The doctor said the extent of the brain damage would be hard to predict while he remained in a coma.

When he came out of the coma, he wasn't the man the boys remembered. He looked at them in a weird way, like he didn't recognize them, which turned out to be true. This was especially crushing for Timmy because he couldn't fully grasp what was happening. This was one of the hardest parts for Craig. He watched Timmy, always so full of spirit and joy, spiral into an emotionally confusing place. Before the shooting, Timmy played off of the excitement of others. When their dad told stories, they were really colorful and full of animated motion, and both sons loved it.

Once their father was released from the hospital, he also began receiving chemotherapy for the cancer. Craig said their lives felt like something out of a Stephen King novel. They hired a full-time nurse, but their father would scream at the nurse, break dishes, curse constantly, and roam around the apartment. Timmy went to a special school, so Craig would pick him up each day and then they would do whatever was needed to avoid going home.

> We often went to the library, where Timmy would watch stuff on my computer while I did my homework. If it had to be done on the computer, which most of it did, I would wait until after dad went to bed. Timmy began wetting the bed, which gives you a pretty good idea what life was like for him. My father would just look at Timmy with disgust. I have no idea what my father was thinking; what I knew is that it was devastating for Timmy.

Adding insult to injury, Craig's mother was offered a lucrative job with an international firm, which meant now she was gone even more. As Craig described it, she was never home. She would say, "Oh, seeing me is just too hard for your father, so staying away is best."

> I mean are you f---ing kidding me? It was like, yeah, no shit lady, everything upsets him. Another interesting thing about my mother. She had no pictures of us in her office. She bailed and left Tim and me to pick up the pieces. You know, we didn't see my mother a lot before the shooting; however, our nanny was great. And when dad was there, he was fully there. Tia just couldn't bear to see my father's transformation. So, she quit. I honestly have never seen true anguish in someone's face before that moment Tia said she was leaving. It is kinda like people in the rescue boats of the *Titanic* watching all these people die who remained on the ship. Tia knew she was our last remaining lifeline. I could not blame her, not one bit.

Craig was only 15 and Timmy was 19, with one of them wetting the bed and both abandoned on an island by themselves. Their mother called every other day out of some sense of obligation. Craig stopped taking the calls because she had nothing interesting to say, she didn't ask about her husband, and the whole routine felt like a farce. They finally decided to just text if either needed anything. Craig never once texted her.

Their mother filed successfully for divorce when Craig was 16. She put money in an account so the boys would have food, but that was the extent of how she perceived her obligation. "I mean, how f---ed up is all this? Who does this? Who abandons their kids? It felt like she was punishing me and Timmy. For what, I don't know. She has always been like this phantom, so why would this be any different?" Their mother—who hit the gym every day and was very lean and fit—met a younger man. He was an artist and had custody of his three children. Instead of bringing her almost-grown kids with her to the new marriage, she simply abandoned them.

Besides the escapism of it all, Craig suspected that she was ashamed of having a Down syndrome child. High school became a much-needed sanctuary for Craig. He studied hard and took Timmy with him to the local library to study. It was an excellent way to achieve two goals: First, Craig wanted to do well academically to have choices about where to go to college, and second, it kept both sons out of the house and away from their father as long as possible.

Craig's hard work paid off when he learned he had been accepted into Columbia University. He did not date because his anger was too high. The one date he did go on, the girl said something that triggered his anger, so he simply walked away from her. He had a significant and understandable chip on his shoulder, and he drank and smoked a lot of weed. Timmy noticed Craig's self-medication, and in his own way asked him to stop. Craig self-medicated so much that it got in the way of his schoolwork, and he took six years to finish college. Once he graduated college, he wanted nothing to do with their mother, even though she did pay for his tuition at Columbia. He had taken care of Timmy himself, and he now felt they were both better off without her permanently. Timmy never once asked about her. He did ask about their father, but only after he died.

Craig had been in the paralegal position for three months before coming to see me. After our fourth session, I asked if Craig would take the EQ-i 2.0. I explained to him the key aspects of emotional intelligence, after which I sent him a sample Comprehensive Feedback Report, which I send to anyone interested in taking the assessment.

What was clear is that after 13 years of drinking and smoking, Craig no longer wanted to live a life often "dazed and confused," to quote a popular nineties movie about pot. He wanted to be there fully for his brother, who still wet the bed. He wanted to explore the notion of dating, which meant learning to communicate more of what he was feeling. So, we mapped out precisely what it would look and feel like to be more balanced and a better brother to Timmy.

I said, "Timmy obviously knows you drink and smoke [pot] heavily. My sense is this deeply impacts him. So, I would like to test a theory. The more Timmy sees you sober, engaged, and actually more emotionally balanced, the less he will wet the bed or be depressed. All of this may allow his light to shine again."

The only person to really stand by the boys after the shooting was their uncle, who was their father's brother. He asked Craig and Timmy to move in after the shooting, but Craig said no. He did this because his uncle's daughter—the boys' cousin—had severe brain trauma from an accident. Craig worried that introducing Timmy into the equation would be too much. But he made that decision under the influence of alcohol and pot. As Craig began thinking more clearly, he realized there were a number of mistakes he made after the shooting. His priority was to numb the pain and take care of Timmy. Numbing the pain also numbed his critical thinking capacity, disrupting his ability to be more rational and even-tempered.

With the EQ-i 2.0 as Your Tool, What Would You Do Clinically?

Now, take time to address the issues associated with this case. What competencies are underutilized, overused, or working well in Craig's daily life? What story do these competencies tell as they interact with each other, often challenging Craig's personal perspective and choices? My observations and interaction with Craig around these issues can be found after the competencies chart (page 3 from the comprehensive feedback report). Remember, each of us will use our own beliefs, clinical training, and desire to help Craig—and in doing so, allow Tim to heal. There is no right or perfect way. The EQ-i 2.0 is just one tool, but it is a critical one nonetheless.

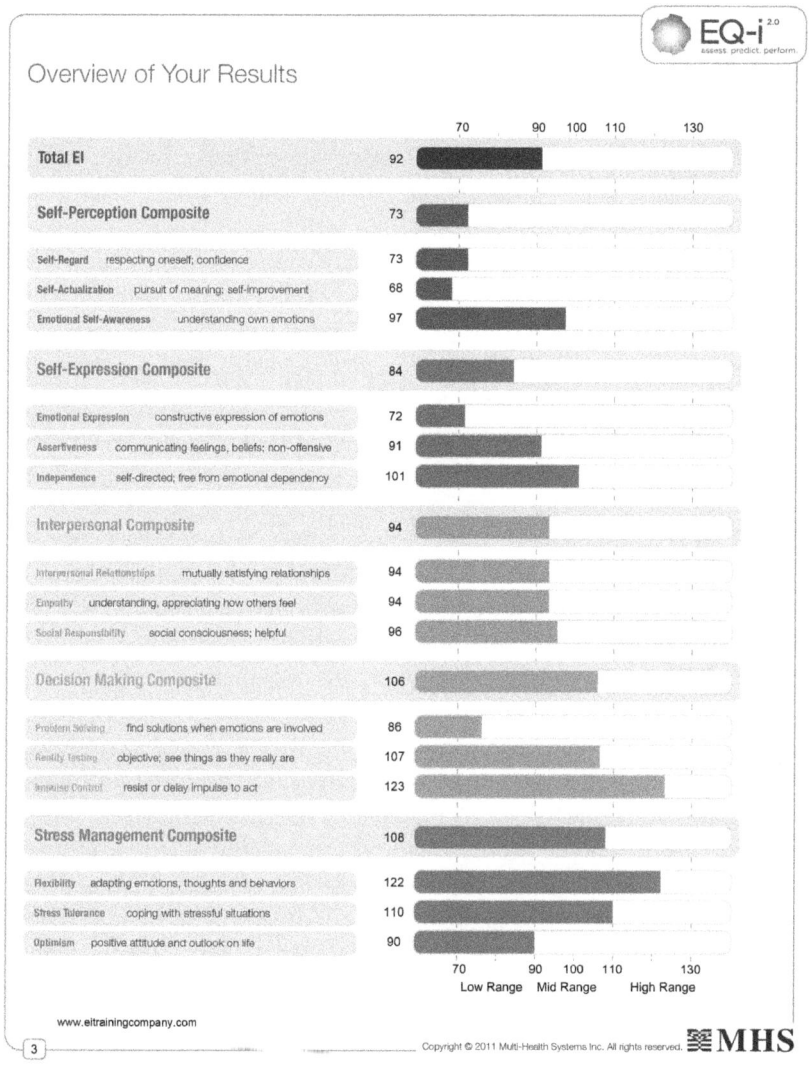

Figure 7.1.

My Analysis

It is evident that Craig feels things very deeply (Emotional Self-Awareness 97), though his ability to talk about or share his feelings is exceedingly low (Emotional Expression 72). In fact, the latter is almost two standard deviations lower than the former. And remember, anything below 85 suggests the competency needs attention.

His Impulse Control score of 123 suppresses his Emotional Expression even further. He rarely did anything spontaneously, making this an overused competency, which also serves to reinforce his Stress Tolerance (110), which was also strong from having to adjust to constant change.

Craig's Flexibility score was 122, but it was less of a strength than an overused competency, because if you consistently go with the flow of what others are doing or want, your expectations will be lower and disappointment minimal. Craig made few demands, and, in doing so, rarely felt disillusioned. With work, he would do exactly what was asked of him. He did not show initiative or anticipate the needs of colleagues, which meant he did his job and nothing more.

His Self-Actualization score of 68 was surprising at first blush, given that he worked exceedingly hard in high school and college. However, academics became a form of escape for him. He placed a great deal of importance on his academic endeavors, without a real sense of what he wanted out of life or knowing how he wanted to contribute.

His abuse of alcohol and marijuana are documented killers of personal motivation and a belief in one's abilities. His Assertiveness was strong enough, considering some of the other scores. His Independence was appropriately on the higher side, since he cared for himself and Timmy for years. Once Craig decided to go to Columbia, friends stopped calling, and he stopped calling them. He worked two jobs to afford a fairly nice place in Brooklyn for the two of them. Timmy would watch TV and color while Craig was in school. At night, he would help Timmy with some educational studies for people with developmental delays. Timmy really looked forward to these classes.

Craig wanted nothing to do with his mother or her life with the artist. He had not spoken to her or had any interaction since the day she paid the last bill before he finally graduated from college. He wasn't quite sure how to feel about her, and whatever feelings he did have were negative, verging on hostile.

In this particular case, Reality-Testing affects (or infects, as the case may be) Craig's ability to see things as they are. He does tend to sugarcoat things with Timmy, because positivity is really the only thing Timmy responds well to. After the shooting, Timmy just couldn't understand what happened to his father or why their mother disappeared. Timmy would often sob in his room because their father was yelling and breaking things.

Imagine for a moment what Craig experienced: He knew precisely what his mother was doing and why. His only solution was evicting her from his thoughts and memories. This also coincided nicely with his resolve to never really talk about what had happened with anyone. He felt things deeply (Emotional Self-Awareness) but had not shared these feelings with anyone until coming in for therapy.

His emotions and appraisals of situations were rooted in reality. He did not make things up, positively or negatively. He spoke with a sense of conviction and purposefulness. However, his low Problem-Solving competency suggested the boiling magma of anger was just below the surface. Both of us were uncertain if or when it would erupt.

The lack of Emotional Self-Expression coupled with high Stress Tolerance, low emotional Problem-Solving, and a strong sense of right and wrong suggested to me that Craig could continue his lifestyle for quite some time, provided everything went smoothly and the booze and drugs didn't create a social or emotional crisis. In my experience, however, the drinking and weed smoking would inevitably catch up with him. "What if you are arrested for disorderly conduct and in the process hit a cop with his own night stick?" I asked, spinning a scenario that I knew from years of the work I do was actually possible for a man that angry. "What happens to Timmy?"

He answered that a woman comes in twice a week, and he told her if anything ever happened to him that she could find money in the envelope, along with his uncle's contact information. His uncle was the one person he could say he loved. I asked him if he really thought this was a plan, and he knew the answer was no.

Craig made it clear he did not want to live this way anymore. Before all this, Timmy was such a bright light, but now Craig couldn't remember the last time either of them smiled. Based on his desire to be the best version of himself, we mapped out what it would look like.

The program that Timmy used twice a week was, to use Craig's term, "dynamite," but he couldn't afford to put him in for six days a week. We discussed asking his mother to pay for the program, which then would free Craig up to work. He would be far less worried and could even consider dating once his after-work hours were free, since the program had evening adult care. It was doubly tough for Craig to think about asking his mother for anything. However, he finally agreed and even saw the benefit of it.

We did not become too existential about his mother participating financially. I believe it may have given her some form of hope that a relationship could occur, but Craig was clear that was not going to happen. She asked Craig if she could call and talk to me, but he said, "If I don't want to talk with you, why do you think I would want him to?"

Craig's substance use was more than just an escape. It had risen to the level where he needed to go to rehab. Fortunately, Timmy's program also had a residential component. Craig's insurance was very good, and his mother paid for the out-of-pocket costs.

Nine months after coming to see me and three months after leaving treatment to come back home, I asked Craig to retake the EQ-i 2.0. The results are pictured in figure 7.2. Take the time to really see the differences. While not every competency changed, the ones most essential to living a socially and emotionally balanced life did. He had begun to live his life, and on our last visit he even had plans to take a girl to the beach for four days. He felt she was just incredible, and he wanted to be sure he was the complete gentleman, so he invited a chaperone. It was Timmy.

Some Stories in Summary

Clients who seize upon the revelations offered by the EQ-i 2.0 Feedback Report are served best through a sustained therapeutic or coaching relationship, where they can build and enhance their emotional intelligence. Many have found it a transformative process. Considering the changes it has produced in people's lives, the more clinicians and coaches that utilize this approach, the quicker clients will achieve their desired goals. As noted before, the EQ-i 2.0 is not a clinical panacea. It is one spoke in the wheel of a clinician's/coach's many different therapeutic tools. It is my hope you can see the benefit of learning and knowing how the competencies impact our daily life. Deciding how

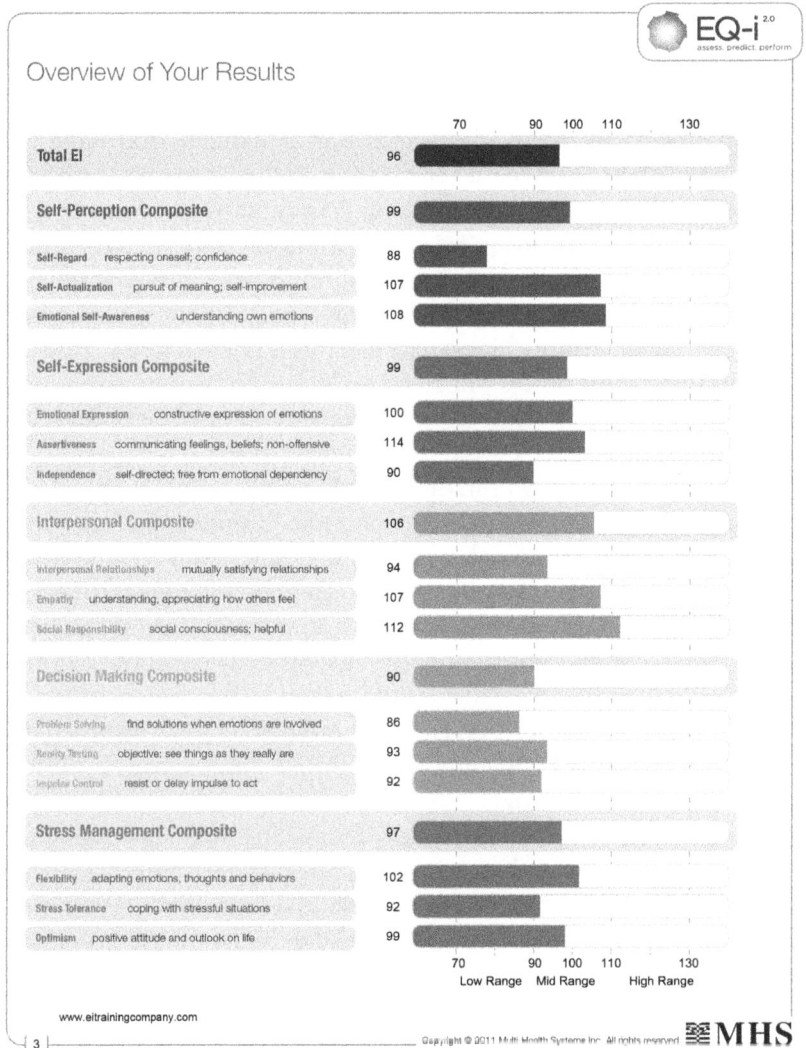

Figure 7.2.

to use the EQ-i 2.0 and the competencies in your practice takes some consideration. Sometimes it helps to just dive in. One of my favorite phrases for this has also become popular in success literature, "Ready, fire, aim!"

The Essence of Courage

This book, based on the courage of those represented in it, provides a blueprint of how to recognize how our clients can expand their social and emotional repertoires. Transformation is difficult, and more for some than others. Leaving a relationship, telling someone how you truly feel, risking ridicule for speaking your mind (even from a well-thought-out place), letting people know who you really are rather than what they expect or want you to be—all of this requires courage and some aspect of change. These stories have covered many topics and much emotional territory. Some may feel this is uncomfortably close to our own lives, while others will be more distant. Every narrative leaves its clues about how to create the characters we want to be in this play called life. Good therapeutic questions often shift the axis of our discussions to spin more slowly or in different directions.

Therapy or coaching can serve to emotionally protect a client while addressing various emotional, physical, and psychological invectives experienced over time. When it works, it reinforces protective factors that allow us to overcome years of doubt, omnipresent pain, and fractured self-esteem. By consistently introducing what has gone well in a person's life or what is imaginable with regard to their talents, we can help quiet the client's noise of self-doubt often accompanying a deficit-oriented paradigm (i.e., "I am not enough," "I won't succeed," "What is the point of even trying?" "I am just not talented," "The abuse was my fault—I deserve what I get," etc.). Enhancing individual resilience begins with empathy and emotional Self-Awareness, resulting in the person consistently living the life they want. This requires recognizing and shedding pessimistic attitudes that hold us back from being our best selves. It requires a reorientation to view life through the lens of optimism rather than as a foregone negative conclusion. Is this easier said than done? Not if we respectfully develop a plan around an individual's unique strengths and build upon their personal vision, which unfolds in the therapeutic relationship. We must honor their pain and acknowledge it before any real healing can take hold. If we are taking a wall down, it must be done brick by brick. Resolve is the key to managing perseverance, especially when emotional fatigue sets in. As in chess, each move takes the player that much closer to capturing the coveted King. The person moves even closer to what they want, widening the gap between "What's the use?" to "This path is precisely where I need to be to achieve the outcomes I want."

Our Inner Dialogue: Jenny

Even in the face of tremendous emotional and psychological challenge, people can learn to thrive while making consistent and life-affirming choices. Some clients have been through so much that they compare their life to the Greek mythological figure Sisyphus, pushing a rock up a mountain each day, going to bed exhausted, and then waking the next day to see it has tumbled back to the bottom. Now, they have to push it up all over again.

Whoever came up with "sticks and stones can break my bones, but words will never hurt me" must have been working with a small sample size! Words matter, and, if words were used to consistently eviscerate someone's emotional life and belief in self, all the ability to achieve a balanced life seems bleak. Those who try to limit us through their words in fact bully us, projecting onto others their own insecurity and pain. In terms of normal parenting (whatever that may be), mom or dad can occasionally lose their cool and say something mean to one another or their children. That is hurtful, but it may well not be abuse. I'm talking about parents who use their children as emotional shields to deflect their own insecurities. This abuse extends beyond hurt and actually undermines character development and has the capacity to destroy self-regard.

Jenny grew up in a serially abusive home where her earliest memories are of her parents using profanities and vulgar phrases, "Just what the f--- is wrong with you?" "You are the singularly most worthless piece of s--- I have ever, ever seen." Her parents were professionals with high incomes who were intensely stressed. They wanted children who were seen and not heard. If they heard the children, then they verbally annihilated them.

She had a loving nanny (which seems to be a trend in this book) whose gentle words and touch served to counterbalance this avalanche of verbal abuse. Connecting with such constructive and affirming people can create hope. Hope then nourishes the person's optimism, resulting in motivation and a life well lived! (as we have seen previously). We learn to believe what we hear, whether that is positive or negative. Once we realize we can pay attention to positive influences, we can develop our own inner strength and power and drown out negative ones.

When I looked at the beautiful woman sitting in front of me, I also saw her littler self, a small person surviving such a barrage of pain. She inched closer on the couch toward my chair and said, "Thank you for coming into that darkness with me. Thank you for protecting the little me."

It was authentic and heartfelt.

"No one has ever been brave enough to be in that place with me," she continued. "This is where I will heal, Doctor P."

Introducing the EQ-i 2.0 into the therapeutic process is a potential harbinger of hope, opportunity, and definable solutions. Instead of the initial negative phrases that began this section, together we focus on "You can do anything you put your mind to"; "The invisible string of love that connects us is never broken"; "If you see it, you can achieve it"; and, "I am so proud to know you and be your parent." These types of messages have the capacity to burrow into the woundedness, releasing an antidote that allows us to rise above a less accommodating world.

The magnitude of early negative messages can leave us reeling from what seem like nonstop aftershocks. The aftershocks come in the form of "triggers." The more unaddressed triggers that exist in our life, the greater the likelihood of building our lives on socially and emotionally shaky ground. If I don't feel at home in my own skin, how can I possibly feel good around others? It is understandable that individuals emotionally terrorized or psychologically abused in childhood would feel very little hope in the world. This is what many bring to the therapeutic table. They ante up, but with no real expectation of winning. Life has suggested they won't win, at least, not emotionally. Our challenge as therapists and coaches lies in ushering our clients through the early, negative childhood experiences with an eye on encouraging them to author a whole new inner script.

Helping others is an important part of embracing our strengths and moving toward what we want to achieve. This can be through service work, volunteering in the community, or launching something simple yet impactful to a targeted population. One client who worked long hours and could not direct her time to service work nevertheless tended a garden and gave the fruits and vegetables to a local food bank. Gardening was therapeutic for her, and the food was beautiful and nutritious for those relying on the kindness of others for meals. This gift of "paying it forward" is powerful (we have been extremely fortunate and want to share with those who at this moment are not), and it confirms our positive forward movement. A positive therapeutic relationship supports individuals to move toward what has been missing, what matters in their personal development, and what is necessary to sustain growth or movement over time. Giving back to others less fortunate is the pinnacle in recognizing our own gratitude for what we have and what we have accomplished. On the EQ-i 2.0, this competency is called Social Responsibility.

A Tool for Organizations, Applied to Individuals

Many come to therapy with an invisible brand on their body. This mark asserts they belong to someone else, so there is nothing they can do.

> "My parents pay for my college tuition, so there is no way I can tell them who I really am."
>
> "I am like my partner's trophy. Great at this, first in that, always on top . . ."
>
> "You know until we started talking, I had no idea what I wanted."
>
> "I heard my mom last year tell my father that she will do everything in her power to make sure I don't suffer in this world. But I am suffering because I can't tell them who I am in love with."
>
> "I'll do all the right things for this important job, but when I am done with this assignment, I am done pretending."

The EQ-i 2.0 and attending competencies offer an important perspective on personal growth. This assessment can be an essential aspect of the clinician's strategic playbook to help someone gain freedom from these invisible brands or tattoos. I have witnessed astonishing growth with individuals who are committed to understanding the psychic and emotional pain they have carried so long. While that hurt comes from different places over the development of a life, we can significantly reduce it until someone actually feels emotional freedom. This is true even if a person's inner fire was all but extinguished during a troubled childhood or young adulthood.

As noted before, this assessment was created largely to benefit organizations. When used in a clinical setting, it generates an interesting discussion when people feel they are different at work than at home. We talk about this in relation to their results. If they did not take the assessment, I ask specific questions about their competencies; I ask them what it would look like to be more balanced or socially and emotionally consistent at work and home. The notion of our many selves in professional versus private settings is quite real. A minister's son recalled his father's dual selves. He spoke of how much concern and devotion his father had for the congregation, yet when he was home he wasn't really communicative and didn't want to talk about his day. Seeing by all accounts your parent being loving toward others while you don't feel it can leave a deep, unhealed wound.

Another client who demonstrated this had been a volunteer for Teach for America. I could see that her Social Responsibility was through the roof, even before she thought of taking the EQ-i 2.0. She did everything for everyone and asked nothing of others. She felt invisible in the world because no one really knew her. She was kind and caring, though she rarely socialized with colleagues or anyone. She did not feel worthy of having fun and getting to know people. Knowing her backstory, this made a lot of sense. Learning how the competencies intersect gives a person a new lens through which to view self and others.

The EQ-i 2.0 often validated things I was already hearing from the client. They tell me that what helps them the most is hearing the narrative I offer after analyzing their EQ-i 2.0 competencies. How does strong Emotional Self-Awareness but low Emotional Expression impact a person? This person is deeply frustrated, feeling many things, but only letting them out with great irregularity.

I once had a client say, "I have been forced to take so many personal and team building assessments through work that I can't even remember them all. The reason is they had very little impact. So is this tool really going to be any different?" Six months later, however, he was a believer. He took a second assessment to see if he had achieved the changes we discussed after the first one. After seeing the results he said,

> Understanding the impact of these competencies day to day, I can honestly say I am now a better father to my children, a better boss to my direct reports, a more loving and thoughtful husband, and last, though certainly not least . . . I really like who I am becoming.

There are many assessments and tools for personal change out there, and I am sure they can be helpful. I choose this tool, the EQ-i 2.0, because I know it well, and I have witnessed its power to change people who stay with the process. I occasionally use it when teaching, and one of my students said she took it at her high school. After taking it again and referring to the results of the instrument throughout the semester, she said, "This has been incredible. But, why is it so amazing now and it really wasn't when I took it before?" I said it's because she got to know herself much better through the Comprehensive Feedback Report, rather than simply being introduced to it through professional trainers who are limited in the amount of time they can spend on any tool they are using. This limited amount of time is something I encounter in the certification trainings I facilitate for clinicians and coaches who want to use this tool in their practice.

Using the EQ-i 2.0 in a Work Setting

While this has been a book for practitioners, anyone interested in their own personal growth can read this book, understand how the competencies operate in their life, and begin making shifts and changes to live a more balanced and authentic life.

But what if you are in an organization where you know you and your colleagues could benefit from this work? Or what if you are part of leadership at a university or college? Can the EQ-i 2.0 make a difference there as well? Absolutely, and I invite you to reach out to discuss it with me. To decide whether my approach is right for you, we can consider two stories. In the first story, I was hired to work with an international organization that did enviable global work with some of the world's poorest and most deserving. It was a pleasure to sit down with these intelligent, hardworking, dedicated professionals. They were all great to me, but through interviews I learned that they would not talk to each other! There was so much passive-aggressive behavior and purposeful nonsharing of information. They were dedicated to their worthy mission, yet they didn't trust each other, and many felt threatened.

I asked the leadership team if I could give all the participants, about 25 people, the EQ-i 2.0 in the first training session I facilitated, and then have four one-on-one, 45-minute sessions with each of them. This would get them all working in the same direction while being clear on their motivations. After which, we would have a second training session incorporating all the pieces they talked about wanting as a group.

Although they believed the training sessions would be useful, the CEO objected to the one-on-one strategy. I insisted that if you want to see group cohesiveness and positive change, the one-on-one is a critical first step. He wanted me to just do the full group training. I said, "No thank you, not worth it." I believe the CEO knew that if I spent enough time with individuals, it would become clear that he was the problem! He did not want to hear it. Keeping them in a large, distrustful group felt like the safest thing for him, which is why I turned down the contract.

Now, for the second story. It was a similar organization, but instead of resisting my wish to work with the individuals, the leadership team said fine. Let's put together a schedule. We met as a group for a day to take the EQ-i 2.0, and then over the course of two and a half months I met with each person four times for 45 minutes each. Unlike in the first story, this CEO agreed to be a participant like everybody else.

After our one-on-one sessions were complete, we came back together as a group for a full day to assess where we were and lessons learned. Where do people want to go with what they've learned in terms of their own competencies? How will teammates ask for support from one another? Where will trust within this organization come from and what does trust actually mean? The focus of the organization was generating personal and organizational growth through interdependence and defining what that looked like individually and collectively. It's about a dedicated willingness to work with me and the assessment as I provide it, leading to the development of mutual rapport and a shared vision. When it works, it's fantastic.

Even though this is not a book about communication per se, it is a skill that is vital to everything we do in these corporate, university, and other institutional settings. When the group in the second story worked with me on my terms with the EQ-i 2.0, they learned how to communicate, how to say no in a way that someone else can accept, how to discuss their own personal needs so that other people can understand, or how to deal with difficult information that might seem off-putting or could easily make others close down. I've done this with scores of clients, and it has a way of creating change. We see both micro and macro changes within individuals.

Future Use of the EQ-i 2.0

I believe people will continue to use this assessment in the boardroom and classrooms. It makes great sense to me, and I have seen it clear new pathways for those who take the assessment and are dedicated to getting as much out of it as possible. Probably one of our most useful idioms is, "You get out what you put in." This is true of this assessment when you understand the power of the competencies.

There is nothing magical about the EQ-i 2.0 itself. But magic occurs when people see the powerful interaction of their competencies, expressed through their socioemotional behaviors and relationships. They can track how a low competency moves them away from what they want. They can see how a high one can push others away because the client overuses it and becomes a difficult person to be around. I hope as you consider this tool as a practitioner, as a potential client, or as part of a leadership team thinking about bringing in someone like me to run a training, you'll remember the individuals in this book and their true stories of courage. Every person who takes the EQ-i is unique, with their own specific perceptions of how their life can be better if they allow themselves to go deep into what the competencies reflect.

When I look at it, it tells a story to me that I then share with the client, and they tend to say something like, "Wow, it's right. What it shows is really what is happening." Herein lies the fulcrum of change.

The life-changing impact the 15 competencies have had on personal and professional outcomes is always remarkable for me to witness. Rekindling a person's belief in self means living another idiom, "If you believe it, you can achieve it."

Index

AA. *See* Alcoholics Anonymous
Aaron, 20–22, *21*
abandonment, 72
abuse: of alcohol, 204; by brother, 132–33; by Carl, 183; in childhood, 98, 210–11; client experiencing, 17; nanny counterbalancing, 210; self destroyed by, 209. *See also* substance abuse
achievement, 23
action: Carl dismissing, 182; contemplation followed by, 55; feeling basing, 195; knowledge reconciling, 4; social responsibility involving, 49
Adams, Shelby Lee, 49–50, 53
addiction, 23–25, 27
ADHD. *See* attention deficit hyperactivity disorder
advocate, 5
aggression, 45, 99, 113–14

alcohol, 38–39, 92–93, 204
Alcoholics Anonymous (AA), 15, 27–28
anger, 3–4; alcohol with, 92–93; Chas understanding, 97–98; Ellie in, 99–100; emotional independence controlling, 129; of father, 92; with love, 121; pain fueling, 99, 110; therapy managing, 81; Thom managing, 99
angst, 193–94
anxiety, 132, 138
Appalachia, 49–50, 53
assertiveness: aggression contrasted with, 45, 113–14; communication requiring, 101; emotional expression and, 143; emotional independence sustained by, 88; by Leslie, 95–97; Steve overutilizing, 43
assumption, 60

217

attention deficit hyperactivity disorder (ADHD), 30, 108; with BPD, 109, 117, 184, 187; father on, 71; pain with, 24; parent challenged by, 70; Ray impacted by, 71
autism spectrum, 140–42
awareness, 97–98; change contrasted with, 4, 109, 153–59, 187–88; client rating, 98; of pain, 65; of Ray, 73; with self-actualization, 190–91. *See also* emotional self-awareness

balance: change for, 213; choice emanating, 5; competencies overpowering, 103, 112–14, *113*; decision-making measuring, 55; Denny achieving, 90–93, *91*; EI keeping, 128; of emotion, 98; empathy seeking, 48–49; honesty allowing, 44–45; impulse control measuring, 59; independence maintaining, 46; parents disrupting, 146; Pete considering, 168; as priority, 116–17; in relationship, 47, 150; resentment caused by, 151–52; in therapy, 154
Bar-On, Reuven, 183
Beck, Aaron T., 7
behavior, 48; emotion impacted by, 106; EQ-i 2.0 expressing, 215; of Grant, 111; Mara modifying, 158; by mother, 146; parents teaching, 38–39; as passive aggressive, 99; reinforcement of, 170
Borderline Personality Disorder (BPD): ADHD with, 109, 117, 184, 187; DBT managing, 112, 185; narrative influenced by, 110
boundary, 31, 109
BPD. *See* Borderline Personality Disorder
Brackett, Marc, 153
brother: abuse by, 132–33; Craig and, 199; with Down syndrome, 197–98, 201; family impacted by, 119; flexibility without, 123; friendship with, 74; pain and, 72; parents monopolized by, 159; relationship with, 71–72, 120; support by, 120
bullying, 134–35
business, 65

Carl: abuse by, 183; action dismissed by, 182; drinking by, 178–83; EQ-i 2.0 of, 179–80, *181*; flexibility of, 182; independence overutilized by, 182; self-actualization of, 180; self-regard of, 180; wife dismissed by, 179, 180
change: awareness contrasted with, 4, 109, 153–59, 187–88; for balance, 213; with competencies, 216; death motivating, 73; EI creating, 32, 97; from EQ-i 2.0, 92; flexibility navigating, 66, 84; Mara resisting, 154; plan for, 5; preparation for, 115, 116; relationship and, 175; with strength, 19; stress management exploring, 65; support for, 5; in therapy, 153–54, 167
Chas, 83; anger understood by, 97–98; EQ-i 2.0 of, 81–82,

83, 85; reality-testing by, 82; relationship reinforcing, 84; social responsibility of, 81–82; Taliban hunted by, 80

childbirth, 33–34

childhood: abuse in, 98, 210–11; doubt from, 60–61; empathy born of, 22; mechanisms from, 3; privacy in, 94; stress tolerance lowered in, 157; in therapy, 42

choice: balance emanated by, 5; control of, 193; drinking and, 92–93; Grant connected with, 112; of Jean, 187; pain of, 109–10; Sisyphus representing, 209

client: abuse experienced by, 17; awareness rated by, 98; EQ-i 2.0 impacting, 167; goal understood by, 16; obstacles to, 193–94; opportunity perceived by, 193; order created by, 61; pattern by, 103; relationship healing, 192; support of, 192; therapy monitoring, 153. *See also specific client*

Clinton, Bill, 119

Coach Report, 90

cocooning, 11

college, 155, 168–69, 201

Columbia University, 201

coma, 199

combat, 80–81

comfort, 35, 127–28

communication, 38, 101

community, 51

competencies: Aaron exploring, 20–22, *21*; balance overpowered by, 103, 112–14, *113*; change with, 216; EI measured by, 14, 18; interpretation of, 130; knowledge of, 19–20; pain recalibrated by, 16; Paul explaining, 15; power of, 16–19; recovery told by, 28–29; relationship expressed by, 215–16; strength reframed by, 20; sturdiness created with, 68; in therapy, 191–93; well-being created by, 34. *See also specific competencies*

composites, 17–18

Comprehensive Feedback Report, 131, 145, 189, 202

connection: empathy deepening, 48; Karla establishing, 165; through reading, 196–97; trauma challenging, 157

Connor, Kathryn M., 7

contact, 159–60

contemplation, 58

control: of choice, 193; death guiding, 72; of father, 94; need for, 150; stress heightened by, 24. *See also impulse control*

courage, 31–32, 208–9

Craig: brother and, 199; at Columbia University, 201; drinking of, 201–2; EQ-i 2.0 of, 196, 203, *203*, 204, 206, *207*; father of, 198; flexibility overused by, 204; mother leaving, 200, 204–5; pain numbed by, 202; problem-solving of, 205; reality-testing impacting, 205

creativity, 106

Damien: AA centralized by, 27; EQ-i 2.0 of, 25, 29; faith connected to, 28; in recovery, 22–30, 25, 29; relationship of, 24; self-actualization of, 23; sobriety entered by, 30

Darren, 187, 190, *190*; Comprehensive Feedback Report ignored by, 189; EQ-i 2.0 of, 189, *191*; lying by, 189; methamphetamine used by, 188–89; optimism of, 191; in therapy, 188

dating, 45, 95

David: EQ-i 2.0 of, 75, 76, 79; integrity displayed by, 78; on lying, 76, 78; behind persona, 75; self-regard of, 77; self reinvented by, 75; stress of, 76

DBT. *See* Dialectical Behavior Therapy

death, 72–74, 124

decision, 60, 123

decision-making, 18, 58–61, *57, 58*, 62–65, *64*

Deirdre, 151–52; EQ-i 2.0 of, 147, *148*; impulse control overused by, 150; mother overridden by, 147; reality-testing by, 148–49

Denny: balance achieved by, 90–93, *91*; Coach Report for, 90; EQ-i 2.0 of, 90, *91*; therapy sought by, 92

depression, 6, 7, 10, 34, 120

Descartes, René, 111

development, 40, 74, 115–16

Dialectical Behavior Therapy (DBT), 112, 185

Diane, 127–28; emotional self-awareness by, 124; EQ-i 2.0 of, 122, *125*, 126; impulse control overused by, 123; problem-solving underutilizing, 123–24; self-regard of, 124–25; strength of, 118–19; stress tolerance of, 123; suicide impacting, 120–21

disability, 138

disappointment, 154; Marsha and, 61–65; Paul impacted by, 8; in relationship, 39; in support, 197

distraction, 33

divorce, 50, 201

Doran, George, 115

doubt: from childhood, 61–63; after death, 124; disability with, 138; pain and, 122, 208; relationship creating, 47; talking about, 146; at work, 139

Down syndrome, 197–98, 201

drinking: by Carl, 178–83; choice and, 92–93; of Craig, 201–2; lying protecting, 169; mental health complicated by, 169–70; Pete influenced by, 168–71; stress alleviated by, 182–83; triggers to, 28

Driven to Distraction (Hollowell), 108–9

Ellie, 99–100

emotion, 2; balance of, 98; behavior impacting, 106; emotional self-awareness overwhelmed by, 38; perception fluctuating, 58; rationality contrasted with, 58; reason for, 144–45. *See also* anger; disappointment; doubt; fear

emotional expression, 44–45; assertiveness and, 143; emotional self-awareness contrasted with,

Index ～ 221

42, 134, 140, 180–81, 185–86; empathy with, 131; impulse control suppressing, 204; inclusivity developed by, 164; of Mara, 155; of Steve, 41–42
emotional independence: anger controlled with, 129; assertiveness sustaining, 88; Grant overusing, 114; of Pete, 173; with problem-solving, 130
emotional intelligence (EI), 2, 183; balance kept by, 128; change created by, 32, 97; childbirth and, 33–34; competencies measuring, 14, 18; EQ-i 2.0 testing, 12; happiness and, 33; kindness with, 151; stress rooted in, 6; well-being evaluated by, 3
emotional regulation, 98
emotional self-awareness, 8, 9, 40, 168; by Diane, 124; emotional expression contrasted with, 42, 134, 140, 180–81, 185–86; emotion overwhelming, 38; with empathy, 163; feeling understood with, 37; lying limiting, 77; pain and, 147, 163; self-actualization combined with, 143; strength of, 155
empathy, 168; balance sought with, 48–49; childhood birthing, 22; Comprehensive Feedback Report defining, 145; connection deepened by, 48; with emotional expression, 131; emotional self-awareness with, 163; through experience, 47; improvisation and, 155; of Jeb, 145; Jennifer leveraging, 54; in relationship,

100–101; social responsibility compared with, 49
emptiness, 104
environment, 5
EQ-i 2.0, 2, 7–9, 15–16, 40; of Aaron, 21; angst pierced by, 193–94; behavior expressed in, 215; card game contrasted with, 195–96; of Carl, 179–80, *181*; change from, 92; of Chas, 81–82, *83*, *85*; client impacted by, 167; of Craig, 196, 203, *203*, 206, *207*; of Damien, *25*, *29*; of Darren, 189, *191*; of David, 75, 76, *79*; of Deirdre, 147, *148*; of Denny, 90, *91*; depression suggested by, 10; of Diane, 122, *125*, 126; EI tested by, 12; garden compared to, 195; of Grant, 112, 117; growth offered by, 212; of Irene, 86, 89; of Jean, 185, *186*; of Jeb, 140, *141*, 143–44, *144*; of Jennifer, 54, 55, *56*, *57*; of Jon, 133–34, *135*; of Karla, 161, *162*; leadership taken by, 214; of Leslie, 95, 96; of Mara, 155, *156*; of Marsha, 63, 64; MSCEIT compared with, 152; narrative within, 13, 212–13; organization utilizing, 214; pattern of, 129–65; of Paul, 9; of Peg, 174–75, *177*; of Pete, 171–73, *172*; power of, 213; of Ray, 68, 69; relationship with, 206–8; of Rene, 106, *107*; on social responsibility, 211; in therapy, 42, 210; as tool, 167, 202–3, *203*; of Willy, 130; in work, 213–15. See *also* composites; Comprehensive Feedback Report

eulogy, 26–27
experience: empathy through, 47; friendship impacted by, 11; knowledge in, 36; of suffering, 1; therapy addressing, 208–9
explaining, 54

faith, 27, 28, 82, 127–28
family, 119; abandonment in, 72; knowledge inherited by, 50; of Peg, 174–78, *177*; relationship with, 110–11. *See also* brother; mother
father: on ADHD, 71; anger of, 92; coma of, 199; control of, 94; of Craig, 198; divorce impacting, 50; Jennifer appreciating, 50–51; Positive Parenting by, 70–71; privacy denied by, 94; values instilled by, 51
fear, 119; anxiety and, 132; Leslie guided by, 93; optimism suppressed by, 140; rehearsal minimizing, 100. *See also* doubt
feedback, 13–14, 24–25
feeling: action based on, 195; emotional self-awareness understanding, 37; independence silencing, 54; Jon connecting, 136; talking contrasted with, 77; after therapy, 84; tolerance lacked by, 43–44. *See also* emotion
flexibility, 124; without brother, 123; of Carl, 182; change navigated with, 66, 84; Craig overusing, 204; development influencing, 116; independence contrasted with, 136; of Paul, 8; about perspective, 67; relationship reinforced by, 114; as strength, 173
flourishing, 5
friendship, 11, 74, 169

Gabi, 131–32
gaslighting, 63
goals, 16, 122, 192
Goleman, Daniel, 152
Grant, 109–10, 113, *113*, 115, 118; behavior of, 111; choice connecting, 112; emotional independence overused by, 114; EQ-i 2.0 of, 112, 117; time centered by, 116
growth, 212
guilt, 73
Gwen, 34

happiness, 33, 105
healing, 192; from improvisation, 157; at mosque, 82; pain contrasted with, 30; with risk, 22; through talking, 15
Hesse, Hermann, 23
Hollowell, Ned, 108–9
home, 103–9
honesty, 44–45
hope, 10
humor, 20
husband, 108–9, 174, 176

identity, 35
imposter syndrome, 36
improvisation, 155, 157
impulse control: balance measured by, 60; Deirdre overusing, 150; Diane overusing, 123; emotional expression suppressed by,

204; of Paul, 8; predictability establishing, 60
impulsivity, 19, 65
inclusivity, 164
independence: balance maintained with, 46; Carl overutilizing, 182; decision impacted by, 123; feeling silenced with, 54; flexibility contrasted with, 136; mother countered by, 149; in relationship, 46; self-actualization with, 176. *See also* emotional independence
Infinite Jest (Wallace), 121
insecurity, 146–47
integrity, 78
intentionality, 66–67
interpersonal relationships, 18, 46–47, 49–55, 140, 191
interpretation, 130
Irene: as doctor, 86–87; EQ-i 2.0 of, 86, 89; reality-testing by, 88; social responsibility of, 87; stress tolerance of, 87; support for, 88

Jean, 183–87, *186*
Jeb: on autism spectrum, 140–42; empathy of, 145; EQ-i 2.0 of, 140, *141*, 143–44, *144*; pattern seen by, 142; strength demonstrated by, 143; at work, 142–43
Jeffers, Robinson, 196
Jennifer, 49; Appalachia depicted by, 53; community considered by, 51; empathy leveraged by, 55; EQ-i 2.0 of, 54, 55, 56, *57*; father appreciated by, 50–51; judgment and, 51–53; profiling by, 52; self-regard of, 54; in therapy, 55
Jenny, 209–11

Jerome, 48
job, 117
Jon, 132; EQ-i 2.0 of, 133–34, *135*; feeling connected by, 136; optimism of, 135–36; self-actualization leveraged by, 135–36
journal, 164
joy, 137
judgment, 51–53
Jung, Carl, 23

Kal, 37
Kant, Immanuel, 112
Karla, 159, 162–64; connection established by, 165; EQ-i 2.0 of, 161, *162*; as intellectual, 160; stress tolerance of, 165; thinking concealed by, 161
kids, 176
Kilcarr, Patrick J., 70
kindness, 151
King, Stephen, 200
knowledge: action reconciled with, 4; of competencies, 19–20; in experience, 36; family inheriting, 50; through pain, 14; power of, 30–31; of self, 4–5, 82

laziness, 117
leadership, 214
Leslie: assertiveness by, 95–97; EQ-i 2.0 of, 95, *96*; fear guiding, 93; music aiding, 94–95
Linehan, Marsha, 112, 185
"Little Bird," 194
love, 74, 121, 127
lying, 90; by Darren, 189; David on, 76, 78; drinking protected by, 169; emotional self-awareness

limited by, 77; reality-testing damaged by, 75; relationship suffocated by, 178

Mara, 153, 156–57, 159; behavior modified by, 158; change resisted by, 154; emotional expression of, 155; EQ-i 2.0 of, 155, *156*
marriage, 104, 176
Marsha: business created by, 65; decision-making of, 60–65, *64*; disappointment and, 63–64; EQ-i 2.0 of, *63, 64*; strength considered by, 62
Matilda (movie), 10, 62
Mayer-Salovey-Caruso Emotional Intelligence Test (MSCEIT), 152, 153
mechanisms, 3, 183
mental health, 169–70
methamphetamine, 188–89
mosque, 82
mother: behavior by, 146; Craig left by, 200, 204–5; Deirdre overriding, 147; divorce filed for by, 201; independence countering, 149; pain and, 155; relationship with, 205–6; socialization prevented by, 61; wife as, 187–88
MSCEIT. *See* Mayer-Salovey-Caruso Emotional Intelligence Test
Mulcahy, Dylan, 194
music, 94–95

nanny, 198, 210
narrative, 13–14, 110, 212–13
need: for control, 150; Peg recognizing, 178; in relationship, 104–5; responsibility compared with, 188; social responsibility and, 54, 150; stress from, 132
North Korea, 114–15

objectivity, 60, 118, 152–53
observation, 60
obstacles, 193–94
opportunity, 93, 193
optimism, 7, 9, 10, 12, 67–68; of Darren, 191; fear suppressing, 140; of Jon, 135–36; possibility focusing, 68; relationship connected with, 140
order, 61
organization, 13–14, 16, 211–15

pain, 39–40, 98, 136; with ADHD, 24; anger fueled by, 99, 110; awareness of, 65; brother and, 72; of choice, 109–10; competencies recalibrating, 16; contact limited by, 159–60; Craig numbing, 202; creativity from, 106; depression masking, 6; doubt and, 122, 208; emotional self-awareness and, 147, 163; healing contrasted with, 30; humor through, 20; husband hearing, 108; journal capturing, 164; joy contrasted with, 137; knowledge through, 14; mother and, 155; strength challenged by, 63; therapy healing, 30; trauma creating, 16; of Willy, 129. *See also* abuse
Paradox (Zeno), 178
parents: ADHD challenging, 70; anxiety created by, 138; balance disrupted by, 146; behavior taught by, 38–39; brother monopolizing, 159; husband impacted by, 108;

of Jenny, 209–10; Peg impacted by, 175; Pete protecting, 170; relationship with, 173; school influenced by, 63. *See also* father; mother
partner, 63
past, 35–36
pattern: by client, 103; of EQ-i 2.0, 129–65; Jeb seeing, 142; marriage impacted by, 176; of self-expression, 44; of thinking, 158
Paul, 6–7, 9–10, 12; competencies explained by, 15; disappointment impacting, 8; EQ-i 2.0 of, 9; flexibility of, 8; friendship of, 11; impulse control of, 8
Peck, M. Scott, 158
Peg: EQ-i 2.0 of, 174–75, *177*; family of, 174–78, *177*; need recognized by, 178; parents impacting, 175; strength of, 176
perception, 58
persona, 75
perspective, 67
Pete, 174; balance considered by, 168; in college, 168–69; drinking influencing, 168–71; emotional independence of, 173; EQ-i 2.0 of, 171–73, *172*; friendship with, 169; parents protected by, 170; reality-testing by, 172
plan, for sustained change, 5
poem, 103–4
Positive Parenting, 71
possibility, 68
postpartum depression, 34
power, 16–19, 30–31, 132, 213
predictability, 60
The Prelude (Wordsworth), 124, 126
premenstrual dysphoric disorder, 48

preparation, 115, 116
present, 35–36
priority, 65, 116–17
privacy, 94
problem-solving, 8, 19, 59; of Craig, 205; Diane underutilized by, 123–24; emotional independence with, 130; impulsivity without, 63; relationship strengthened by, 58
profiling, 52

Quinn, Patricia, 70

rage, 80–81, 90
Rand, Ayn, 104, 105
rationality, 58
Ray: ADHD impacting, 71; awareness of, 73; EQ-i 2.0 of, 68, 69; guilt of, 73; self-incriminated by, 70; stress management by, 68–74, 69
readiness, 93
reading, 10, 196–97
reality-testing: by Chas, 82; Craig impacted by, 205; by Deirdre, 148–49; by Irene, 88; lying damaging, 75; objectivity revealed with, 59; by Pete, 172
reason, 144–45
recovery, 93, 174; from addiction, 27; competencies telling, 28–29; faith within, 27; responsibility in, 79; of self, 78–79, 79; substance abuse contrasted with, 171
rehab, 206
rehearsal, 100
reinforcement, 170
relationship, 18, 49–55, 87, 134, 139, 191; balance in, 47, 150;

with brother, 71–72, 120; change
and, 175; Chas reinforced by, 84;
client healed by, 192; in college,
155; communication in, 38;
competencies expressing, 215–16;
courage altering, 31–32; of
Damien, 24; disappointment in,
39; doubt created by, 47; empathy
in, 100–101; with EQ-i 2.0, 206–
8; with family, 110–11; flexibility
reinforcing, 114; independence
in, 46; lying suffocating, 178;
with mother, 205–6; need in,
104–5; optimism connecting,
140; with parents, 173; problem-
solving strengthening, 58–59;
responsibility in, 180; Steve
reflecting on, 42; therapy
practicing, 42–43
relaxing, 74
Rena, 33–34
Rene: EQ-i 2.0 of, 106, *107*; home
impacting, 103–9; poem shared
by, 103–4; strength overused by,
106; support of, 106
resentment, 151–52
responsibility: need compared
with, 188; in recovery, 79; in
relationship, 180; safety without,
198. *See also* social responsibility
risk, 11, 22
The Road Less Traveled (Peck), 158

safety, 198
Salovey, Peter, 152, 153
school, 61, 155, 168–69, 201
self: abuse destroying, 209;
advocating for, 5; David
reinventing, 75; knowledge of,
4–5, 82; Ray incriminating, 70;
recovery of, 78–79, *79*. *See also*
emotional self-awareness
self-actualization, 36, 40; awareness
with, 190–91; of Carl, 180; of
Damien, 23; emotional self-
awareness combined with,
143; goals achieved with,
122; with independence, 176;
Jon leveraging, 135–36; Kal
embodying, 37
self-expression, 18, 44–46, 101, 205
selfishness, 121–22
self-perception, 17, 35–43, *44*
self-protection, 10
self-regard, 7, 9–10, 12, 36, 40, 75; of
Carl, 180; of David, 77; of Diane,
124–25; about identity, 35; of
Jennifer, 54
showing, 53
sister, 100
Sisyphus (myth), 209
S.M.A.R.T. *See* Specific,
Measurable, Achievable,
Realistic, Time-bound
sobriety, 30, 137
socialization, 61
social responsibility, 168; action
involved by, 49; of Chas, 81–82;
empathy compared with, 49;
EQ-i 2.0 on, 211; of Irene, 87;
need and, 54, 150; North Korea
inspiring, 114–15; with stress
tolerance, 149–50
Social Skills, 101
Specific, Measurable, Achievable,
Realistic, Time-bound
(S.M.A.R.T.), 115
Steve: assertiveness overutilized
by, 43; development of, 40;
emotional expression of, 41–42;

relationship reflected on by, 42; self-perception of, 38–43
strategy, 53, 192
strength, 68–69, 103–5, 107–18, 120–28, 211; change with, 19; competencies reframing, 20; of Diane, 118–19; of emotional self-awareness, 155; flexibility as, 173; Jeb demonstrating, 143; Marsha considering, 62; pain challenging, 63; of Peg, 176; Rene overusing, 106; stress tolerance relying on, 67; in therapy, 145–46
stress, 34; from bullying, 134–35; control heightening, 24; of David, 76; drinking alleviating, 182–83; EI rooting, 6; with intentionality, 66–67; from need, 132
stress management, 18, 67; change explored by, 65; priority aligning, 65; by Ray, 68–74, 69; support required with, 66
stress tolerance: childhood lowering, 157; dating testing, 95; of Diane, 123; interpersonal relations exacerbated by, 140; of Irene, 87; of Karla, 165; with self-expression, 205; social responsibility with, 149–50; strength relied on by, 67
sturdiness, 67
subjectivity, 152–53
substance abuse: interpersonal relationships reinforced by, 191; recovery contrasted with, 171; rehab for, 206; sobriety contrasted with, 137; treatment for, 26. *See also* drinking

suffering, 1
suicide, 120–22, 127
support: by brother, 120; for change, 5; of client, 192; disappointment in, 197; for Irene, 88; of Rene, 106; stress management requiring, 66. *See also* therapy
Sylvia, 100

talent, 26–27
Taliban, 80
talking: about doubt, 146; feeling contrasted with, 77; healing through, 15; power of, 132
therapy, 211; Aaron in, 22; anger managed in, 81; balance in, 154; boundary fortified by, 31; change in, 153–54, 167; childhood in, 42; client monitored in, 153; competencies in, 191–93; Darren in, 188; Denny seeking, 92; EQ-i 2.0 in, 42, 210; experience addressed in, 208–9; feeling after, 84; husband in, 174; insecurity in, 146–47; Jean without, 184–85; Jennifer in, 55; objectivity offered by, 118; pain healed by, 30; relationship practiced in, 42–43; strength in, 145–46
thinking, 158, 161
Thom, 99
Thunberg, Greta, 197
time, 35–36, 116
tolerance, 43–44
trauma, 16, 157
treatment, 26
triggers, 28, 210–11
trust, 111

values, 51
vision, 53
Voices from Fatherhood (Quinn and Kilcarr), 70

Wallace, David Foster, 121
well-being, 3, 7, 34
wife, 179, 180, 187–88

The Wild God of the World (Jeffers), 196
Willy, 129–30
Wordsworth, William, 124, 126
work, 139, 142–43, 213–15
wounding, 1, 33

Zara, 19–20
Zeno of Elea (philosopher), 178

About the Author

Patrick Kilcarr, PhD, has been the director of Georgetown University's Center for Personal Development since 1999. The Center offers direct clinical services, workshops, and trainings on a variety of topics related to enhancing mental health and personal well-being, especially related to emotional intelligence, leadership, and motivation. His research studies the intersection of risk-taking behavior and emotional intelligence in the college-age population. He is a master trainer in emotional intelligence, certifying professionals to use the EQ-i 2.0 (the most valid and reliable self-assessment of emotional intelligence) to assess and evaluate the social and emotional competencies of individuals in a variety of professional venues. He has acquired a number of certifications in the field of mental health, along with being an adjunct professor in the School of Health Science at Georgetown University, teaching interactive courses on personal development, sexual health, and emotional intelligence. He completed his PhD in human development, through the acclaimed Institute of Child Study at the University of Maryland College Park. All of his work is directed toward strengthening the individual with respect to their innate talents and abilities. He has written extensively on emotional intelligence, addiction, and Attention Deficit Hyperactivity Disorder, and he has coauthored an award-winning book, *Voices From Fatherhood: Fathers, Sons and ADHD*. Dr. Kilcarr maintains a private practice in Washington, DC, where he offers individual, couples, group, and family therapy to local residents.

www.ingramcontent.com/pod-product-compliance
Ingram Content Group UK Ltd.
Pitfield, Milton Keynes, MK11 3LW, UK
UKHW040201230326
469203UK00006B/22